44.50
60 B

D0850854

PLACE IN RETURN BOX to remove this checkout from your record.
TO AVOID FINES return on or before date due.

The integration of West Germany into the North Atlantic Treaty Organisation (NATO) became one of the most important and contentious problems of post-war security. Increasing Cold War tensions during and after 1949 had led Britain to consider the need to rearm West Germany. Yet fears of a resurgent Germany existed both in Britain and on the continent. The timing and manner of German incorporation was crucial and became the subject of lengthy negotiations.

Using extensive archival material, Saki Dockrill explores the paradoxes and dilemmas of British policy between 1950 and 1955. She stresses how the government was forced to react to the constantly changing positions adopted by the USA, France and Germany itself and addresses three main issues: what made Britain accept the need for a German contribution to the defence of Western Europe? why was Britain reluctant to encourage any hasty American and French proposals? and why did Britain eventually put forward proposals that successfully resolved the crisis?

The author argues that, contrary to the accepted view, Britain was not at any time enthusiastic about rearming West Germany. Moreover, as Dr Dockrill shows, Britain's attitude to Western Europe did not result in a radical departure from her traditional opposition to a continental commitment, but led to her persuading her allies to accept Britain's original plan for a West German army controlled through NATO.

This is the first book-length analysis of the formulation of Britain's strategy for rearming West Germany and will be of interest to specialists and students of international politics, with special reference to post-war diplomatic history, NATO and European security.

BRITAIN'S POLICY FOR WEST GERMAN REARMAMENT 1950–1955

Editorial Board

STEVE SMITH *(Managing editor)*
LAWRENCE FREEDMAN FRED HALLIDAY KAL HOLSTI
ROY JONES ROBERT S. LITWAK PETER NAILOR
WILLIAM OLSON ADAM ROBERTS JOHN SIMPSON
JACK SPENCE ROGER TOOZE JOHN A. VASQUEZ

Cambridge Studies in International Relations is a joint initiative of Cambridge University Press and the British International Studies Association (BISA). The series will include a wide range of material, from undergraduate textbooks and surveys to research-based monographs and collaborative volumes. The aim of the series is to publish the best new scholarship in International Studies from Europe, North America and the rest of the world.

BRITAIN'S POLICY FOR WEST GERMAN REARMAMENT 1950–1955

SAKI DOCKRILL
Department of War Studies
Kings College London

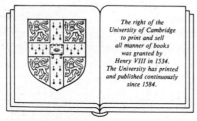

The right of the
University of Cambridge
to print and sell
all manner of books
was granted by
Henry VIII in 1534.
The University has printed
and published continuously
since 1584.

CAMBRIDGE UNIVERSITY PRESS
Cambridge
New York   Port Chester   Melbourne   Sydney

Published by the Press Syndicate of the University of Cambridge
The Pitt Building, Trumpington Street, Cambridge CB2 1RP
40 West 20th Street, New York, NY 10011, USA
10 Stamford Road, Oakleigh, Melbourne 3166, Australia

© Cambridge University Press 1991

First published in 1991

Printed in Great Britain at the University Press, Cambridge

British Library cataloguing in publication data

Dockrill, Saki
Britain's policy for West German rearmament 1950–1955 –
(Cambridge studies in international relations; 13).
1. Great Britain. Foreign relations with Germany. Policies of
government, history 2. Germany. Foreign relations with Great
Britain. Policies of British government, history
I. Title
327.41043

Library of Congress cataloguing in publications data

Dockrill, Saki
Britain's policy for West German rearmament, 1950–1955/ Saki
Dockrill.
p. ca. – (Cambridge studies in international relations; 13)
Revision of the author's thesis (Ph.D – London University),
1988: under title: Britain and a West German contribution to
NATO.
1950–1955.
Includes bibliographical references.
ISBN 0-52-38111-8
1. Europe – Military relations – Great Britain. 2. Great Britain –
Military relations – Europe. 3. Germany (West) – Defenses. 4.
Great Britain – Military relations – Germany (West) 5. Germany
(West) – Military relations – Great Britain 6. Great Britain –
Foreign relations – 1945- I. Title. II. Series.
D1065.G7D63 1991
327.41043 – dc20   90–33132

ISBN 0 521 38111 8 hardback

wv

0269

For my mother, Setsuko

CONTENTS

ACKNOWLEDGEMENTS

This project could not have been completed without my being allowed access to several archives. I wish to thank the archivists at the British Library, the Air Historical Branch at the Ministry of Defence, London, and the Royal Air Force Museum, Hendon, for permitting me to examine and to quote from the papers listed in the bibliography. I am also indebted to Lady Younger for allowing me to consult and quote from the diaries of Kenneth Younger and to Professor Geoffrey Warner of the Open University, who kindly made the diaries available to me. I would like to thank the Trustees of the Liddell Hart Centre for Military Archives, King's College, London, for their permission to examine and reproduce extracts from the papers of Sir Basil Liddell Hart and Sir William Elliot. Copyright material from the Public Record Office, Kew, appears by permission of Her Majesty's Stationery Office.

I appreciate the help and advice given by the staff of the Public Record Office, Kew, and of the National Archives, Washington D.C., and by the archivists at the British Library Manuscripts Department, the British Library of Political and Economic Science, the Churchill College Archives Centre, Cambridge, the Library of Nuffield College, Oxford, the Seeley G. Mudd Manuscript Library, Princeton University, the Department of Aviation Records, the RAF Museum, London, the Department of Documents, the Imperial War Museum, London, the Department of Western Manuscripts, the Bodleian Library, Oxford, and the Department of Manuscripts and Archives, the Sterling Memorial Library, Yale University.

I am particular grateful to Patricia Methven, the archivist at the Liddell Hart Centre for Military Archives, King's College, London, James Leyerzaph, the archivist at the Dwight D. Eisenhower Library, Kansas, and Air Commodore H. A. Probert, the Air Historical Branch, the Ministry of Defence, London, for their invaluable assistance.

This book grew out of my thesis 'Britain and a West German contribution to NATO, 1950–1955', which was awarded a PhD from London University in the summer of 1988, and I wish to express my gratitude to my thesis supervisor, Professor Lawrence Freedman of King's College, London, for his judicious advice during the preparation of the thesis. I am also grateful to Professor D. Cameron Watt of the London School of Economics and Political Science and to Dr John Baylis of the University College of Wales, Aberystwyth for their helpful suggestions about transforming the thesis into this book.

Although it is impossible to mention all those who assisted this project directly or indirectly, I would like to express my thanks to Professor Geoffrey Warner of the Open University, Dr John Young of the London School of the Economics and Political Science, Professor Thomas Schwartz of Harvard University, Professor Richard Immerman of the University of Hawaii, and Dr Günter Bischof of the University of New Orleans, all of whom read parts or the whole of my earlier drafts, for their encouragement and useful comments. Sir Andrew Gilchrist was kind enough to discuss his experiences in the Foreign Office during the earlier stages of Britain's involvement with the question of West Germany's military integration with the West, when I visited him at his home, Arthur's Crag, Lanark in September 1985. Colonel Norbert Wiggershaus of MGFA, Freiburg and Heather Yasamee of the Foreign Office Library and Records Department have been most helpful in providing me with both information and copies of their recent publications dealing with aspects of this subject. I am also grateful to the patient efforts of Michael Holdsworth of the Cambridge University Press in arranging for the publication of this, and to the John M. Olin Foundation and the Department of History, Yale University, for providing me with a stimulating academic environment during the 1988–9 year and for the generous research funding which enabled me to complete this project. I would like to express my gratitude to Professor Paul Kennedy of Yale University for doing so much to ensure that my working environment there was comfortable and pleasant.

Finally, writing this book was a long, fascinating and often rather stressful experience stretching over five years and I thank my husband, Michael, for his moral support and for helping me correct typing and grammatical errors in the manuscript. My greatest debt is to my mother, Setsuko, to whom this book is dedicated, and who, being the most understanding supporter of my project, provided me with much needed financial assistance without which I could not have finished this book. While I owe a great debt to many people for their assistance and advice, the views expressed in this book are solely my own.

Saki Dockrill
London

ABBREVIATIONS

(1) *Public Record Office references*
CAB   Cabinet
COS   Chiefs of Staff
CP   Cabinet Memoranda
DEFE   Defence
DO   Defence Committee of the Cabinet
FO   Foreign Office
JP   Joint Planning Staff
PREM   Prime Minister's Office
PHP   Post Hostilities Planning
PUSC   Permanent Under-Secretary's Committee at the Foreign Office

(2) *Other references*
Cmd   Command Papers
DBPOI   Documents of British Policy Overseas Series 2 Vol. I
DBPO III Documents of British Policy Overseas Series 2 Vol. III
DDEL   Dwight D. Eisenhower Library, Kansas
DNSC   Documents of the National Security Council
FRUS   Foreign Relations of the United States
JIC   Joint Intelligence Committee (United States)
MGFA   Militärgeschichtliches Forschungsamt (West Germany)
NAW   National Archives Washington
Parl Deb H of C
    House of Commons Debates
PPS   Policy Planning Staff (United States)
RJCS   Records of the Joint Chiefs of Staff

INTRODUCTION

This book will deal with one of the most important and contentious problems of post-war security in Europe. Having formed the
North Atlantic Treaty Organisation (NATO), the central issue for the
Western allies during this period was how and when West Germany
was to be integrated into the Western defence system. The main
theme of this study is the evolution of Britain's strategy and foreign
policy for the post-war defence of Western Europe during and after
the Korean War, and to assess the impact on this strategy of other
problems with which Britain was confronted during the period – her
fear of a rearmed and independent West Germany and the impact of
the Cold War on Europe. Britain's search for a satisfactory solution to
these problems led to her increasing commitment to European
security. There is a dearth of original archival research on this subject.
This book, which is based largely on research in British and American
archives, both public and private, is intended to fill that gap.[1]

Clearly the difficulties which Britain faced in Europe after 1945
were by no means new. For instance, after 1915 Britain and her allies
had become dependent on American loans to sustain their colossal
war effort. Just as the unification of Germany became the central issue
in Europe in the mid nineteenth century so the reunification of that
country became a major concern for the great powers in the mid
twentieth century, especially after the death of Stalin in March 1953
and Churchill's proposal for summit talks about Germany two
months later. Similarly, the problem of German rearmament and the
threat a resurgent Germany posed to European stability had been a
constant factor in shaping Britain's continental policy between 1930
and 1939. Traditionally Britain had resisted involvement in European
conflicts, preferring to devote her resources to imperial concerns and
the protection of her world-wide commercial interests. Britain's
geographical separation from Europe and her naval supremacy made
such a strategy possible. As a result the British army had increasingly
become an imperial police force during and after the second half of

1

the nineteenth century, although, following Haldane's post-1906 reforms, a comparatively well-trained and well-equipped British expeditionary force of 166,000 became available by 1914 as an 'optional luxury'.[2]

While historians continue to disagree as to whether Britain should have committed herself decisively to a European strategy during the interwar period,[3] the situation after 1945 had become more complex, in that Britain now recognised that she must concern herself with the security of Western Europe if she wished to avoid becoming involved in another war on the Continent. Equally important was that she was now totally dependent on United States military and economic support in order to retain her great-power status. The difference was also the result of a unique combination of circumstances in which Western policy towards a defeated Germany was influenced by the evolution of the Cold War in Europe, while Britain's European policy, after 1949, was guided by her determination to re-establish the war-time special relationship with the United States and by her unwillingness to be allied to a rearmed West Germany in the absence of American participation in a European defence system.

The origins of the Cold War and the formation of NATO have been subject to continuous historical reinterpretation during the last three decades. Most recent studies have concentrated on the period from 1945 to 1950, reflecting the availability of archival resources which have, in turn, persuaded American historians to take greater account of the role of United States' allies in influencing and modifying her foreign and military policies towards Europe. They also suggest that American post-war European policy was much more subtle and cautious than earlier scholars had surmised, in that American policy makers sought to cooperate with the Europeans and not to dictate to them. Two reasons have been put forward for this.

The first was based on American idealism which believed that the European powers should be encouraged, and not forced by, the United States to reform themselves and that they should resolve their long-standing conflicts of interest without external interference. The second reason was that before 1949 she was confident that European security was sufficiently provided for by the American nuclear umbrella, and that, as a result, she could take a relatively relaxed attitude towards Europe's problems.[4] Nor was it obvious before 1950 that the United States should feel it necessary, as a matter of urgency, to undertake any deep commitment to European security merely because the Soviet Union began to adopt a more threatening policy towards Eastern and Central Europe, a policy which, in any case, was

2

bound to have a much greater impact on the minds of European leaders than on their American counterparts. This study takes account of this American tendency to follow a cautious policy towards Europe, which helps to explain why the United States, after proposing the rearmament of West Germany at the NATO Council meeting in New York in September 1950, became more receptive to British and European pressure which persuaded Washington to adopt a 'wait and see' policy until the Europeans had worked out their own solution to this controversial issue.

Thus, while recent studies have tended to downgrade the United States' role in Europe after 1945, there has also been a tendency to concentrate more on the significance of Britain's influence on the formulation of allied policy towards the Cold War in Europe, and especially in establishing the Western alliance.[5] This has been partially attributed, notably by Geoffrey Warner and John Young, to Ernest Bevin's enthusiasm for British cooperation with West European countries – hitherto Bevin was regarded as a committed Atlanticist.[6] This still leaves a number of questions unanswered – to what extent was Bevin prepared to commit Britain to the cause of European unity and why, after 1948, did he begin to work for a wider Atlantic community instead of for an exclusively European arrangement as his preferred instrument, from the point of view of Britain's interests, for promoting European stability? While this aspect of British policy is not the main theme of this study, I have attempted to suggest, in broad terms, the motives for Bevin's apparent change of emphasis in Chapter 1.

Finally, and most importantly, historians have reached a consensus that the Cold War was not the sole explanation for the course which Western policy followed after 1945. There were other factors – British and European anxiety about the decline of their influence, economically and politically, in world affairs as a result of the immense strains imposed upon them by the Second World War, and their relative impotence in the face of the predominance of the two superpowers in the settlement of the problems of post-war Europe and, in particular, the crucial question of the future status of Germany as a divided or reunified country. All these factors are now regarded by contemporary historians as essential to understanding how the West was able to formulate a foreign and strategic policy for Europe.[7] Equally important, this book is concerned to explain what D. Cameron Watt has described as 'the almost inextricable interactions between the twin problems of controlling Germany and containing the Soviet Union.[8]

3

1 INITIAL PLANS TO REARM WEST GERMANY

The defeat of Germany in 1945 created a vacuum in Central Europe. The question of how this could be filled was a major concern for the victorious allied powers in the immediate aftermath of the Second World War. According to the Potsdam Agreement on Germany in August 1945, the United States, Britain, France and the Soviet Union were to make concerted efforts through an Allied Control Council to establish economic unity throughout Germany. Moreover, the four occupying powers were to prepare for the eventual reconstruction of an independent and democratic Germany which must never again become a menace to world peace. To this end, the Potsdam Agreement laid down strict guidelines for ensuring the complete disarmament and demilitarisation of Germany. Within a year, however, the Soviet zone was sealed off from the rest of Germany and the initial aim of dealing with Germany as an economic 'whole' became questionable. By the autumn of 1949 the major objective of the Potsdam Agreement collapsed as two German governments emerged, one in the East and one in the West.

Many of the leading ministers in Britain's Labour government, which came to power at the end of July 1945, were well acquainted with European power politics. While the Prime Minister, Clement Attlee, was a reserved man, he was an astute politician, who had served as deputy Prime Minister under Churchill between 1942 and 1945. Ernest Bevin, the Foreign Secretary, was a pragmatic, able and cautious ex-trade union leader. His Foreign Office advisers, Sir Ivone Kirkpatrick, Sir William Strang, and Sir Donald Gainer, were experienced diplomats, who were well versed in German affairs. Similarly, the senior military officials, – Field Marshal Sir William Slim, Field Marshal Sir Bernard Montgomery and Air Chief Marshal Sir John Slessor – were actively involved in formulating Britain's strategy for the defence of post-war Europe.[1] They were all anxious to preserve Britain's position as a global power, which meant her adjustment to a rapid development of the Cold War in Europe. As a result,

4

Britain's policy for Germany and for Europe as a whole evolved in stages between 1945 and 1950.

While Britain gained a sharper insight than the United States into what she saw as the ambitions of the Soviet Union, Britain did not want to be seen as the main instigator of the Cold War – as Bevin stated in May 1946, it was 'most important' to 'ensure' that 'responsibility' for splitting Europe and particularly Germany, was 'put squarely on the Russians'.[2] Unfortunately for Britain, her occupation zone in Germany was the most economically handicapped of the four zones and her desperate need to reduce her huge occupation costs of nearly £90 million in 1946 left her with 'no alternative' but to join her zone economically with that of the US in January 1947.[3] However, Britain moved only cautiously towards the political unification of the Anglo-American zones, while the French remained opposed to any measure that might lead to a centralised Germany.[4]

The second stage, between 1948 and 1949, was one in which Britain's misgivings about Soviet policy in Czechoslovakia, towards Norway and finally in Berlin, increased, and Whitehall's European policy sought more consciously to counter these Soviet pressures.[5] By that time France had been brought to accept, however reluctantly, the need for consolidating the three Western occupation zones economically as well as politically. Consequently, the London talks on Germany between the three Western powers in spring 1948 laid the foundations for the establishment of a Federal government in West Germany. The growing Cold War tension in Europe helped Britain to secure close American cooperation in the defence of Western Europe, which culminated in the creation of the North Atlantic Treaty Organisation (NATO) in April 1949.

The last stage, from the autumn of 1949 to the outbreak of the Korean War in June 1950, was one of a further steady deterioration in East–West relations on a global scale. The Soviet Union's large conventional ground forces in Eastern Europe were now regarded by the Western Europeans as a serious military threat to their security. Accordingly NATO began to press for the improvement of Europe's defence capabilities. However, while the three Western occupying powers assured the Federal Republic of Germany that they hoped to secure her close association with the West in the future, this was expressed in economic and political terms, thereby avoiding the question of her military recovery. During the first and second stages, from 1946 and 1949, Britain's policy for Western Europe and for Germany was greatly influenced by the evolution of the Cold War in Europe and it was only during the last phase that a gap between the two began to emerge.

1. Britain's long-term strategy for the rearmament of Germany

As early as July 1944, military planners pointed out that:

> the two European countries which could constitute serious threats to our strategic interests are a resurgent Germany and Russia...if Russia does become hostile, Germany is the only country whose geographical position, manpower and resources could provide the aid which might be essential to our preservation.[6]

During 1946, the Chiefs of Staff identified the Soviet Union as 'a much more dangerous potential enemy than Germany; and suggested that '[O]ur long term policy with regard to Germany...cannot be shaped solely from the point of view of preventing a revival of a threat from Germany'. What the military feared most (this fear was shared by Bevin) was a resurgent Germany 'dominated by Russia'.[7]

The breakdown of the Council of Foreign Ministers' meeting in London in December 1947 ended any lingering expectation in the Foreign Office that collaboration between the United States, Britain and the Soviet Union could provide the basis for the reconstruction of the post-war world.[8] In a minute for the Cabinet on 4 January 1948, Bevin suggested the idea of drawing Germany into a 'Western democratic system' backed by the US and the Commonwealth.[9] The potential Brussels powers referred to the possibility that West Germany might eventually be included in the Brussels Treaty Organisation (which was formed in March 1948).[10] Germany's future role was spelled out in more specific terms in proposals drawn up as a result of British–Canadian–American talks at the Pentagon in Washington in March and April 1948:

> When circumstances permitted, Germany (or the three Western zones) and Spain should be invited to adhere to the Brussels five-power treaty and to the North Atlantic Defense Agreement. This objective, however, should not be publicly disclosed.[11]

As the Cold War heightened, Britain and her allies (with the important exception of France) began to contemplate ultimately including West Germany in the defence of Western Europe. However, the Labour Government was unable to establish a consensus on this question by the end of 1948. Some anti-German Ministers, like Hugh Dalton, the Chancellor of the Duchy of Lancaster, believed that a rearmed West Germany would constitute 'the greatest danger to World peace',[12] while on the other hand, both Field Marshal Montgomery, the Chief of the Imperial General Staff, in February, and Lord Pakenham, the Minister of Civil Aviation, in October, proposed a radical reversal of allied occupation policy by building up a strong West Germany allied to the West.[13] The Foreign Secretary concluded at the end of a Cabinet meeting on 22 December 1948 that it was 'premature' to make any hasty decision on the future defence relationship between West Germany and the allies.[14] Indeed, throughout the years between 1945 and 1949, there were ample reasons why the concept of a remilitarised West Germany were both politically unacceptable and militarily unnecessary.

First, Britain's fear of a resurgent Germany, as well as her strong suspicions of the German people, while felt less intensely than in France, remained strong. The First Sea Lord, Sir John Cunningham, doubted whether 'Germany would ever be a contented nation even when she had regained her old boundaries and once again rebuilt her military power'. However, Bevin doubted that strengthening West Germany would ensure the safety of Western Europe.[15] The Cabinet view on Germany which emerged by 1948 was that the association of the three Western zones of occupied Germany in a non-military sense with the West was essential not only as a counter to any further Communist infringements of the Western sphere of influence but also as a safeguard against a resurgent West Germany.

Secondly, despite strained relations with Moscow, Britain did not perceive an imminent military threat from the Soviet Union. Given her technological backwardness and her exhausted economy as a result of the enormous losses she had incurred during the recent war, British intelligence did not believe that the USSR was in any condition to resort to war with the West until 1957 at the earliest.[16]

Finally, and in relation to the above, there was no comprehensive defence plan for Western Europe between Britain, the Brussels powers and the United States which could take account of West Germany's possible role. Indeed Anglo-American military planners assumed that in the event of a war with Russia, the territory of West Germany would be abandoned by allied forces, who would try to hold the line of the Rhine.[17]

2. Britain's strategy for the defence of Western Europe from 1945 to March 1950

Western Europe was utterly defenceless and its security depended upon the American possession of the atomic bomb to deter any Russian military threat. In August 1948, the Chief of Staff warned the Cabinet that in the event of a major confrontation with the Soviet Union, the military situation would 'become critical by about six months after the outbreak of the war'.[18] That Western Europe should become politically stable and militarily strong was essential for Britain if she wished to avoid involvement in another war on the Continent.[19] Field Marshal Montgomery was a lone voice in advocating in February 1948 that Britain should send two divisions to the Continent to encourage the morale of her European friends. The Chief of the Air Staff, Lord Tedder, the First Sea Lord and the Prime Minister all rejected this proposal.[20] The underlying principle behind these objections was that: 'the plan for the defence of Europe…was, in fact, only a part of our overall strategy'.[21]

This reluctance to undertake a binding commitment to Europe reflected Britain's traditional posture and her recent costly involvement in land warfare in Europe.[22] Britain also aspired to remain a great world power.[23] Following the collapse of the war-time triumvirate, Bevin tried to secure European cooperation through his concept for Western Union which, as he stated in January 1948, was to be 'some form of union in Western Europe…backed by the Americans [sic] and the Dominions'. He had then hoped that a successful Western Union might become an independent third force, which would allow Britain to avoid subordinating her interests to those of the United States, while enabling Western Europe effectively to resist Communist threats. Although Bevin's idea for creating a third force was superseded by the American decision to participate in NATO, his consistent efforts to preserve Britain's global status were not merely based on outdated assumptions.[24] Despite granting independence to India and Ceylon in 1947, she still retained a large number of overseas colonies and military commitments. Her presence in the Middle East, according to the Foreign Secretary, 'served a purpose other than a military purpose which is vital to our position as a Great Power'.[25]

The real and growing problem she confronted was how she could reconcile these responsibilities with her limited resources. Britain's initial optimistic assumptions about post-war reconstruction notwithstanding, her own economic and financial difficulties in meeting her pressing internal, foreign and imperial problems were likely to continue and her first priority was, like those of the other Western European countries, the recovery of her economic and industrial strength at the expense of her defence preparations.[26] Indeed, her early experiences with the Brussels Treaty Organisation soon proved that Britain and the other Western European states were unable to do much towards building up their defences.[27] The core of Britain's strategy for Western Europe became inevitably one of securing American economic and military assistance, but the United States was reluctant to rescue Western Europe unless the latter demonstrated its willingness to defend itself.[28] Bevin's painstaking efforts to break the 'vicious circle' culminated in the formation of NATO.[29]

The prime virtue of NATO to Britain lay not so much in its effectiveness as a military organisation designed to 'stop a Russian armed attack', but as a political and psychological means of uniting the Western democracies in the face of Soviet threats[30] and later for containing a rearmed West Germany.[31]

Furthermore, Britain's membership of the Atlantic alliance and her emphasis on the 'special relationship' within that body, would secure her position as an extra European power.[32] Nor did this require her to make any drastic change to her traditional strategy: her contribution to Western European defence comprised air power, the defence of sea communications and the security of the Middle East, while the major responsibility for providing ground forces was left to France.[33]

It was not until the spring of 1950 that Britain embarked on a serious reexamination of her strategy for the defence of Western Europe. This resulted from Britain's perception of the declining deterrent effect of US nuclear capability, as a result of the Soviet Union's test explosion of an atomic bomb in August 1949. This sense of insecurity was increased by the rise of Communist China on the Asian mainland in the autumn. United States attention would be diverted from Central Europe towards Asia, while at the same time a large number of French troops were tied down in Indochina.[34]

It was in this context that in March 1950 the Chiefs of Staff suggested a major shift in British defence priorities away from the Middle East to Western Europe. '[T]o hold the enemy East of the Rhine' was now regarded as 'vital to our first pillar, the defence of the United Kingdom'. A subsequent Cabinet defence committee meeting agreed that Britain should send two infantry divisions as a reinforcement to the British Army of the Rhine (BAOR) in the event of a war with the Soviet Union and that this would be at the expense of reinforcements for the Middle East.[35]

The proposed reinforcements would not meet the military

demands of the situation and it was, as Montgomery, now chairman of the Commander-in-Chief Committee of the Brussels pact, put it, 'utterly futile to pretend that we can delay the Russians east of the Rhine for longer than a period of two or three days'.[36] Although Soviet forces were believed to be too deficient in training and equipment to mount a serious military invasion of the West, the Soviet Union reportedly had 25 divisions stationed in Eastern Europe out of a total ground force strength in excess of 175 divisions. Western European forces numbered a mere 12 divisions, including $2\frac{1}{3}$ American divisions, $2\frac{1}{3}$ British divisions and 3 French divisions in West Germany, all intended for occupation duties.[37] Nevertheless, the shift in Britain's strategy towards the defence of Western Europe was a harbinger of her closer involvement in European security questions after September 1950. Equally important was the change in the proposed line of defence from 'on the River Rhine', NATO's existing plan, to 'east of the Rhine'. This modification was bound to raise the question of what to do about West Germany: would she be abandoned by the West in the event of war, or should she be encouraged to fight for the West against the Soviet Union? In the latter case this would mean that the West would have to confront the question of her rearmament.

3.   An actual Soviet threat vis-à-vis an eventual German threat

The creation of NATO, the heightening Cold War tension and the formation of the Federal Republic of Germany in 1949 resulted in the emergence of the question of the integration of a rearmed West Germany into the Western camp after 1950. While the policy of disarmament and demilitarisation of the Federal Republic was continued by the three Allied High Commissioners (who had replaced the former Allied Military Governors), the German Chancellor, Dr Konrad Adenauer and his military advisers, notably Hans Speidel, had reached their main conclusions about West Germany's future security commitment to the West.[38] Given West Germany's strategically exposed position in Europe and given that Western military strength fell far short of that of the Soviet Union, her sense of insecurity increased and her leaders became convinced that West Germany's immediate interests would be best served by her assimilation with the Western democracies. West Germany's military integration into Western Europe, rather than her possession of an independent armed force of her own, would not only prevent West Germany from being once again dominated by a dictatorship, but would also help her to achieve her full sovereignty and her reestablishment as an equal member of the European community. To this end, by April 1949 German military planners contemplated raising some 15 German divisions equipped with modern American weapons for service in NATO, and who would be equal in status to the other NATO countries. This plan was accepted by the West German Chancellor and provided that foundation for West Germany's negotiating position at the Bonn talks later in 1951.

The success of these objectives, however, depended upon West Germany being able to persuade her Western allies to accept the axiom that Europe was 'nur ein Torso ohne Deutschland', that is, the defence of West Germany was central to the defence of Western Europe.[39] Their acceptance of the crucial importance of West Germany to the security of Western Europe would enable the Federal Republic to extract better conditions for her future independence, as well as to ensure the defence of her territory. At the same time, the Federal Republic was well aware that her military contribution must not appear to be a potential threat to the other Western Europeans, and particularly to the French. While Bonn looked to the United States as the mainstay of deterrence in Europe, the problem of a West German defence contribution was regarded as essentially a European one, which was to be resolved through close European cooperation, particularly with France.[40] Indeed, prior to the birth of NATO, Speidel envisaged the idea of organising a European common defence system or a European army in which West Germany military effectiveness would be included.[41] The Cold War provided West Germany with a greater chance of achieving her political aims in Europe, since the more the Western Europeans feared the threat from the East, the more they would be prepared to accept a West German military contribution to the West. The German Chancellor, a former Mayor of Cologne, although 75 years old, was an astute and self-assured Catholic conservative politician.[42] He warned the Western occupying powers of the danger of losing West Germany to Communism if NATO was only willing to defend Europe as far as the River Rhine, but he was unlikely to offer West Germany's military assistance to NATO unless, as he stated in an interview with an American journalist on 3 December 1949, the West 'insist[ed] on [a] German participation in the defence of Western Europe'.[43]

Conversely, Benelux leaders thought it unfair to allow West Germany, with a population of about 40 million, to escape from the

11

military burdens which were being forced on her Western neighbours. In the course of the final negotiations for setting up NATO in the autumn of 1948, West Germany and Spain were mentioned as possible future members, but it was recognised that the time was not yet ripe for determining the defence role of West Germany, a decision confirmed at the meeting of the NATO Council in May 1950.[44] France, on the other hand, feared the rise of a future revanchist Germany as much as the Soviet threat to West Europe. Occupied three times by Germany since 1871, she would have preferred to put off the question of Germany's remilitarisation for good, but she realised that the formation of NATO was bound eventually to cause this question to be raised – Le Monde aptly described German rearmament as 'the yoke of the egg' of the Atlantic alliance.[45]

4. *Britain's initial policy for a West German defence contribution, May 1950*

Although by the end of May 1950 Britain had concluded that the Federal Republic of Germany must eventually join NATO, preliminary studies by British military and civilian leaders, undertaken after November 1949, revealed that this would be fraught with numerous strategic and political difficulties.

First, in order to contain the possible threat arising from the restoration of West Germany's military power, the armed forces of the other Western European powers, and above all those of France, would have to be fully rebuilt before West German rearmament could begin. It would also be necessary to impose a number of safeguards upon West Germany, such as a ban on her use of tanks and aircraft.[46]

Secondly, in view of the strong anti-rearmament mood prevailing in West Germany, it would be undesirable for the West to press too enthusiastically for West German rearmament, since this would increase West Germany's bargaining position *vis-à-vis* the allies. On the other hand, Britain appreciated that it was unlikely, as Attlee told Bevin on 2 May 1950, that West Germany would 'settle down without some armed forces'. At the very least, the West should deal with West Germany circumspectly on this question.[47]

A third consideration was the crucial political one of the effect of Britain's post-war relationship with Western Europe on West Germany's military integration. Whitehall became fully convinced by May 1950 that European security problems must be dealt with in the wider context of the Atlantic alliance in order not only to contain a

Soviet military threat but also to control a future rearmed West Germany. Britain feared that in the absence of a US military presence, a rearmed West Germany might eventually come to dominate Europe or enter into an alliance with the Soviet Union.[48] Clearly, Britain's approach to European issues and particularly to the problem of Germany, was in conflict with that of France: the Council of Europe was reduced to a consultative body mainly because of Britain's opposition to the creation of a federal political institution, which France wanted. However genuine Bevin's concern for the unification of Western Europe might have been in early 1948, the Labour Government and especially the Treasury did not believe that Britain could afford to become involved in European schemes of federation, since this would affect her ability to uphold her responsibilities overseas as well as to maintain the sterling area.[49] Moreover, Britain's approach to European unity differed from that of France: Bevin preferred a practical step by step approach to the solution of problem, instead of 'advocating ambitious schemes of European unity'.[50]

By May 1950 the issue of German rearmament had not been formally raised by the three occupying powers. Britain did, however, possess some indications of the thinking of her two allies on this subject: France would probably prefer to involve West Germany in a purely European arrangement on the lines of the Schuman plan, which was designed to contain Germany's economic recovery through supranational control over her production of coal and steel,[51] while Washington also encouraged close European integration.[52] Nevertheless, Bevin was convinced that the Federal Republic, if she was to be rearmed, must be included in NATO, a view which received the full support of the Cabinet on 8 May 1950.[53]

Finally, Britain's most delicate and exhausting task would be to deal with the repercussions of West Germany's rearmament on the Soviet Union, and on the question of Germany's reunification. Although the Soviet Union had already set up a para-military formation, the *Volkpolizei*, in her zone which was reported to be armed and organised to undertake limited military operations, no measures equivalent to the incorporation of West Germany into NATO had been taken by Moscow with respect to East Germany.[54] Nevertheless, future West German military cooperation with the West became inevitable in British eyes, because 'unless Western Germany becomes politically and militarily an integral part of the West the whole of Germany may become an integral part of the East'.[55]

This implied that the rearmament issue could have been postponed if there had been no Cold War in Europe. The hesitant British attitude

13

towards the rearmament of West Germany was more deeply rooted in the Foreign Office than in the Chiefs of Staff Committee, mainly because the former appreciated more clearly than the latter that the partition of Germany reflected 'the impasse' in international affairs between the Soviet Union and the Western powers.[56] While Britain's long-term aim was to secure Germany's reunification, Bevin, the Foreign Office and the Cabinet were in agreement with the Chiefs of Staff that the time was not yet ripe for extracting favourable conditions for German reunification from the USSR. Meanwhile the West should continue to draw West Germany into its orbit and this in turn would constitute an important source of strength for the West in any future negotiations with the Soviet Union.[57]

This roundabout approach to German reunification was both deceptive and confusing, and it caused the question of German unity to be revived in the middle of the negotiations on the European Defence Community (EDC) in 1953.[58] Indeed, the Permanent Under-Secretary's Committee,[59] while agreeing to this proposed sequence of events, also realised that the full participation of the Federal Republic in the West as a sovereign state would sharpen the division of Germany, thereby making reunification more difficult. However, Britain did not seriously examine the interplay between the question of rearming West Germany and the issue of German reunification at that time. In any case, the Foreign Office accepted that it would be extremely difficult for Britain to ignore a Soviet proposal for the resumption of four-power negotiations on Germany, given German aspirations for reunification.[60] Nor did the Chiefs of Staff overlook the danger of inciting the Soviet Union to launch a preventive war if the West took any irrevocable steps towards obtaining a West German military contribution.[61]

These factors – the desire to contain a rearmed West Germany effectively, the need for diplomatic subtlety in dealing with the Federal Republic, the importance of obtaining American and French support for Britain's approach to this question and the fear of adverse Soviet reactions – were at the centre of Britain's thinking on the question of West Germany's military integration into the West from 1950 to 1954. On the eve of the Korean War, Britain regarded the NATO solution as a long-term objective. Politically it was desirable to involve West Germany in Western Europe in stages 'as part of a European organism', first in the Organisation for European Economic Cooperation (OEEC) – in which West Germany had been included in 1948 – then in the Council of Europe and eventually in NATO in the belief that this process would provide the West with the opportunity, over a long period, to test German trustworthiness. By the time this programme was completed, the defences of the other West European powers would be fully developed and fears of a rearmed West Germany would be correspondingly diminished.[62] Field Marshal Slim, the Chief of the Imperial General Staff after March 1948, anticipated, correctly as it turned out, that 'any useful [military] contribution' from the Federal Republic could not be achieved before 1954.[63]

It was of course sensible for Britain to explore short-term and safer means of obtaining a West German defence contribution to the West through the modification of the existing allied occupation policy. The three Allied High Commissioners agreed to study a request by Adenauer, on 25 April 1950, for the formation of a centralised police formation of 25,000 men to be controlled by the Federal government.[64] A German civilian police force of some 87,000 men (nearly half of whom were equipped with pistols) had already been formed in West Germany. These were organised on a local basis in each of the three occupation zones and, consequently, the Federal government was deprived of any central police power.[65] Britain was ready to agree to the creation of a Federal police force, which would help to reduce the heavy burdens on the Allied occupation forces in West Germany. However, it was uncertain what was to be the exact purpose of this police force: while the British Chiefs of Staff wanted it deployed as a counter to East Germany's police force and thus regarded it as a means of applying some German resources to the defence of Western Europe, the Prime Minister and the Foreign Office remained dubious about its use for this purpose.[66]

5. The American approach to the West German rearmament question

Different significantly from Europe in terms of her historical orientation, geopolitics and political beliefs, it was, of course, less painful for the United States than Britain to consider the remilitarisation of West Germany. United States' policy towards post-war Germany was, at first, strongly punitive in nature as the abortive 'Morgenthau Plan' and the notorious JCS 1067 directive of April 1945 testified.[67] Suspicions about future German revanchism dominated American thinking towards the end of the Second World War, with Franklin Roosevelt minuting in September 1944 that 'I just cannot go along with the idea of seeing the British Empire collapse financially,

15

and Germany at the same time building up a potential re-armament machine to make another war possible in twenty years.'[68] However, the anti-German mood in the US softened more quickly than it did in Western Europe after 1945 and by 1947 US civilian and military leaders were in agreement on the need to promote German economic growth. This shift in attitude reflected United States recognition that Germany's resources should be utilised for the restoration of Western Europe's war-ravaged economy.[69] It was this that inspired the Marshall plan and US insistence on the inclusion of Germany in the European Recovery Programme. Thus in Washington, European economic unification, to include West Germany, was regarded as a first step towards the restoration of Europe.[70] Other than this, the US had no comprehensive plan for post-war Europe or for post-war Germany in the immediate aftermath of the Second World War.[71]

With the growing impact of the Soviet threat, United States' policy for West Germany evolved accordingly and the State Department had, at the end of 1947, dismissed German unification through negotiations as impracticable.[72] Similarly, Washington tended to see the conclusion of the Dunkirk and Brussels treaties, both of which were directed against a possible resurgent Germany as 'outmoded and unrealistic'.[73] In American eyes, the Soviet Union now posed a direct and real danger to post-war Western society and to counter this, West Germany, if she was to be rearmed, must be associated with the Western community. In JCS 1769/1 in April 1947, the service chiefs explained that:

> Potentially, the strongest military power in this area is Germany. Without German aid the rearming countries of Western Europe could scarcely be expected to withstand the armies of our idealogical opponents.[74]

By the summer of 1948 George F. Kennan, the State Department's Director of Policy Planning Staff, and the Pentagon accepted that '[W]hen circumstances permit', West Germany should be incorporated into the planned North Atlantic Defence system or into the Brussels Treaty Organisation, but when NATO was formed they agreed that 'it was too early to attempt it at this particular moment'.[75]

As in Britain and Western Europe, US interest in the German question revived in the autumn of 1949, when the US Army General Staff drafted a plan for the incorporation of German conventional ground forces into the NATO framework. This plan also included rather vague provisions for preventing the Germans from acquiring certain types of weapons.[76] It was endorsed by the JCS in document 2124 of

April 1950, in which they urged the US government to move away from the policy of West German disarmament and demilitarisation:

> The Western Germans should now be given real and substantial opportunity to participate politically, economically and militarily in Western Europe and North Atlantic region arrangements and on a basis of equality and of being integrated rapidly into the North Atlantic Community.[77]

In the period up to the Korean War a number of other suggestions were made by the JCS about German rearmament. Although these were not developed into an elaborate policy, the following points are worth noting. First, the US JCS and British leaders were in agreement about the desirability of forming a Federal police force. To this end, the JCS recommended the raising of 5,000 men as a 'Republican Guard', but the nature and the form of this force had yet to be explored.[78] Second, the JCS were more sanguine about West Germany's willingness to rearm, while Britain was more cautious about assuming West Germany's wholehearted readiness to join the Western defence system. Lastly, the JCS were more straightforward in their approach to this problem than British leaders. They took for granted that: 'France [can] be persuaded to recognize that the USSR is a greater menace to the independence of France than is Germany', but they did not examine, as Britain did, the question of priorities for European rearmament or whether there would be genuine apprehension on the part of the Soviet Union about the military recovery of the Federal Republic.[79]

In response to the JCS proposal, the State Department argued that

(1) the economy of the Federal Republic was still too weak to be able to finance any military contribution to European defence;

(2) the majority of West Germans were content to leave their security to the Western forces of occupation and did not wish to rearm themselves;

(3) nor were the Europeans, especially the French, ready to accept a rearmed West Germany as a future ally while their fears of German militarism prevailed; and

(4) the creation of a Federal police should not be regarded as a first step towards rearmament.

It was therefore important to gain time to build mutual confidence between the Germans and the other Europeans by continuing the existing policy of promoting the economic and political association of West Germany with the European community, which would outweigh 'the risk we may be taking by not adding German manpower in a military sense to the West'.[80]

17

The disagreement between the State Department and the Joint Chiefs of Staff did not come into the open prior to the Korean War. While Washington tried to interpret the JCS proposals as the basis for a future programme, which might be employed when circumstances permitted, the Pentagon did not press their views further.[81] The US decision to adopt a cautious approach to this issue conformed to the wishes of Britain and the other European countries. At a meeting in London in early May, Bevin and Dean Acheson, the American Secretary of State and an enthusiast for European integration,[82] agreed that the question of West Germany's military integration was too 'premature' to be discussed fully within the Western alliance.[83]

However, Washington was not as decisive as London about the question of ultimately including West Germany in NATO. Kennan expressed his opposition to the NATO solution in April 1950, describing it as 'unsound' and 'confusing the present Western European objectives'.[84] Moreover, the State Department, as Bevin feared, regarded the proposed Schuman plan as a 'real encouragement' to the policy of 'firmly cementing Germany into the West'.[85] In Washington's eyes, this might open the way to a Franco-German reconciliation and eventually lead Western Europe to support West German rearmament, while suspecting correctly that France preferred this approach to the idea of directly including Germany in NATO.[86] In other words, American leaders expected the Europeans to solve the question voluntarily on the basis of European ideas.

Washington's wait and see policy in part reflected a traditional American reluctance to be involved in European power politics. Although the Cold War persuaded Congress to accept a peace-time alliance commitment to Western Europe through NATO, US membership was intended to provide psychological and material support in order to inject a new momentum into a demoralised Europe.[87] She was careful lest her participation in NATO should dampen European aspirations for closer unity and was not enthusiastic about British and Canadian hopes that the North Atlantic forum would eventually deal with European economic and political as well as military issues.[88] The Americans anticipated that once the Western Europeans and West Germans became sufficiently united to contain further Communist advances, the initial American objective in Europe would be achieved. As Britain correctly suspected, Americans expected that a full West German defence contribution would enable them to withdraw American forces stationed in that country.[89] Conversely, Britain looked to the US to be the counterweight to a rearmed West Germany. The NATO solution was therefore more suited to Britain's interests than to those of the United States. To make matters even more complicated, the Americans also looked to Britain to counterbalance a rearmed West Germany.

By the early summer of 1950 the State Department had developed far-sighted views on the nature of the problem with which Western Europe was confronted in the immediate aftermath of the Second World War.

> We can never forget that we have a double problem. Even confronted with the Soviet menace as we are, we cannot ignore from the long-range point of view the vital importance of obtaining the right kind of Germany.[90]

The problem was how to contain a resurgent Germany without keeping American forces permanently in Europe. In the eyes of the State Department and its diplomats in Europe, Continental Europe, lacking 'potential economic and military strength', was unlikely, without British support, to deter possible West German military revanchism. Charles E. Bohlen, the senior State Department expert on Soviet affairs and then US Minister in Paris, informed Kennan on 20 October 1949 that:

> It is…in our view completely unrealistic to expect the French to take [the] leadership in the formation of a coalition or union…which would have more than a 50–50 chance of being a German-dominated coalition.[91]

However, Washington was as yet uncertain about the feasibility of Britain's active participation in Continental integration, given that Britain's initial enthusiasm for cooperating with France in the cause of European unity had declined. This tendency in London to disassociate Britain from a purely European organisation was likely to continue. Even more embarrassing to the US was that Britain was now emphasising the 'special relationship' with the US in the wider context of the Atlantic community.[92]

American civilian leaders did not deny that Britain was 'our most dependable and powerful ally',[93] but they felt that Britain tended to abuse this notion of a 'special relationship' in order to bolster her position as a global power, while at the same time using her close ties to the United States to justify her lack of support for European unification. Britain's attitude was regarded by the United States as a serious impediment to the achievement of American aims in Europe.[94] Washington did not fully take into account Britain's increasing concern for the strategic stability of Western Europe. This concern and the recognition of her physical inability to contain both

19

the USSR and a future rearmed West Germany drove Britain to rely on American power.

Thus, while these two powers were in agreement about some form of future West German rearmament, on the need for a slow and careful approach and on the necessity for the containment of a rearmed West Germany, they could not agree as to which of them should act as a counterpoise to a rearmed West Germany, despite their shared anxiety for a strong and stable Europe.

At this stage, however, the United States was not in a hurry to rearm the Germans and she was slower than Britain to react to heightened Cold War tensions after the autumn of 1949. While Britain began to formulate a rearmament programme,[95] the United States, despite the recommendations contained in NSC-68 of April 1950 for an all-round strengthening of US military capabilities to allow for an appropriate response at any level to a Communist assault upon the Western hemisphere, was reluctant to raise the existing defence ceiling of $13.5 billion.[96] In early May Harry S. Truman, the President of the United States, even suggested publicly that there would be less spending on the armed forces in 1951.[97]

2 THE AMERICAN INITIATIVE IN NEW YORK, SEPTEMBER 1950

1. The outbreak of the Korean War

The latent disharmony in the attitudes of Britain and the United States towards the Cold War was revealed after the outbreak of the Korean War on 25 June 1950. For Britain, the Korean crisis increased her uncertainties about Soviet intentions either in risking a major war or in encouraging limited and localised conflicts like that in Korea. Furthermore, the war reinforced her determination to maintain close relations with the United States so that she could persuade Washington to keep the conflict restricted to the Korean peninsula and, above all, encourage the Americans not to divert their attention from Western Europe, which as the Cabinet Defence Committee put it in July, was now 'in a most unsatisfactory and disturbing condition'.[1]

To the United States, on the other hand, the Korean War clearly demonstrated that the Soviet Union intended to use armed force to gain her ends, as had been assumed in NSC–68. Given her new found role as 'world policeman', the United States felt that it was essential for her to act to stem the rising tide of Communist expansionism, as otherwise she would appear to be weak. Accordingly, the Americans embarked upon a massive rearmament programme and altered their forecast of Soviet readiness for war with the West from 1954 to 1951, while at the same time they urged the NATO powers to rearm.[2]

The success of the European NATO countries' rearmament programmes depended upon the provision of American financial assistance, the condition on which France insisted before she would agree to raise a further fifteen divisions. Britain also felt unable to go ahead with her rearmament programme unless she was assured that $550 millions of US aid would be forthcoming.[3]

Washington remained non-committal on the subject, partly because the preliminary rearmament proposals that the European states put forward to the US, 'fell far short', in Acheson's opinion, 'of any candid view of an adequate defense'.[4] The underlying principle behind Congressional approval of the Mutual Defence Assistance programme of 1949 – that further American support would depend upon greater European efforts – remained unchanged. Thus, if Western Europe proved to be incapable of mobilising its own resources sufficiently to resist aggression, Britain was well aware that the next American action would be to propose the utilisation of 'the untapped reserve of German manpower'.[5]

The East German para-military formations (what became known as *Bereitschaften* (alert-units)) of between 50,000 and 60,000 men were believed by the West to be the basis for the formation of an East German army of 150,000 by 1951. To oppose this force the allies disposed of nine battalions in West Berlin (three each from Britain, France and the United States) which were considered to be just adequate to defend West Berlin from an invasion by East German forces for a limited period. Western forces stationed in West Germany were believed to be capable of resisting any East German attack which occurred before the end of 1950, provided that the allied garrisons were brought up to full strength, and that satisfactory arrangements were made for the co-ordination of the allied occupation forces in the event of such an emergency.[6]

In this bleak situation the British were scarcely surprised by the 'wave of panic' which swept over West Germany in the aftermath of the North Korean invasion of South Korea. The Korean War also provided Adenauer with the opportunity to demand that the allies reinforce their troops in West Germany. At the same time he urged the three occupying powers to authorise the Federal government to create an armed police force of 150,000 men, a sharp rise on the figure of 25,000 men he had proposed in April.[7]

Adenauer's démarche was the result of his increasing dissatisfaction with the assurance given by the three Foreign Ministers in May 'that an attack on our [Western] forces in Germany would constitute an armed attack within the meaning of Article 5 of the North Atlantic Treaty'.[8] Although this suggested allied willingness to defend West Germany in the event of Communist aggression, the Korean War greatly reduced the psychological effect of this declaration in West Germany. Adenauer warned the three High Commissioners on 17 August 1950 that 'unless real resolution was shown by the Allies, the West German population would adopt a neutral attitude'.[9] Indeed, the more pronounced West German fear of the threat from the East after Korea, accompanied by their decreasing confidence in allied military capabilities, contributed not only to the weakening of their morale in the mood of 'ohne mich', but also to the renewal of West German press speculation about a possible allied move towards the utilisation of West German manpower for immediate military purposes.[10]

Similar speculation was voiced elsewhere on the Continent. The debate on a European army (which was to include some West German contingents) took place in the Consultative Assembly of the Council of Europe at Strasbourg between 9 and 11 August 1950. West Germany participated in the Assembly for the first time as an associate member. During the debate, the West German Social Democratic party (SPD) emerged as a staunch opponent of West German rearmament. The party's views closely resembled those of the British Labour government in emphasizing that the question could not be considered before the armed forces of the other West European powers had been fully strengthened. This reaction was due in part to the fact that the SPD, headed by Dr Kurt Schumacher, was concerned that the division of Germany would be deepened if the Federal Republic agreed to military involvement with the West. Unlike the pro-integrationist Adenauer and his Christian Democrats, Schumacher's first priority was the reunification of Germany and he insisted more forcefully than did the Federal government that the West must provide immediate and concrete evidence that they were sufficiently prepared militarily to share with the West Germans 'the same risk and the same chances in warding off a Soviet attack' before he would change his mind on the issue.[11]

The French Government of René Pleven also rejected any suggestion that West Germany should recover her military status until France and her allies had completed their rearmament programmes. Thus, Pleven held the same order of priorities as the British Labour leaders. However, the French delegation at Strasbourg made it clear that the French sought a European solution (as opposed to Bevin's interest in an Atlantic alliance) to the military problem of West Germany, although French ideas about a European army ranged from one which was tightly integrated to one which was loosely federated, thus leaving room for further discussion.[12]

Finally, Winston S. Churchill, the leader of Britain's opposition Conservative party, put forward a resolution calling for 'the immediate creation of a unified European Army', which was adopted on 11 August by the Assembly, after nine words, 'under the authority of a European Minister of Defence' were inserted at the request of the French. This amendment was intended to appeal to European

23

federalists by creating the impression that this was the precursor of eventual European military unification.[13] Churchill's motion was received favourably in Paris and was welcomed by Adenauer.[14] Bevin, who also believed that Churchill was trying to steer Western Europe towards federation, commented later that 'Churchill made use of the Assembly as a platform, stealing the show by calling for "the immediate creation of a unified European Army".'[15]

Bevin's conjecture was debatable, as Churchill's European army was to include American contingents. Letters Churchill wrote to Attlee and Truman and a minute he addressed to his son-in-law, Duncan Sandys, during the summer of 1950 envisaged the formation of a European army of at least 36 divisions within the next six months. This force would comprise 15 French, 6 British, 6 American and 5 West German divisions, together with 3 divisions from the Benelux countries. Although about 17 per cent of the total force was to be provided by the United States, Churchill insisted on describing it as 'a European army'. Every national armed unit in this army was to be treated equally and given the same arms. West Germany would not be allowed to create her own national army but was to be provided with equipment and munitions from 'a European pool'. His ideas remained nebulous and he was not much concerned about the political framework in which a European army was to be established.[16]

Churchill's Council of Europe resolution created a wave of excitement among the enthusiasts for a federated Western Europe. More importantly, his initiative brought the West German rearmament question to the fore in a dramatic fashion.

2. *The British proposal for the formation of a Federal police force*

The outbreak of the Korean War did little to reduce Britain's fundamental fear of a rearmed West Germany, and both her civilian and military authorities adhered to the policy towards a future West German military contribution which they had formulated before the War: (1) that the political difficulties must first be overcome; (2) that any move towards rearming West Germany should be 'gradual and unostentatious'; and (3) that priority should be given to the strengthening of other Western military forces, especially the French army. Similarly, both Britain's short- and long-term objectives remained essentially unchanged, that is, for the immediate creation of a West

German Federal police force and for the ultimate incorporation of West Germany into NATO.[17]

With these considerations in mind, the Chiefs of Staff in mid-August completed a study on the military problems involved in utilising West German resources for the West. They proposed that a future West German contribution to Western defence should consist of coastal naval forces, a balanced army of 20 divisions, with a reserve of 10 divisions, a tactical air force of 1,100 fighters and a 'substantial anti-aircraft force' equipped with guided weapons. Equally important were the safeguards on which they insisted in order to prevent a resurgence of German militarism. The Federal Republic would not be allowed to possess: (1) large naval vessels or submarines; (2) airborne forces; (3) heavy and medium bombers and long-range maritime aircraft; and (4) atomic, biological and chemical weapons and long-range missiles. Although their paper containing these recommendations emphasised that the approach to West German rearmament should be on a step by step basis, the Chiefs of Staff recommended that 'His Majesty's Government should take the initiative now in approaching the other Allied Governments chiefly concerned so as to enable the rearmament of West Germany to be started.'[18]

However, when the Foreign Office received the Chiefs' paper, its officials concluded that the Service Chiefs wanted to raise a West German army at once, a proposal which they rejected as totally impracticable.[19] Slim realised that the Foreign Office had 'slightly misunderstood the intention of the Chiefs of Staff', and he attempted to retrieve the situation by informing Bevin at the end of August that 'it was unrealistic to suppose that it would be possible immediately to go ahead with the programme advocated in their [COS] paper'.[20]

There was some truth in Slim's argument: at a COS meeting early in May when the Foreign Office was represented by Andrew Gilchrist, the deputy head of the German political department, the military planners had been asked to draw up a detailed proposal on the method, scale and timetable of a future West German contribution to the West.[21] The COS believed that the ensuing paper fulfilled this request, whereas Bevin and Ivo Mallet, the Assistant Under-Secretary of State in charge of German affairs, had not been made fully aware of what the planners had been originally asked to do.

However, it is also true that, although the Chiefs of Staff did not propose any major alteration of Britain's policy on the question of West Germany's defence contribution, they did go slightly beyond their agreement with the Foreign Office in May. At that stage, the idea of including West German soldiers in NATO was considered

25

merely as a long-term possibility and the British government did not intend to take any initiative on this. The Chiefs of Staff, however, now raised this as an immediate issue, reflecting their greater emphasis on the military necessity for West German rearmament as a result of the Korean War. On the other hand, the Foreign Office was more concerned about the strong political and strategic objections which would be raised to such a proposal by Britain's European allies, and in particular by France. An even more important consideration for the Foreign Office, in the face of the uncertain security situation in Europe after the Korean War, was that any plan to rearm West Germany would require cautious handling in order that Soviet Russia and East Germany were not provoked into taking countermeasures.[22]

As a result of joint discussions between the Chiefs of Staff and the Foreign Office, which took place at least twice towards the end of August, the Minister of Defence, Emmanuel Shinwell, who shared the Foreign Office's apprehensions, eventually adopted the Foreign Office line, and the Chiefs were persuaded to follow suit. There would be no suggestion of an eventual formation of West German contingents within NATO, but other more immediate steps were to be taken in accordance with recommendations put forward by Kirkpatrick and further developed by the Foreign Secretary.[23] The Defence Committee endorsed this procedure on 1 September 1950 and it became the basis for a revised British policy towards West Germany which was to be discussed with the US and other European powers at the forthcoming New York NATO meeting.

The major aspects of this new policy were: (1) the cessation, apart from a few exceptions, of industrial dismantling and demolition in the Western zones; (2) the improvement and expansion of the West German Frontier Customs police force; (3) the transformation of the auxiliary forces (composed of both Germans and displaced people) serving with the occupation armies into properly constituted military formations; (4) the end of restrictions imposed on certain industries to permit a greater West German industrial contribution to the West European economy; and (5) the establishment of an armed, Federally controlled police force of some 100,000 volunteers and a similar force of 3,000 men in West Berlin.[24] Overall this plan did not represent a radical departure from that formulated by Britain's leaders before the Korean War. Thus, the Foreign Office now came to accept a COS recommendation of May 1950 that the demolition programme should be abandoned. Britain was well aware how anxious the US was for the revision of the Prohibited and Limited Industries Agreement. As for points (2) and (3) they were merely regarded as appropriate measures to reinforce West German security forces as a result of Britain's perception of an increasing threat from the East.[25]

An important feature of this proposal was the decision to create, in response to Adenauer's frequent appeals, a Federal police force of 100,000 men. The implications of this were two-fold. The Western High Commissioners had already examined the question after Adenauer had raised it in April 1950. They had, however, decided on 28 July against authorising the creation of a Federal police force, mainly because of French opposition to such a degree of centralised control. However, the Allied High Commission was prepared to approve the setting up of a mobile police force on a *Land* basis, which would be subject to Federal control in an emergency. This force would have an initial strength of 10,000 men (one tenth the figure proposed by Britain).[26]

This projected force would not be designed for action against the East German *Bereitschaften* and was to be deployed entirely for the purpose of internal policing. Neither the British nor the Federal government were satisfied with this proposal, since 10,000 men recruited for internal police duties would do nothing to strengthen West Germany's security in the face of increasing concern in West Germany about the country's vulnerability to Soviet pressure after the onset of the war in Korea.[27] Bevin's proposal was intended to reverse this allied decision. Furthermore, Bevin and the Foreign Office had now been converted to the opinion held by the Service Chiefs since May 1950 that police units on a Federal basis should be organised on the model of the *Bereitschaften* in East Germany, although the 150,000-man force requested by Adenauer was considered to be too large and was reduced to 100,000.[28]

There were a number of arguments put forward by the British in support of their plan for a Federal police force. First the Soviet Union's reaction was unlikely to be very strong in view of the precedent she had already created by establishing the *Bereitschaften* in East Germany in violation of the Potsdam agreements. This special West German police unit was intended to counter increasing East German armed strength, as well as to fulfil a useful role in relieving the allies of some of the burdens of maintaining internal security in West Germany. Secondly, the British wanted to do something to sustain West German morale, and providing them with an armed police force might help them to 'make a beginning with [the] task of defending themselves'. The third argument was a political one: Britain feared that to ignore Adenauer's request might bring about his downfall and his replacement by the radical Schumacher. It was also

27

sensible to take advantage of 'having the Germans ask us [the West] for something'.[29]

Nevertheless, Britain remained uneasy as to whether her proposal would be acceptable to the other allies. Although the French agreed that there should be a police force in West Germany larger than the 10,000 men authorised by the High Commissioners, Britain was uncertain that she could persuade France to consider a Federally controlled rather than a *Land*-based police organisation.[30] As the Chancellor's plan for a Federal police force became public knowledge towards the end of August, there were increasing fears voiced in France and in West Germany that a central police force in West Germany, capable of warding off an East German military attack, might be the precursor of West German rearmament, leading to the possible revival of the *Wehrmacht*.[31] However these fears were not so pronounced as to impel the British Government to reconsider its policy on the subject. Britain still had to reach agreement with the United States on this issue and Washington was as equivocal as ever about West German rearmament.

3.   At the eleventh hour – preparations for the US 'one package' proposal

The American 'one package' proposal placed before the North Atlantic Council in New York had emerged from a rather hasty and haphazard process of resolving what Acheson described as 'an ugly dilemma' facing the Pentagon and the State Department over how to bring about West German rearmament.[32] With the shock of the outbreak of the Korean War, the Pentagon now pressed the Truman administration as a matter of urgency to agree to the rearming of West Germany.[33] The Secretary of State was also converted to the need for securing a West German military contribution to the West – 'the idea that Germany's place in the defence of Europe would be worked out by a process of evolution was outmoded'.[34] During the course of a long discussion with Truman at the end of July, Acheson explained (and Truman generally agreed) that:

> the question was not whether Germany should be brought into the general defensive plan but rather how this could be done without disrupting anything else that we were doing and without putting Germany into a position to act as the balance of power in Europe.[35]

Accordingly, the State Department in mid-August drew up a proposal for the formation of a European defence force which was to contain military contingents from the US and West Germany, under a NATO Supreme Commander. This followed Britain's plan in that the underlying principle behind it was for the inclusion of West Germany in NATO, ultimately as a full member country. The Americans insisted that a means must be found to allay European fears that West Germany might eventually become the dominant military power on the Continent. This meant that West German manpower and resources would have to be assimilated as far as possible into the Western defence system. Furthermore, the State Department intended that this should be achieved under American leadership, which entailed the United States accepting greater responsibility for the military security of Western Europe.[36]

The State Department's proposal required, first, that the production and procurement of major military materials should be placed under central direction, although in fact this process was to be initiated by the US as the major supplier of such materials to the Western European powers. Secondly, Washington wanted the European defence force to be integrated at least up to the level of 'the lowest completely balanced ground, air or naval fighting unit'.[37] An American Supreme Commander was to be appointed, whose task would be to supervise the thorough integration of this force within NATO. He would have absolute control over the national contingents at divisional level and therefore the national general staffs would not be allowed to interfere in the chain of command between the Supreme Commander and the armed units comprising the European defence force.

Finally, West Germany's contribution was to be limited to ground forces in units of divisional size which would be integrated with non-German units at corps and higher levels. West German soldiers would be recruited and paid for by their national government, but West Germany was not to set up a general staff. The Supreme Commander would oversee the training and deployment of these West German military contingents.

The French rearmament programme, which reached Washington early in August, also suggested that NATO establish a 'common defence' plan. At the core of this plan was the pooling of the resources of the NATO members to obtain the standardization of arms and equipment, 'the fairest possible distribution of the financial burdens of the common defence', and the formulation of a joint policy on the allocation of raw materials.[38] The Americans regarded this French suggestion as a clumsy tactic designed to extract as much aid from the US as possible, while at the same time minimising

29

France's commitment to the defence of Western Europe. Nor did Washington consider that it would be possible, given the pressures imposed on its policy makers by the Korean War, to find the time to organise this complex and ambitious French programme.[39] In any case, it was out of the question for the United States to participate in such a supranational organisation unless she was assured of ultimate authority over it. The State Department's proposal thus demonstrated the limitations the United States would impose on her own participation in any new defence organisation in her efforts to further European military unification.

The State Department presented this proposal to the Pentagon on 16 August 1950. The Defense Department, while approving the formation of a European defence force, frowned on the idea of the limitation of national sovereignties on the grounds that this would not only impair the military effectiveness of the armed forces of the participants, but would also create organisational confusion within NATO. Instead, the Joint Chiefs of Staff favoured West German participation in such a defence force on a national basis, although appropriate safeguards against a resurgence of German military power would be imposed upon her. This closely resembled the ideas of the British Service Chiefs.[40] Furthermore, the JCS insisted that preparations for the initial defence of Western Europe were the responsibility of the Europeans and that their acceptance of this must be the prerequisite for the fulfilment of the US commitment to Europe.[41]

In making this demand, the Pentagon differed from the State Department, for the latter did not call for the immediate inclusion of West German units in NATO, but suggested that 'an effective European integration…would provide the basis for [an] eventual German contribution to the common cause in Europe'.[42] In contrast, the Pentagon asserted that priority must be given to West German rearmament over the provision of US aid and US troop reinforcements and the appointment of an American supreme commander, and that in order to ensure this, all these requirements should be incorporated into a single package proposal.[43]

Two weeks of fruitless debate between the State Department and the Pentagon ensued and on 27 August, with the New York NATO conference only two weeks away, Truman ordered the two departments to formulate an agreed policy by 1 September, although he later extended this deadline to 5 September. As a result, Acheson was forced to compromise and on 30 August he told General Omar Bradley, the Army Chief of Staff, that 'German rearmament must be part of any plan to send American forces to Europe'. In effect this meant that Acheson had given in to Pentagon pressure for 'a speedy, frontal assault on the problem of a German armed force'.[44] On 11 September, the State–Defense joint agreement, later circulated as document NSC-82, was finally endorsed by President Truman as US policy for the defence of Western Europe and for future West German rearmament.[45]

In this document, the basic ideas of the State Department were transformed into proposals which met the Pentagon's desiderata. First, the original State Department concept of an integrated European defence force was watered down, with more emphasis now being placed on the role of each European participant in organising and commanding each individual contingent on a national basis, while the Supreme Commander was confined to a supervisory role. Second, American willingness to increase her contribution to European defence was made contingent upon what the Europeans were prepared to offer. The proposed increase in US ground forces from two to six divisions depended upon the Europeans agreeing to substantial increases in their armed forces, and this applied particularly to Britain and France. The United States would appoint an American general as Supreme Commander only if the other participants requested this, and then only if they assured the US that: 'they will provide sufficient forces, including adequate German units, to constitute a command reasonably capable of fulfilling its responsibilities',[46] thus allaying Pentagon fears that a totally inadequate force structure in Europe would 'condemn the American commander...to complete disaster if war broke out'.[47]

Lastly, as a result of this State–Defense compromise, the Americans managed to evade having the onus of rearming the West Germans thrust upon them, since the Europeans now had to make this decision. Indeed, apart from the US demand for immediate West German rearmament, the document put forward a rather random selection of ideas, the inevitable product of the hurried bargaining between the State and the Defense Departments. The initial West German contribution was to be a balanced ground division as a maximum size of national unit and which was to be incorporated into non-West German contingents. No mention was made of the future size of West German forces, either in the joint State–Defense agreement or in the American memorandum presented to the NATO Council on 15 September,[48] but the JCS in fact contemplated an initial strength of 2 to 4 divisions, rising eventually to 10 to 14 divisions.[49] West German resources would also be utilised for the common defence, but 'vital

31

military equipment' necessary for West German armed units would be supplied from non-West German industrial sources.[50] Moreover, the United States did not anticipate that these proposed German forces would be controlled by the Federal government, nor would they be allowed to have their own general staff or their own command system. The implication of all this was that the Americans wanted to extract a few divisions from the Federal Republic of Germany and make use of her industrial resources for the purpose of enhancing European security without allowing West Germany to recover her military status as a sovereign power.

The Secretary of State was now able to present this to the New York conference and to attempt to secure the unanimous approval, at least in principle, of the other allies to its contents. He later confessed that 'he had erred in agreeing to the package formula, and to its presentation at New York'.[51] At the time, however, there were several reasons why he felt impelled to adopt the Pentagon's tactics.

The heated discussions on a European army in the Strasbourg Assembly of the Council of Europe had demonstrated that Europe was now searching for some form of West German contribution to the defence of Western Europe. Adenauer, in his proposal to the three Allied High Commissioners for a centrally controlled police force on 29 August 1950, once again mentioned a possible West German contribution to the defence of Western Europe 'if an international West European army' was 'to be set up'.[52] The progress of European rearmament, despite strong US pressure, was far below US expectations. Furthermore, the continuing deterioration of the military situation in South Korea at the beginning of September added to Acheson's difficulties. Convinced that the Korean War was inspired by Moscow, Bradley feared that it was 'a tactical or strategical diversion – tactical to cover a Chinese communist invasion of Formosa, strategical to cover a Soviet invasion of Western Europe'.[53] Faced with savage fighting in Korea, JCS concern about the possible loss of Europe became more acute.[54]

These considerations increased the Pentagon's determination to secure not only greater European defence efforts, but West German rearmament as well. This determination was reinforced by growing Congressional pressure. Elections to the US Congress were due in November and Acheson's competence as Secretary of State was being seriously questioned by Republican Senators like Robert Taft of Ohio, the chairman of the Senate Republican Policy Committee, and Kenneth Wherry of Nebraska, the Senate Floor Leader, both of whom seemed willing to abandon Europe in favour of concentrating US efforts on fighting Communism in the Far East.[55] Accordingly, Acheson had to obtain the military's agreement before he could achieve his aim of providing more US aid and troops to Western Europe,and this meant that he was compelled to accept a package formula which would incorporate military as well as Congressional demands.

Fortunately for the Truman administration, the Joint Chiefs of Staff remained firmly committed to the strategy of 'Europe first' after the outbreak of the Korean War.[56] This strategy was, however, rooted primarily in such military interests as the acquisition of strategic bases in West Europe and US participation in NATO military planning, and was not intended to saddle the United States with 'a long and hazardous commitment to a collective defence effort'.[57] Moreover, the military was faced with the fact that the US could not afford to fight two wars in Asia and Europe at the same time. While Bradley claimed that 'Korea was comparatively a minor irritation', it nevertheless drained US resources away from the European theatre. The Europe-first strategy had to be subordinated to some extent to the requirements of the Korean battle fields.[58] The Pentagon's refusal to contemplate an immediate and increased US commitment to Western Europe stemmed both from their unwillingness and their inability to do so. Consequently, the Pentagon's one-package approach was 'immovable'.[59]

4.   The New York conference of 12–26 September 1950[60]

Given France's continued opposition to the adoption of any measures towards rearming West Germany – beyond the creation of a *Land* police force – and Britain's reluctance to take any positive steps towards securing West Germany's participation in NATO, it was predictable that the New York conference (with Acheson in the chair), which comprised three tripartite talks with two NATO Council sessions, would become an ordeal for the United States. The achievement of American objectives therefore required the US to exercise firm leadership over the conference, but this was unlikely, given that the American Secretary of State himself was not convinced of the wisdom of the Pentagon's 'package' deal. Acheson's doubts in turn suggested that, depending on how the discussions developed at New York, he might agree to modify the American proposal. Indeed, when the three Foreign Ministers met between 12 and 14 September, prior to the opening of the NATO Council meeting, the package proposal soon became the subject of intense controversy.

Both Robert Schuman, the French Foreign Minister, and Bevin welcomed the US decision to reinforce her troops in Europe and her proposal for the establishment of an integrated force, but neither comprehended that an immediate West German contribution to this force was an essential ingredient of the American package. It was not until the second day that Acheson finally elucidated US principles to Bevin, who informed London on 13 September that:

> At today's meeting Acheson made it quite clear that the President's undertaking to station troops in Europe is dependent on the assembly of a sufficient force to make the whole enterprise successful…in the US view this could not be achieved without some German participation in the defence of Europe.[61]

Moreover, Britain's proposal for a Federal police force was brushed aside by the American Secretary of State as merely a peripheral West German contribution, the details of which would have to be further considered in the context of allied occupation policy for West Germany. Bevin was surprised that Acheson had raised the West German military question in such a brusque way,[62] but at the same time he recognised that a great virtue of the package proposal was that the United States was prepared to pledge herself to a deeper and more direct commitment to NATO and, 'consequently', as he explained to London, 'in view of [the] stakes involved I propose to give general concurrence'.[63]

London at first also failed to grasp the full implications of the package proposal. The Cabinet's reaction on the 14th was that Bevin should not at this stage agree in principle to any form of German rearmament which went beyond the measure envisaged in the British proposal. However, on the following day, having belatedly realised that the US demand for West German rearmament was a *sine qua non* of a further American contribution to the defence of Western Europe, the Cabinet reluctantly reversed its policy. It was also appreciated that to approve the proposal in principle would still leave considerable leeway for further procrastination, for it would be some time before any West German armed units were able to participate in the unified European defence force.[64]

Nevertheless, there was an underlying feeling of bitterness in the Cabinet that Britain had been presented with no other choice but to endorse the US proposal in principle. The Korean War increased the importance in British eyes, not only of preserving the Anglo-American 'special relationship', but also of ensuring that the United States remained committed to the defence of Europe. Furthermore, the Cabinet feared that any ostentatious British effort to persuade the Americans to modify their policy might play into the hands of the neo-isolationists in Washington – as Kenneth Younger, the Minister of State at the Foreign Office, commented: 'the enthusiasms of today give place to the enthusiasms of tomorrow'.[65] Sir Donald Gainer, the Permanent Under-Secretary of State for the German section, minuted gloomily:

> While this situation must be regarded as one which was beyond our power to avert and as something which cannot be weighed in the balance against the immensely valuable revolution in US policy in the defence field of which it forms a part, we have to bear the danger in mind and do our best to prepare against it.[66]

As Gainer suggested, even if the 'offer' contained in the US package proposal was irresistible, it carried with it the danger that a decision to rearm West Germany would lead to a further deterioration in Britain's relations with the Soviet Union. Sir William Strang, the Permanent Under-Secretary of State, was apprehensive that:

> By this decision and fateful act, I think that we confess to ourselves that we believe war to be inevitable. Indeed, I fear that we make it inevitable, for Russian reaction must sooner or later be expected, which will force us to make war.[67]

While official opinion in London was deeply depressed that Britain had been forced to support the US proposal to form West German military units, Bevin succeeded in New York in emasculating the Pentagon's rigid formula and transforming it into a more realistic and flexible proposition. During the New York conference the package proposal evolved in four stages. During the opening stage – the preparatory tripartite talks of 12–14 September – Acheson remained ostensibly loyal to the Pentagon's requirements. During the second stage – the NATO Council meeting of 15–18 September – he began to show signs of retreating from the original proposal. While there was unanimous recognition that the inclusion of West German armed elements in NATO was militarily imperative, the majority of the ministers present, including the French, supported Bevin's thesis that, before West Germany could join, a unified force of the other powers under a supreme commander must first be established. The Secretary of State did manage to secure approval in principle from all the representatives, except Schuman, for the US package proposal, but this carried with it a tacit understanding that once the NATO countries had agreed to West Germany's rearmament in principle,

35

but without determining the timing and the form of her rearmament, the United States would undertake additional commitments to Western Europe. Despite Bevin's efforts, the problem of obtaining French agreement, even in principle, remained.[68]

During the third stage – the tripartite talks between the Foreign and Defence ministers of France, Britain and the United States on 22 and 23 September – the United States' attitude softened further. Acheson revealed that the US had no really cut and dried plan for the use of West German forces for Western defence. French intransigence was reinforced by the presence of Jules Moch, the Defence Minister, at the meeting – he represented hard-line French opposition to West German rearmament. When Bevin, Shinwell and Air Marshal Sir William Elliot met him at a dinner party on the 23rd, Moch asserted that:

> if the Americans insisted on making German rearmament a condition of the acceptance of the help which they were offering, he would prefer to forego both and content himself with five instead of ten French divisions, and place these on the French frontier instead of in Germany.[69]

Acheson was, on the other hand, accompanied by General George Marshall, who had been appointed as the US Secretary of State for Defense on 21 September and who shared Acheson's readiness to modify 'the tactic of the rigid and brusque one package proposal'.[70]

At a private meeting of the three Defence Ministers during a tea break on 22 September, Marshall showed Moch a paper which had been 'hurriedly prepared' by the US Joint Chiefs of Staff on the 21st.[71] This paper suggested some immediate steps that could be taken to enable West Germany to play a role in the defence of Europe, in case the three powers failed to reach agreement in principle on the US package proposal. The measures proposed in this paper, which came to be known as 'General Marshall's Eight Points', included the following recommendations: (1) the immediate strengthening of the *Lander* police so that they would reach parity with the East German *Bereitschaften*; (2) an increase in the size and quality of the German labour service units; (3) the formation of Sabotage Security Units as a countermeasure to fifth column activity; (4) the production of light military equipment in West German factories; and (5) the utilisation of German raw materials for the production of heavy equipment outside Germany.[72]

Except that Britain had suggested the formation of such police units under Federal rather than *Lander* control, the rest of 'Marshall's Eight Points' bore a striking resemblance to Britain's earlier proposals. Moch accepted them, thus enabling the Defence and Foreign Ministers to reach agreement on Marshall's Eight Points on the 22nd.[73] In fact, it was no longer clear precisely what form a major West German contribution to the defence of Europe would take. However, Acheson had no intention of withdrawing the package proposal since this would mean the abandonment of the entire US scheme for the formation of an integrated defence force in Europe. Thus, Marshall's concession to the French left the Secretary of State in an awkward position – he could only assert that, despite this agreement on supplementary means of activating West German military resources, 'decisions on the creation of an integrated force in Europe and on German participation in such a force would not be put behind us entirely'.[74] In private talks with Bevin later, on 28 September, Acheson admitted that some 'confusion' had arisen on the American side because Marshall had rushed to the meeting without any preliminary discussions with the Secretary of State.[75]

During the fourth and final stages of the conference, the package proposal, which had been modified slightly during the first NATO Council meeting and had nearly been upset entirely as a result of Marshall's interim proposals during the subsequent tripartite meeting, occupied the central position at the resumed NATO Council session on the 26th. The familiar stalemate emerged: the French remained adamant in their refusal to accept it in principle, while in response the US declined to proceed with her plans to improve European defence capabilities. In the event the final Council session unanimously accepted only the US proposal for creating the unified force, which was to be set up under centralised command – but its finalisation was suspended pending further consideration by the NATO Defence Committee, especially on the question of a West German contribution. The communiqué therefore stated that:

> The Council was in agreement that Germany should be enabled to contribute to the build-up of the defence of Western Europe and, noting that the occupying powers were studying the matter, requested the Defence Committee to make recommendations at the earliest possible date as to the methods by which Germany could most usefully make its contribution.[76]

With this final communiqué, the long, hectic and dramatic New York conference concluded on an anticlimactic note.

5. The New York conference and its aftermath

Although the New York conference did not resolve the problem of West Germany's defence role in the West, the three Foreign Ministers did make some progress on the future of allied occupied West Germany and West Berlin at the tripartite talks of 18 and 19 September, and what they agreed upon was listed in the voluminous communiqué issued on the 19th. These included provisions for ending the state of war with West Germany, the recognition of the Federal Republic of Germany as the sole and legitimate representative of Germany, some relaxation in both the occupation regime and the agreement on prohibited and limited industries, the setting up of a police force under *Land* control of 30,000 men for internal security purposes (thus trebling the number which had been approved by the three Allied High Commissioners in July), and an allied guarantee of West Germany's external security.[77]

Overall agreement on these general questions at least demonstrated allied willingness to allow West Germany progressively to recover her sovereignty, and thus helped to ease tensions between the West Germans and the allies. Both Adenauer and Schumacher welcomed the communiqué. The Chancellor commented that the allied pledge, more strongly worded than previous assurances, to 'treat any attack against the Federal Republic of Berlin [sic] from any quarter as an attack upon themselves' was a 'most gratifying step forward'. At the same time the three allies agreed to increase their forces in West Germany.[78]

Adenauer was embarrassed by the failure of France to agree to a definite contribution of West German military units to West European defence. Although the 'ohne mich' mood prevailed in Bonn, Britain received indications from its diplomatic sources that the idea of West Germany joining in the common European defence was beginning to gain in popularity. However, West Germany's leaders and the West German electorate were determined that her contribution must be 'on terms of equal rights and equal obligations', which would eventually entail equality of rights in other fields as well.[79] The demand for equality was bound to overshadow all future allied negotiations with West Germany, since none of the NATO powers was really prepared to contemplate the inclusion of West Germany in an integrated European force on the basis of complete equality.

The police force issue created further controversy. There appeared to be two approaches to this subject in New York. First, Britain assumed that she had failed to secure her original proposal for the formation of a *Federal* police force of 100,000 men comparable with the *Bereitschaften* of East Germany – as Adenauer had requested – when Bevin accepted the Franco-American agreement of 18 September that the allies should adhere to the original concept of *Lander*-controlled police forces for *internal* security purposes. However, the question became more complicated when, during the tripartite defence and foreign ministers' meeting on 22 September, General Marshall put forward an interim proposal to organise a *Land*-based mobile police force which was to be equipped with automatic weapons so that it could also deal with external aggression.[80] Although the three occupying powers had endorsed Marshall's interim proposal, it remained unclear whether this agreement entailed the abandonment of the allies' earlier decision of 18 September for the creation of a small and lightly equipped *Land*-based mobile police force to preserve internal law and order.

In fact, Britain was now becoming doubtful about the wisdom of her original proposal – which Marshall had revived albeit on a *Land* basis – for the overt rearmament of West Germany through its police force. By the middle of October the Attlee government recognised that the prospect of West German anti-invasion forces disguised as police would have little appeal either to West German public opinion or to her politicians. Schumacher, particularly, was nervous about any suggestion of creating 'the nucleus of a "black" remilitarisation' and he could probably rally sufficient support to prevent the implementation of any such allied scheme.[81] In the meantime, the three High Commissioners, after discussions with Adenauer and Schumacher, agreed to the creation of a relatively strong police force – the two West German politicians wanted a 'considerable strengthening of the police force' – but they (the three High Commissioners) made it clear that its role must be confined to that of internal policing.[82] The subject of the police force was never thereafter emphasised by Britain, the US or the other members of NATO.[83] The significance of this episode rested on the dichotomy between the immediate contritribution to Western security a militarised police force would provide and the long-term danger inherent in setting up such an organisation at all. There was also involved in this issue a conflict of interest between West Germany and the allies: West Germany did not want to fall in with makeshift allied plans designed to exploit her manpower by covert means as a way of compensating for the inability of the allies to protect West Germany adequately against the Soviet bloc. Speidel was not keen on creating this special police force, which would not help the Germans to achieve an equal status in the European community.[84]

Conversely, Britain had hoped that her original scheme for a Federal police force was the safest way of obtaining some form of West German military assistance, thus avoiding the need for immediate and radical measures for achieving an outright West German contribution to NATO. However, these British calculations were upset both by West Germany's aversion to the creation of a police force of the kind Britain and Adenauer had wanted, and by the American initiative at New York in launching a plan for West Germany's integration into the Western defence system.

3 THE SEARCH FOR ALLIED AGREEMENT

1. Britain's response to the Pleven plan

After the New York conference in September 1950 Britain still hoped to resolve the Franco-American deadlock over the question of West Germany's defence role in the West by persuading the French to follow the British example and accept the American package proposal in principle. If France agreed to this, Britain and France could then press the United States to move cautiously on the West German rearmament question. Bevin conveyed Britain's real feelings on this subject to Schuman on 9 October 1950:

> It was with no enthusiasm that I accepted in New York the principle of German participation in the integrated force for the defence of Europe. My attitude reflected that of the Cabinet. We do not like the idea of German re-armament any more than the French do.[1]

Despite this disclaimer, the French believed that the British had genuinely changed their minds on the German problem and that France had been betrayed by Britain for the sake of her connection with the United States.[2] France was faced with a dilemma: while she was anxious to see the American offers contained in the package proposal finalised at an early date, she was unable to endorse the American thesis on West German rearmament, which was part of that proposal. France felt that she had to put forward an alternative to the American plan, since otherwise, as Jean Monnet, the author of the Schuman plan, explained to Pleven, on 14 October: 'Our resistance will have proved futile. We shall lose face, and lose the political initiative.'[3] Monnet was assigned the task of producing a French counter proposal 'in the same spirit and by the same methods' as the Schuman coal and steel plan.[4]

On 24 October the draft text of the Pleven plan was presented to the French National Assembly. The plan entailed the creation of a European army of a supranational character by merging military units 'at the level of the smallest possible unit', (presumably a battalion), financed by a common budget, under the leadership of 'a European Minister of Defence, responsible to a Council of Ministers and a Common Assembly'. Two days later the Assembly approved both the Pleven plan (by 343 votes to 220) and a government resolution which opposed the creation of a German army and a German Defence Minister (by 402 votes to 168).[5]

Under the Pleven plan a European army of an initial strength of some 100,000 men, including West German units, would be created, while a European NATO integrated force, excluding West Germany, would be established on the basis of existing national armies, as was provided for in the US package proposal. The European army would eventually be merged as 'a federal unit' with the other national forces of NATO. The existing European NATO members who would participate in the Pleven plan would continue to retain control over their national forces, which would not be part of the European army, while West Germany would be denied such a right.[6] According to the French Defence Minister, in the initial stage the French contribution to the European army would number some 50,000 men, nearly half the planned strength of that army and, as a result, the West German contingent would be tightly controlled by the French *cadres*.[7]

Thus, the Pleven plan was intended to prevent West Germany either acting independently in the future, or becoming militarily threatening. This was where it differed fundamentally from the American plan, which would allow the West Germans eventually to have a general staff, a national army and even membership of NATO in their own right.[8]

Bonn, London and Washington were well aware of the motives behind the Pleven plan and their initial reactions were negative. Adenauer was, of course, opposed to a plan designed to keep West Germany in a subordinate status and was depressed by the continuing French distrust of the Germans.[9]

Bevin dismissed the plan as unrealistic. His opinion was shared by Shinwell, Marshall and Acheson, who all regarded it as a French device to postpone consideration of the German defence contribution and separate it from the rest of the package proposal.[10] The tone of the official comments in London and Washington was guarded: the British government received it 'with great interest', while the US government gave it a 'cautiously favorable response'. Both countries expressed the hope that the plan could be successfully implemented within the NATO framework and emphasised that such a far-reaching proposal would require further study.[11]

This diplomatic language concealed significant differences of opinion between the British and the Americans about the plan. Within a month of the conclusion of the New York conference, General Marshall persuaded the Joint Chiefs of Staff to move closer to the State Department's position by agreeing to the appointment of an American Supreme Commander as soon as possible rather than to continue to insist on their original demand that 'sufficient forces will be provided to constitute a command reasonably capable of fulfilling its responsibilities'.[12] Accordingly General Dwight Eisenhower agreed to undertake this task when Truman suggested his nomination on 28 October.[13] The Pentagon also reversed its decision on the timing of West German rearmament and now endorsed the British view that West German participation in a European defence force should follow the strengthening of allied forces and that the formation of German units should be 'initiated immediately *upon the establishment of the integrated force*'. Thus the creation of West German military contingents would not now be undertaken until after Eisenhower's appointment, nor would they contribute to the defence of Western Europe until the Western powers had become militarily stronger. Nevertheless, the Pentagon continued to insist that these concessions would not be put into operation until the other NATO powers unanimously accepted the US package proposal in principle.[14]

Consequently, the Pleven plan placed the Americans in a quandary since its rejection would leave them faced with the same deadlock as before, while on the other hand its acceptance would lead to a long delay in securing German participation in Western European defence. However to proceed at once with the organisation of integrated NATO forces with full American participation would make it doubtful that German armed units would ever be created under the 'hopeless' French plan.[15]

For her part, Britain was concerned that the French counter plan would result in the further postponement of the American decision to put her package proposal into effect. The Foreign Office doubted (correctly) that the Americans would be satisfied with the Pleven plan as a practical solution to the deadlock. However the British believed that, if the Americans were 'to make the best use of the implicit admission in the French plan that some German contribution to Western defence is necessary and acceptable', German rearmament could be unanimously accepted in principle without defining the means by which Germany would contribute armed forces either directly through NATO or through a European army.[16]

The three-day debate in the NATO Defence Committee between 28 and 31 October revealed the inability of both the United States and Britain to resolve the dilemma. The French adopted a 'take it or leave it' attitude to the Pleven plan, with Moch insisting throughout the conference that the French government would not discuss the German question except within the context of the plan.[17] Only Belgium and Luxembourg expressed an interest in studying it: the majority expressed doubts about its political and military soundness and therefore about the prospects for its successful implementation.[18] Finally the issue of a German contribution was referred to a joint meeting of the NATO Council of Deputies and the NATO Military Committee, who were instructed to try to find an agreed solution to the problem and report back to the NATO Defence Committee as soon as possible. Although this compromise satisfied French and American *amour propre*, the US Defense Secretary continued to insist that his government would not implement its package proposal for an integrated force in Europe until the question of the participation of West Germany 'had been decided'. Thus there had been no change in the attitudes of the two powers: the American package proposal was held up, while the French maintained their refusal to accept the American thesis on German rearmament.[19]

Given Britain's opposition to schemes for European federation, the French government appreciated that the proposed European army would probably have to be constituted without Britain's participation.[20] Of the other European allies, the Netherlands was anxious that Britain should participate, otherwise the army would be dominated by what Dirk Stikker, the Dutch Foreign Minister, described as a 'continental bloc'.[21] Clearly the Pleven plan balance was in jeopardy although, on 30 October, the British Cabinet agreed that, while Britain would not participate in a European army, she would not object to its formation if the French secured the agreement of her Western European neighbours.[22] This reluctant approval reflected Britain's basic attitude towards the whole question of European federation: she did not want to become too closely involved in such schemes but, at the same time, she did not wish to appear too hostile to any European initiatives on the subject in case this resulted in the loss of her influence in Western Europe.

2. Bonn's price for a West German military contribution

The continuing deadlock over the German defence issue adversely affected the relations between the Western allies and the Federal Republic. NATO disunity hardened West German public opinion against West Germany's participation in Western European defence and increased West German receptiveness to alternative solutions to the problem of her future role, such as a neutralised and disarmed West Germany.[23] Adenauer fought hard to retain his control over the Cabinet. Early in October his autocratic style of leadership led to the resignation of Dr Gustav Heinemann, the Minister of the Interior, who opposed Adenauer's efforts to achieve an early West German defence contribution.[24]

The Chancellor also faced a strenuous campaign by the SPD party against his plans. The leader of the SPD, Kurt Schumacher, was regarded by the British Labour government as a difficult character, and this had resulted in its eventual decision, after initially supporting 'fellow Social Democrats', to favour Adenauer and his CDU party instead.[25] Twenty years younger than the Chancellor, Schumacher was an intellectual, a reformer and a devoted upholder of the cause of social democracy, a strong contrast to the realist, flexible and father-like figure of Adenauer. While both men detested Communism and were willing to side with the Western allies, they differed in their negotiating tactics in dealing with the Western powers. The SPD did not believe that West Germany should make too many concessions to the West since the inclusion of the Federal Republic in the Western defence organisation was, after all, in the best interests of NATO. Nor did Schumacher agree with Adenauer's 'negotiating from strength' approach – that West Germany's participation in a common European defence force would smooth the way towards the eventual reunification of the two Germanies.[26]

Schumacher wanted to defer the remilitarisation question and await Soviet and East German reactions to NATO proposals for a German defence contribution while at the same time insisting that the Chancellor 'exact the highest possible price' from the West for a German contribution.[27] Consequently, as Adenauer's pro-rearmament posture became more pronounced, Schumacher's opposition to it hardened.

Indeed, opinion polls in 1951 showed that the Social Democratic party was becoming the most popular party in West Germany while support for the Chancellor's Christian Democratic Union had reached its lowest point since the 1949 elections. In his anxiety to thwart the

45

SPD, Adenauer was spurred into seeking further concessions from the Western occupying powers,[28] and on 16 November he presented the Allied High Commissioners with a list of demands for a drastic and speedy relaxation of the allied occupation regime. He also renewed his August proposal for the early introduction of a system of contractual agreements to replace the Occupation Statute. In addition he called for an early allied decision on West Germany's association with Western European defence arrangements and for the rapid reinforcement of the allied occupation forces in West Germany.[29]

Gilchrist noted that 'Adenauer is up to his old game of making conditions' in order to find a way out of his increasingly difficult parliamentary position and in the wake of recent SPD victories in the *Lander* elections in southern Germany.[30] A more important consideration for the West, however, was Adenauer's implication that the immediate granting of political equality to West Germany would make it easier for the Federal Republic to agree to make a subsequent defence contribution. The British Foreign Office was divided between hard-line elements on the West German question like Lord Henderson, the Parliamentary Under-Secretary, and those who advocated a moderate approach, like Gainer and Mallet. The hardliners believed that the West Germans should at first be given equal rights within a Western security arrangement in which they would be allowed to make only a limited contribution: when this had been achieved the West would consider granting them full sovereign status.[31] Mallet, in a minute of 16 November, rejected this approach:

> if we need Germany's help and want Germany to form part of our Western bloc, we must make her a full member of the club and reconcile ourselves to seeing her smoking a large cigar in a big chair in front of the fire in the smoking room.[32]

However, Mallet and Gainer were in agreement with Lord Henderson that this was unacceptable in the immediate future. Gainer was concerned that, once West Germany secured complete political sovereignty, even with her rearmament restricted in scope, it would be difficult for the West to prevent her from once again becoming a predominant European power if the threat from the Soviet Union receded.[33] This was the essence of the German problem: the British were as apprehensive as the French about the emergence of a politically independent and militarily resurgent West Germany.

The longer NATO delayed making a concrete defence proposal to West Germany, the higher the price the West would have to pay for a West German contribution in terms of West Germany's recovery of her full political equality. William D. Allen, the head of the

German political department at the Foreign Office, feared that:

> we have now gone so far along the road towards German rearmament that there is really no going back, except perhaps as part of a genuine world settlement with Russia

while Gilchrist added that 'the real importance of Adenauer's approach' was to remind the West 'of the length of the road we have still to travel before a German contribution can be arranged'.[34]

3. *The origins of the Spofford plan and Bevin's counter proposal*

Britain persisted with her efforts to find a solution to the continued Franco-American deadlock over the West German rearmament question. On 17 November the Chiefs of Staff put forward a compromise plan which made two major recommendations. The first was that the basic German military unit should be reduced from the US proposal for a 'balanced ground division' to a 'Brigade Group' or 'Regimental Combat Team' (equivalent roughly to one-third of the size of a division). The Chiefs recognised that, while this was not a militarily ideal solution, it did conform to the spirit of the Pleven plan. The second, and perhaps more important, recommendation was based on a suggestion made by Slessor that the French should be allowed to experiment with the formation of the proposed European army in parallel with the adoption of the British-modified US plan, i.e., the organisation of a brigade group.[35] However, before this COS compromise proposal could be referred to the Cabinet, the allies were already examining a similar scheme at the NATO Council of Deputies,[36] which became known as the Spofford plan or the Spofford compromise.

Charles Spofford, the American chairman of the NATO Council of Deputies, was the originator of this plan, but the final draft which emerged in mid-December was the result of the collective efforts of the Military Committee and the Council of Deputies of NATO. The main purpose of the Spofford plan was to introduce provisional arrangements for the utilisation of West German effectives, pending a final decision on a permanent framework for a German contribution, whereby the US project for a European integrated force would be put into operation, to include the recruitment and training of German troops to form lightly armed land forces on the level of a regimental combat team, together with a small German contribution to NATO tactical air and naval units. The proposal set out in some detail how this initial German rearmament could be achieved, but its main recommendation was for the opening of two sets of negotiations: the first, between the three occupying powers and the Federal Republic for the immediate, but provisional, remilitarisation of West Germany as suggested in the Spofford plan, and the second for a conference on a European army, to be convened by the French.[37] Hence the Spofford plan was intended to be a face-saving political arrangement designed to paper over the disagreement between the French and the Americans about the method and timing of a German defence contribution.

The Americans anticipated that if, as they thought likely, the French scheme was found to be unworkable at the conference on the European army, the combat-ready German units could be converted into balanced divisions and integrated directly into NATO as the US had originally planned.[38] The US would lose nothing as a result of the adoption of this procedure since the intention behind the Spofford plan was to provide a method of raising German units for eventual association within a Western defence system in whatever form was finally agreed upon.

British influence at these Council of Deputies meetings between mid-November and mid-December was minimal: they offered no constructive ideas either against or in support of the Spofford initiative. Sir Frederick Hoyer Millar, the British representative on the Council of Deputies, merely expressed his country's concern at the continued delay in developing a common European defence system and repeated British criticisms of the political features of the Pleven plan.[39] It was therefore doubtful whether the COS proposal would have been presented to NATO as a British compromise solution if the Spofford plan had not been formulated, as the Cabinet would probably not have approved it. This lack of interest on the part of Britain's politicians, and particularly of Bevin, reflected significant differences in the attitudes of her civilian and the military leaders towards the Pleven plan.

The Chiefs of Staff thought that the French plan contained 'a better means' to remove 'the bogey of the creation of a German National Army',[40] than anything else that had hitherto been put forward. Slim explained the Army's position at a COS meeting on 9 November;

> to be militarily practicable, any proposals for German re-armament must accept the formation of German divisions...This would in fact mean that there would have to be a German War Office to organise and administer it. Furthermore, no matter what safeguards were

given, Germany should she so desire would without great difficulty be able to clandestinely re-form the German General Staff.[41]

Of course, the *raison d'être* of the Pleven plan was to prevent this from happening. Indeed this was its sole virtue, since otherwise the plan suffered from two fatal shortcomings – it was both militarily impracticable and unpopular with the other European NATO allies.[42] Thus the British military leaders were in agreement with their American counterparts that, since there would appear to be no chance of the French creating a European army along the lines of the Pleven plan, no harm would be done by letting the French try it out.[43] When the French experiment failed, Britain would be able to persuade them to accept the only alternative, the Anglo-American proposal for a NATO solution.[44]

Bevin could not agree with the Chiefs' proposal. Perhaps because of his poor health, Bevin tended to contemplate the French approach in the gloomiest terms. He wrote on 24 November that a European army under French leadership 'would be too feeble to defend itself and yet strong enough to assert itself in world politics', and that 'it would thus be a sort of cancer in the Atlantic body'. Bevin had devoted much energy to the establishment and consolidation of NATO and he was anxious that, before 'the European federal concept' gained 'a foothold within NATO', 'we must nip it in the bud'.[45]

Accordingly the Foreign Secretary suggested a new British initiative, the concept of 'an Atlantic Confederate Force', a self-contained Atlantic system whereby an Atlantic army would not only be subject operationally to the NATO Supreme Commander but would also be controlled administratively by a high authority under the NATO council. The idea was to prevent the creation of an exclusively European federation by substituting instead an Atlantic framework which would be looser than the French system but would have more centralised political and military authority over the Atlantic force than that proposed in the American scheme for a NATO integrated force. Mallet had suggested a similar plan for an Atlantic confederated force a week earlier, and the Foreign Secretary, despite his awareness of the likely objections to it, was keen to present it as a counter to the French plan.[46]

The proposed Atlantic army would create a similar dilemma to that of the Pleven plan – the surrender of military sovereignty in the cause of Atlantic defence, an area which was, furthermore, much broader than that covered by the Pleven plan. It was highly unlikely that the Americans would accept it, while the British COS were not prepared to abrogate Britain's military sovereignty by committing Britain to a scheme of federation, even if this was within an Atlantic framework.[47]

Moreover the presentation of this plan to the Cabinet occurred almost at the same time as the emergence of the Spofford compromise, and Attlee, Shinwell and other ministers could not regard this grandiose and impractical design for an Atlantic confederated army as a promising alternative to the Spofford solution. Not that they saw the Spofford approach as an ideal solution to the German rearmament question either, since it would give the West Germans a lever with which to explore two methods of participating, either directly through NATO or within a European army, and it might open the way to the creation of a powerful European army, although ministers were more dubious than the Foreign Secretary about the latter possibility.[48] Bevin's opposition, which bordered on an obsession, to the Pleven plan seemed to have made him incapable of formulating a concrete policy towards the German problem. The initiative was again lost to the Americans: neither the COS compromise nor Bevin's Atlantic counter proposal were put forward as official British recommendations.

4. Reversal or acceptance? Britain's attitude towards the Spofford plan

The ambiguities and doubts surrounding German rearmament made it vulnerable to external influences, and in particular to Soviet opposition. The Soviet Union had good reason to fear the remilitarisation of Germany and she became even more alarmed when she discovered that the Western allies were seeking not only to rearm West Germany, but also to create an enlarged transatlantic defence system by associating West Germany with NATO.[49]

Moscow therefore made a series of protests about Western plans, the first of which, on 19 October, was followed in more definite form by the Prague communiqué issued on 21 October by the Soviet Union and her seven European satellites.[50] It was timed deliberately to disturb France, the NATO partner most opposed to the American plan for a German defence participation and whose government was on the point of finalising the Pleven plan. The Prague communiqué was followed by a Soviet note to the other three allied occupying powers on 3 November, proposing a meeting of the Council of Foreign Ministers (which had adjourned *sine die* during the spring of 1949) to examine the question of the demilitarisation of Germany. In response

Bevin took the initiative in persuading France and the US, whose initial reactions differed, to join Britain in working out a tripartite reply to the Soviet Union. The basis of this reply was that the West would agree to a meeting of the Council of Foreign Ministers provided that the Soviets were prepared to discuss broader issues than the German question and which would lead to a relaxation of Cold War tensions.[51]

Washington regarded the Soviet protest as the usual anti-Western propaganda campaign which should not be taken seriously. However, the United States did respond to Bevin's appeal for allied unity in the hope of pleasing the French and thus encouraging them to help solve the German question.[52] Paris, on the other hand, regarded the Soviet move as a sign of a more conciliatory attitude towards the West and intended to use this as a justification for French reluctance to move ahead on the German rearmament issue.[53]

The British Labour government occupied the middle ground between the US and France: while they were as suspicious of the Russians as were the Americans, they were also more sensitive than the USA to the calculated risk of provoking the Soviets by rearming the West Germans. Thus, while Britain perceived no major change in Soviet foreign policy which would cause the West to modify their search for improved NATO defences, she did feel it worthwhile to invite the Russians to talks with the three Western powers to see 'whether they have really any genuine desire for peace'. If such a meeting contributed to the reduction of international tensions, even on minor issues such as an agreement on an Austrian peace treaty which had been held up since 1949, so much the better. In order to gain a better negotiating position with the Soviet Union, it was essential for the West to act in unison. Bevin therefore urged the French Foreign Minister to be reasonable about the German question (this was shortly before the Spofford plan became known).[54] At the same time he had been trying to prevent the United States from engaging in any provocative action, hence his strong opposition to an American proposal for reinforcing West Berlin.[55] The British leadership thus exercised a moderating influence on allied policy towards the Soviet Union.

However, Cold War tensions heightened when the Chinese launched a second offensive in Korea and 'the United States forces in Korea were being pushed right back and things looked black'.[56] Attlee flew to Washington (Bevin was not well enough to accompany him) for a conference with President Truman between 4 and 8 December 1950. The immediate cause of this visit was a British scare about an apparent suggestion by Truman, at a press conference on 28 November, that the atomic bomb might be used in Korea. The Americans, however, hurriedly denied any such intention and the urgency attached to the subject had disappeared by the time the talks opened.[57] The thorny question of a German defence contribution was bound to arise during the discussions on the defence of Western Europe.[58]

The worsening situation in Korea had a dramatic impact on Bevin's thinking on the German rearmament question: in his view the present circumstances were 'entirely different from those which obtained when we first agreed with the Americans that it was safe to embark on German rearmament'.[59] The Spofford plan had not yet been finalised, since it needed a few finishing touches before being presented to the NATO Deputies on 7 December. Theoretically it was still possible for the British government to avoid further involvement in this issue, an idea which occurred to Bevin on 4 December, just after Attlee had left London for the United States, when the Foreign Secretary wanted to telegraph to the Prime Minister that NATO should postpone making any approach to the government of the Federal Republic or announcing publicly any agreement on the issue of German rearmament until the Western powers had fully built up their military strength.[60] This implied that otherwise Britain would not support the Spofford plan and might even withdraw her acceptance in principle to German rearmament, although the Foreign Secretary might have wanted this to be a temporary measure until the international climate had improved.

Bevin also feared that the US would not send reinforcements to Europe since they would be required in Korea and, as a result, Western Europe would be placed in an even more precarious position, as the Russians might, as a result, be tempted to react sharply to any irrevocable step on the part of NATO towards securing a West German defence contribution. This argument was reinforced by a suggestion by Sir David Kelly, the British ambassador to Moscow, that the settlement of the German problem should be deferred until the West discovered what could be achieved by the four power talks, for which the three occupying powers were now drafting an invitation to the Soviet Union.[61]

Bevin's thesis was debatable. Although Attlee was told by the Pentagon that the plan to transfer two divisions from Korea to the European theatre by the autumn of 1951 would not now take place owing to the situation in the Far East, the Americans did agree to send instead, within the following year, some National Guard divisions, who, although they needed training, were the only troops available in the United States.[62] Given that American forces were intended to strengthen the deterrence in Western Europe, the quality of the actual forces deployed was relatively unimportant to the West.[63] Furthermore, when the Soviet Union had protested, in the autumn, to the West about the provocative nature of the proposed German defence participation, the Foreign Secretary had shown no sign then of modifying his attitude towards the German question. If the West now reversed its policy, this would be seen by the Soviet Union as evidence of indecisiveness on the part of the NATO allies. More to the point, the political effects of a British change of heart about German rearmament would be deplorable: it would upset the Americans, confuse the French and irritate the West German Chancellor. It was hardly surprising, under these circumstances, that the Minister of Defence and the Chiefs of Staff opposed the sending of Bevin's telegram to Attlee, and that there were four heated discussions on the subject between the COS and the Foreign Office between 4 and 6 December.[64] Finally, the Foreign Secretary agreed to tone down the initial draft in order to make it clear that there would be no going back on the British agreement on the principle of German rearmament. All his proposal now amounted to was a suggestion that the NATO ministerial talks be postponed in order to avoid an early decision on the issue. The COS views were also inserted at their request in the final draft and the telegram was sent to the Prime Minister on 6 December.[65]

Attlee rejected this suggestion on the same day, using the same arguments that had been put forward by the Chiefs of Staff. The Prime Minister told Bevin that the French were now moving towards accepting the Spofford plan, while Truman had reassured him that General Eisenhower would be sent to Europe as Supreme Commander as soon as NATO accepted the Spofford plan. In the light of these developments, Attlee described it as 'unthinkable' that 'we now wished to pause and draw back'. The Prime Minister tried to calm Bevin's 'apprehensions' by telling him that 'the French proposals will almost certainly fail and that we should not worry too much about them'.[66]

In reply, Bevin 'naturally' accepted Attlee's 'judgement and have authorised Sir F. Hoyer Millar to agree to the Spofford plan' at the next meeting of the Council of Deputies. However, the Foreign Secretary insisted on making two reservations to this authorisation. First, the British government was not to be committed to a precise timetable for an approach to the Federal Republic and, secondly, he questioned whether the formal NATO meetings were the correct forum in which to discuss the plan.[67]

These reservations were obviously designed to delay the progress of NATO discussions about German rearmament but, in the event, they did not succeed in their intention. The Spofford proposal stipulated that negotiations with Adenauer should commence once the plan had been approved by NATO. Secondly, at the NATO Defence Committee meeting in Washington in October, the NATO Defence Ministers had asked the NATO Council of Deputies (dealing mainly with the political aspects of the plan) and the Military Committee (consisting of the Chiefs of Staff of the NATO members under the authority of the NATO Defence Committee) to produce a joint report on the question of a German contribution.[68] If the two NATO Committees agreed to the Spofford proposal, it would then be referred to the NATO Defence Committee and thereafter to the NATO Council of Foreign Ministers. The most important hurdle to overcome in this process would be to reach agreement in the Council of Deputies – and Bevin had now instructed the UK Deputy to approve the Spofford plan. Once this happened the higher committees would give it automatic support.[69] It would thus be impossible to discuss the Spofford plan without using the formal NATO meetings and equally impossible to avoid a public announcement after such meetings.

Thus Bevin's reservations did not have any practical effect and, indeed, when Attlee mentioned them to Truman, the President not surprisingly made no comment and merely noted that the British agreed to the Spofford plan.[70] The French also agreed to accept the plan,[71] and the way was now clear for its presentation to the NATO Council meeting in Brussels.

The Brussels conference on 18 and 19 December resulted in the United States finally agreeing to increase its defence efforts in Western Europe in return for NATO's approval of the Spofford plan. The unanimous support of the NATO powers both for the setting up of the integrated NATO defence force and for increased rearmament programmes by all the members of NATO was followed by Truman's public announcement about the appointment of General Eisenhower as the Supreme Commander and also by the debates in the US Congress over the despatch of US troop reinforcements to Western Europe.[72] Compared with the long drawn-out New York conference in September, the December assembly meeting went so smoothly that it appeared to confirm the solidarity of the North Atlantic powers in their determination to defend Western Europe.

On the other hand, these developments seemed to diminish NATO's interest in the German rearmament question. There was no specific reference to the French proposal for a European army in the final communiqué, and the conference merely gave tacit approval to it as part of NATO's general support for the Spofford recommendations, which included a conference on a European army to be convened by the French. As for the transitional arrangements, the final communiqué stated that the three Allied High Commissioners were to 'explore...in discussion with the Government of the Federal Republic' the question of including West Germany within NATO 'on the basis of the Council's proposals'.[73]

This somewhat less prominent treatment of the German question resulted from allied concern about the likely difficulties they would face in negotiating with Bonn, where the two leading German political leaders were now vying with each other in demanding ever more allied concessions in return for West Germany's agreement to make a contribution towards the defence of Western Europe – in the words of the British High Commissioner, '[t]hey expect us to woo them and behave like a woman scorned if we do not approach them as suitors'.[74] In an interview with an American journalist on 11 December, Adenauer made it clear that the Federal government could not accept the unequal status conferred on it by the Spofford plan and that, if it was presented to him officially, he would have to reject it. He also clarified his definition of equality – by this he meant not 'numerical equality' but 'complete equality for the German military forces'.[75] It was evident that Adenauer sought to achieve for West Germany the most generous terms on which to acquire membership of the Western club, whereby the West Germans would sacrifice fewer resources for the defence of Western Europe than the other NATO members but, in return, they could justify this as a safeguard for the West Europeans against the reemergence of a militarily strong Germany.

The Spofford plan stated that the West German contribution should not exceed 20 per cent of the total of the NATO forces, and this numerical restriction was to serve Adenauer's interest in a small West German contribution to the defence of Western Europe. However, he insisted that the German contingents should be treated on equal terms with the other NATO forces in the quality of their weaponry and of their command authority. The Spofford proposal did not provide for such equality for the West German soldiers. For instance, the size of a German unit would be restricted to a brigade group, whereas the other NATO units would be at divisional level.

Furthermore, the plan discriminated against Germans in terms both of their equipment and the weapons they would be allowed to manufacture, while the raising of West German armed units would be supervised by the three allied occupying powers and would also be subject to the authority of the NATO Supreme Commander in Europe, against whose decisions the Federal Republic would have no legitimate right of appeal, as she would not be a member of NATO.[76]

Acheson was compelled to admit that the West German attitude to the question of their rearmament was now crucial. In a memorandum of 19 December he wrote that: 'the crux of the matter is not the French but the Germans. If the Germans do not want to fight how are we going to hold east of the Rhine?'[77] Eisenhower was equally pessimistic[78] and, in consequence, the three Foreign Ministers agreed that they should approach the Federal Government cautiously, without creating the impression that the Western powers wanted to rush the rearmament issue. The three allies also appreciated that they should progressively move towards granting West Germany full sovereignty and that 'progress on the part of Germany in defence matters would entitle her to corresponding advances in freedom and equality'.[79]

Although the timing and method of West Germany's defence contribution remained unsettled, the Brussels conference succeeded in giving NATO greater military credibility as well as in separating the German question from the urgent problem of setting up a European integrated force. Despite Bevin's overreaction to the Spofford plan and the rising international tension, the British government obtained what it had sought in September.

5. Attlee's four conditions

In the House of Commons on 12 February 1951, Attlee set out four conditions for a German contribution to the defence of Western Europe. First, the rearmament of NATO countries must precede that of West Germany; second, allied forces must be significantly strengthened before West German armed units could be raised; third, West German units must be associated with the other NATO forces in such a way as to preclude the reemergence of a West German military threat; and, lastly, there must be agreement with the West Germans on the level of their contribution.[80] Although Attlee's four conditions did not represent a radical departure from existing government policy, the timing of the statement was significant.

The Western allies now embarked on a new phase of negotiations with the Federal Republic about West German rearmament.[81] It would therefore be some time before the three occupying powers could examine West Germany's conditions for her participation in Western European defence and before they could reach an agreed policy on the subject. The impact of the cumbersome package deal on the German problem had now been softened. Furthermore, the Franco-American divergence on the remilitarisation of West Germany had also been buried by the Spofford compromise. At the same time, after a further exchange of notes between the three Western powers and the Soviet Union, there was now a definite prospect of preliminary talks with the Russians to discuss an eventual meeting of the Council of Foreign Ministers. The question of a German defence contribution to Western Europe might then prove to be a useful bargaining counter in negotiating with the USSR and, until then, the British government was anxious to postpone any practical steps towards German rearmament. Hence, Attlee was in a better position to urge a cautious approach towards this controversial problem.[82]

Domestically, the Prime Minister's speech also demonstrated that, contrary to the popular impression, the British government was not rushing to rearm the West Germans and, moreover, helped to clear up, in the Minister of State's words, 'an unholy muddle', which had resulted from the British involvement in the German question.[83] Labour party MPs were confused and divided over this issue. Although those who opposed West German rearmament were mostly on the left of the party, the motives for their opposition were mixed. Some, like Hugh Dalton were anti-German but not anti-American, others on the 'Bevanite' wing, like John Freeman, were anti-British rearmament and anti-American, while Jim Griffiths and Philip Noel-Baker were pacifists.[84] The Attlee initiative also provided guidelines for the Foreign Office and the Chiefs of Staff in coping with Bevin's doubts about the subject: Kenneth Younger, the Minister of State at the Foreign Office who, although relatively junior, often acted as deputy Foreign Secretary during Bevin's frequent illnesses, complained that:

> He [Bevin] wavered from one view to another on German rearmament, first trying to delay it, then joining the Americans in bullying the French for greater speed, then having cold feet about it and vainly thinking of going back.[85]

Some of Younger's criticism about Bevin's conduct may be accurate, but Bevin's attitude generally reflected the mainstream of his Foreign Office officials' thinking, that is their reluctance to rearm the Germans and concern about possible Russian reactions to a West German military contribution to the West.

However, the Labour government achieved some of its goals not by taking positive action, such as putting forward her abortive counter proposal for an Atlantic confederate force and seeking modifications to the Spofford agreement as Bevin originally suggested, but by adopting a wait and see policy. During his last weeks as Foreign Secretary, Bevin saw the Americans becoming more deeply entangled in the European defence system, with General Eisenhower's appointment as NATO Supreme Commander, followed later by the despatch of four additional American divisions to Western Europe.

This coincided with the growing American realisation that their support for the defence of Western Europe was likely to be an expensive undertaking. The implications of both the 'Great Debate' over the assignment of ground forces to Western Europe, which had been precipitated by the famous 'Gibraltar' speech on 25 December 1950 by former President Herbert Hoover, and by the National Security Resources Board's report to the National Security Council on US global strategy (NSC 100) of 11 January 1951, were that the Americans might revise their European strategy by reducing their land forces in Central Europe and concentrate instead on providing air and naval reinforcements to the European theatre. Among other things, these proposals questioned the wisdom of the Truman administration's commitment to Europe, especially in view of the allegedly half-hearted cooperation of the Europeans with the American crusade against Communism in the Far East.[86] Together with growing American realisation of the close connection between West Germany's sovereignty and the West German military problem, these considerations could lead to the further loosening of the linkage between the defence of Western Europe and West Germany's military contribution.

Alternatively, more cordial Franco-American relations suggested that the Americans might support the French concept of European unity, with German rearmament an essential part of the process. Although Adenauer's preliminary response had reduced the prospects for agreement on the Spofford proposal for intermediate arrangements for a defence contribution from West Germany, what the West Germans would actually suggest when negotiations with the allied powers began in earnest remained to be seen.

4 THE DECISION TO SUPPORT THE PLEVEN PLAN

1. The Bonn talks (9 January to 4 June 1951)

As a result of the Franco-American compromise at Brussels in December 1950, France accepted the American demand for the immediate remilitarisation of West Germany on an interim basis as defined under the Spofford plan, and this culminated in the Bonn (or Petersberg) talks between the deputies of the Allied High Commissioners and a German delegation headed by Theodore Blank, Adenauer's close adviser on defence matters, and Generals Speidel and Heusinger.[1] In return for this concession, the Americans agreed that France should convene a conference in Paris on the formation of a European army.

A third set of negotiations on greater political freedom for West Germany was the product of a compromise between the three occupying powers and the Federal Republic of Germany whereby the Allied High Commissioners were authorised to examine with the West German authorities the establishment of a new political relationship for the Republic on as wide a contractual basis as possible. This meant that the Western allies now accepted Adenauer's 'trade-off' policy of acquiring West Germany's political independence in exchange for her military co-operation with the West. The negotiations about this contractual agreement with West Germany did not start in Bonn until May 1951,[2] and the linkage between the rearmament and sovereignty questions was not as clearly defined at this stage as it was to be later in September 1951.

However, these two compromises (one between the French and the Americans and the other between the allies and the Germans) were to some extent incompatible. Was the value of the French concession to the Americans, i.e., her approval of the Spofford plan for the early raising of German formations, eroded by the second compromise, i.e., that a West German defence contribution would be the price for her political equality? West Germany would not rearm unless she was assured that she would be treated as an equal partner of the West, and would hence not agree to her remilitarisation under the Spofford plan before the conclusion of the discussions on West Germany's political status.[3] Thus the allied–German compromise was bound to delay a West German defence contribution to the West. Nevertheless the allies went ahead with the Bonn talks on the Spofford plan, although they agreed that the Germans were to be encouraged to express their views 'freely' on 'the scale and manner' of a German military contribution. The Allied High Commissioners informed Adenauer to this effect on 21 December 1950.[4]

However, the three occupying powers were to negotiate at Bonn on behalf of the NATO powers and, as a result, the allied representatives of the High Commissioners' deputies could not discuss anything not contained in the Spofford plan without reference back to the High Commissioners, their three respective governments, and ultimately the Council of NATO, but neither the three allied delegations nor the West German authorities seemed to understand this cumbersome procedure fully.[5]

Thus, while the Germans were expected to talk 'freely' on West Germany's defence contribution, this would in reality apply only in a narrow sense to the specific military aspects of a German contribution – the preparations for the recruitment, training and setting up of the limited formations of German soldiers who were to be temporarily incorporated into Eisenhower's command pending the outcome of the Paris conference. In this context, if the West German delegation, as seemed likely, disagreed with the notion of an interim solution, the Bonn talks would become deadlocked. Alternatively, 'freely' could be so interpreted as to give the Germans the right to express their general ideas about a West German defence contribution and to allow the allies to listen to them. If such discussions were to take place at Bonn, what was the point of encouraging the French to start negotiations with the West Germans (who had accepted the French invitation to attend the Paris conference)[6] on the specific form of a West German defence participation through a European army before the allied powers had ascertained the views of the Germans about their defence contribution? Thus the *raison d'être* for the Bonn talks was far from clear.

By the end of January the first three meetings at Bonn had demonstrated that West Germany would not accept the Spofford plan. From February onwards only nine meetings took place at about the rate of two a month, which were characterised by allied silence and West

German eloquence.[7] While the German rejection of the Spofford plan was predictable, their delegation defined the conditions for their participation in absolute terms. Most of these were already familiar to the West, such as (1) the substantial reinforcement of allied forces in West Germany, (2) the termination of the existing occupation regime, and (3) the treatment of future German contingents on the basis of equality with those of the other powers.

On the technical and operational aspects, West German representatives envisaged a carefully prepared rearmament programme, the essential components of which had been originally formulated by Speidel and Heusinger[8] and which were finalised at the Himmeroder conference in October 1950. The German plan was based on their twin demands for a significant and efficient German military role and for equality of rights and called for the creation of a force of 250,000 men consisting of twelve ground divisions of 10,000 men each, with the division as the smallest effective unit, preferably in an armoured formation. Thus Bonn rejected the *infantry brigade groups* proposed under the Spofford plan. This ground force was to be supported by 1,900 tactical aircraft, while West Germany would also possess coastal defence forces whose role would be determined by NATO naval planners. These West German defence forces were to be incorporated into a NATO integrated force under the Supreme Commander.[9] Speidel emphasised that the creation of a homogeneous armoured division was 'common practice' in all armies and he warned the conference that if 'the infantry were French, and the armoured were German, artillery Italian...each telephone man or signal man would have to be tri-lingual' and 'there would be difficulties over food as Bavarians would want sauerkraut and beer, French troops white bread and red wine, and the Italians spaghetti and chianti'.[10]

The West Germans also insisted on having a Ministry of Defence on the same basis as the other Western countries, which would be under the control of the *Bundestag* with a civilian Defence Minister at its head. An *Inspekteur*, subordinate to the Defence Minister and whose duties would be analogous to those of a general staff would be in command of all German soldiers. The Spofford plan had, on the other hand, envisaged only the setting up of a German civilian agency to administer the West German contingents, while planning, intelligence, operations and staffing would be the responsibility of the NATO allies, an arrangement designed to prevent the rebirth of a complete West German Defence Ministry.[11]

The West German timetable for participation envisaged the raising of her contingents by the autumn of 1952, provided that the *Bundestag* passed the rearmament bill in May 1951. The training of the nucleus troops would begin in September 1951 and the training of divisions in April 1952. This clashed with the American hope that West Germany would take preparatory steps immediately towards drafting laws governing the recruitment and conscription of West German military personnel, and would select accommodation areas for the German soldiers before *Bundestag* approval, so that a ground force of 100,000 men would be available by the end of 1951.[12]

The large-scale tactical air support proposed by the West German government – the Chiefs of Staff had suggested that the German air force should be limited to less than a thousand aircraft – was a function of German operational plans which depended heavily upon a tactical air doctrine which was no longer accepted by the NATO powers.[13] This doctrine required the appointment of a German army corps commander who would be responsible for two German divisions supported by a tactical air force. British military planners considered that West Germany's main air contribution should be to the aerial defence of her territory with tactical air support as a secondary mission. The German air contingent should be integrated into a NATO air force under the Supreme Commander, as was envisaged in the Spofford plan.[14] The German demand for a separate West German corps commander also violated the Spofford plan, which provided that higher commands above the authorised level of a basic size of German national units (i.e., the brigade group) should be assigned in the initial stages to non-German officers, with gradual modifications to this restriction as and when recommended by the Supreme Commander.[15]

The Chiefs of Staff could not deny that from a technical and military standpoint, the German insistence on the formation of divisions and on a Minister of Defence was based on militarily sound principles.[16] The allies and West Germany diverged on political rather than on military factors: that is, while the allies insisted on specific controls being placed on West German armed units, the West Germans demanded that there should be no discrimination against their forces. On the other hand, the virtue of the NATO solution lay in its progressive approach towards incorporating West Germany into NATO as a full member by allowing for the gradual modification of the safeguards imposed on her, depending upon the quality and quantity of the West German defence contribution, although the Americans were willing to see this process completed in the near future while the French were not.[17]

This division did not, however, threaten an early collapse of the conference. In part this was because, as has already been discussed, the allied representatives had been given only limited discretion in the discussions with the Germans. When the Germans put forward demands which went beyond the conditions laid down under the Spofford plan, they were met in Blank's words, with a 'negative silence by the Allies'. Since the German side suspected that the Spofford plan covered all aspects of the German defence contribution, they found it extremely frustrating that the allied delegates were unable to put forward realistic and specific proposals about the nature of the military contribution that West Germany was expected to make.[18] In fact, the NATO powers had no clear perspective either on the German issue or on the NATO strategic situation. Under the Spofford plan, the final decision on the basic size of a German formation and on the form of allied control over the German defence administration was left to the NATO Supreme Commander. Eisenhower was travelling around Europe and it was not until 2 April 1951 that he formally took over the NATO command in Europe.[19]

Moreover, there were great difficulties early in 1951 in allocating United States military material to Europe owing to heavy American purchases of raw materials as a result of the fighting in Korea.[20] Britain presumed that, as a result, it would be impossible to provide the necessary equipment for West German contingents for at least two years[21] – which tended to encourage a more relaxed attitude on her part to the German rearmament question in this period. When the West German delegation sought an allied estimate of what the total German strength should be in 1952, the year in which German combat-ready soldiers were supposed to appear on the front line under the German schedule, they discovered that the NATO powers had not yet examined a possible German force level for 1952. Britain, then chairman of the NATO Standing Group, hurriedly worked out a projected figure on the basis of the NATO medium-term plan (which had not, of course, taken a possible German contribution into account). However, the Standing Group did not present this figure to the allied representatives in Bonn, mainly because, given the shortage of resources, it was felt that it would be unrealistic to try to forecast the timing or the scale of a German contribution in advance.[22]

In the light of these political and military disagreements, it was hardly surprising that there were no meaningful exchanges of views, or any developments conducive to a Franco-German *rapprochement*, during the twelve meetings between the occupying powers and West Germany at Petersberg. These talks culminated in the unpublished allied 'factual' report of 6 June 1951. This 'Bonn Report', as it was called, was presented for consideration by the three occupying governments before being referred to the NATO Council. In substance it was an account of the German proposals on the technical and military aspects of their rearmament plan, which was about all the Bonn talks had achieved.[23]

2. The European army conference in Paris (15 February to June 1951)

The Paris conference proceeded during the early months of 1951 in parallel with the unsatisfactory Bonn talks. The conference was opened on 15 February 1951 by the French chairman, Hervé Alphand, amid considerable NATO and West German scepticism about the French project.[24] Henry Stikker, the Dutch Foreign Minister, pointed out to Eisenhower in January 1951 at The Hague that NATO, or more precisely the Americans, were in 'error' in permitting the French to organise the Paris conference at that time. The Netherlands government was dubious about the practicability of the European army project and did not believe that it would help to improve Franco-German relations.[25] The Dutch remained as observers at the conference, while the other five powers (France, West Germany, Belgium, Luxembourg and Italy) were the principal participants. Britain, although refusing to become involved in the European army, had to take account of two responsibilities, one for NATO, of which a European army was to be part, and the other as an occupying power in Germany. Accordingly, she also decided to be an observer, with Sir Oliver Harvey, the British ambassador in France, as the chief British representative. The other observer countries were the US, Canada, Denmark, Norway and Portugal, each represented by their ambassadors to France. David Bruce was appointed as the representative for the United States.[26]

Unlike the Bonn talks, which were informal and exploratory, with no written documents exchanged, the Paris conference was a formal body with plenary sessions for general discussions, three military, financial and juridical sub-committees and a steering committee responsible for supervising the subcommittees and reporting back to the plenary session. The French had prepared more detailed memoranda on their concept of a European army than when they had first proposed the project in the autumn of 1950. They were ready to discuss practical problems at Paris, whereas in Bonn they never articulated French views. Conversely, the German delegation intimated that since their views originated from the discussions in Bonn they could only repeat at Paris almost the same proposals as they had at Bonn.[27]

The initial phase of the Paris conference was marked by verbal duels between the French chairman and the German delegation. In his report to Acheson on 9 March 1951, Bruce described the scene as follows: 'French and Germans seem to have locked horns.'[28] The main arguments were over the basic size of a West German military unit and the level of integration in which the West German contingents should be organised, that is, between the French proposal for creating mixed dividions of 16,000–17,000, each consisting of two or three national regimental combat teams, and the West German scheme for organising European corps as the basic European unit to be made up of two or three national divisions of 10,000–12,000 men each. Although the German delegate tried to persuade the French that the difference between them was only one of degree, Alphand denounced the German proposal as 'nothing Europe [sic: European] 'and insisted that the point at issue was one of political importance as well as of principle.[29] What affected French sensibilities most was the implication of the word 'division', rather than the actual size of a division, since, in their minds, 'division' implied the eventual rebirth of an independent German military establishment.[30]

Apart from this, the Germans were dissatisfied with the unequal treatment accorded to them during the first stage of the setting up of a European army (approximately eighteen months after the ratification of the treaty).[31] The Italian delegation, who generally favoured the idea of a European army, proposed the appointment of European Defence Commissioners or a Defence Committee instead of the French concept of a single, powerful Commissioner as the sole supra-national authority, mainly because it would be most unlikely that an Italian would ever be nominated to such a post, which was clearly intended by the French to be occupied by one of their nationals.[32] Moreover, the key question of the relationship between NATO and a European army remained undefined. The other participants said little. Thus, the initial phase of the Paris conference was, as Harvey expressed it, 'in the doldrums'.[33]

3. Sovereignty and/or rearmament?

While the two sets of negotiations over German rearmament were proceeding in Bonn and Paris, the three allied powers had made a number of concessions towards increasing West Germany's political freedom in preparation for the conclusion of a contractual agreement with her. For instance, the Federal Republic could now establish a Ministry of Foreign Affairs, and the Chancellor appointed himself Foreign Minister on 15 March.[34]

In essence, the contractual agreement presupposed the conclusion of a partial peace treaty between the three Western occupying countries and the Federal Republic of Germany, separate from an eventual peace treaty between the four powers and the whole of Germany. Accordingly, there were matters such as the allied control of the Western sector of Berlin, the reunification of Germany, and the legal basis for the presence of allied occupation forces in West Germany, which could not be covered by the contractual treaty. Moreover, the Western allies would need to determine how to maintain their control over the manufacture by West Germany of offensive weapons, over military research and development, particularly in atomic energy, and over heavy industry and civil aviation, but the settlement of such problems would depend upon the scale and the nature of the German defence contribution. It would thus be impossible to complete a contractural agreement with the Federal Republic without resolving the rearmament question.[35]

France informed Washington that priority should be given to a satisfactory arrangement on a German defence contribution through a European army before the solution of the German political question. In contrast, the United States felt that the restoration of West Germany's political sovereignty should come first in order to facilitate an early settlement of the rearmament question.[36] Bevin and his successor after 9 March, Herbert Morrison, supported a simultaneous settlement of the military and political questions. In view of the complexity of the process involved in restoring sovereignty to the Federal Republic, the political negotiations would require careful handling.[37] The same considerations applied to the military problem of West Germany: Britain regarded the Bonn talks as ill-timed, since there seemed to be no immediate possibility of reconciling German demands for political and military equality with the Spofford plan. Now that the West German delegation had confirmed this suspicion, and the Americans had apparently abandoned the attempt to impose the Spofford plan on the West Germans, Britain took less interest in the course of the negotiations in Bonn.[38] The longer these exploratory discussions continued, the more would Britain be pleased since, until these talks were concluded, it would be unlikely that she would be pressed to go further than her 'moral commitment' to the Spofford concept.[39]

The Paris conference on a European army proved to be equally contentious. Indeed, Kirkpatrick and Evelyn Shuckburgh (the head of the Western Organisations Department at the Foreign Office) thought it better to let the West Germans 'kill' the French scheme in Paris and thus destroy the French initiative on the European army.[40] Such an outcome would be highly satisfactory to Britain. As the conference proceeded at a snail's pace in May, Morrison began to appreciate that the French and Germans were at last beginning to tackle the West German rearmament issue seriously and that the Federal Republic might modify France's plan in a more realistic direction. Yet these developments did not cause Britain's political and military leaders to reconsider Britain's position as a 'passive observer'.[41]

Britain and, to a greater degree, France were also reluctant to proceed any further with the German problem until they had learned the outcome of the preliminary talks with the Soviet Union. The meetings of the four Foreign Ministers' deputies, which consisted of seventy-four sessions, were held at the Palais Rose in Paris between 5 March and 21 June, and ended without even reaching agreement on an agenda for a conference of the Foreign Ministers of the four governments. That these talks were likely to collapse was clear by mid-May when the British representative, Ernest Davies, the Parliamentary Under-Secretary of State for Foreign Affairs, reported that, at the fifty-ninth meeting on 23 May, 'No one spoke.'[42] Despite this stalemate, the conference of deputies continued to meet mainly because the French wanted to avoid a breakdown of the talks before the French general elections in June – they feared that the communists would exploit any open disagreement between the powers. The British were equally anxious to convince public opinion in the West that the three Western powers had explored every avenue of agreement patiently and positively with the Soviet Union.[43]

The internal disharmony among the three allied powers over the negotiations with the USSR continued after November 1950, when the Soviets had made their first approach. However, clumsy Russian tactics during the four-power preliminary conference enabled the Western delegates to preserve a degree of unity. Instead of concentrating solely on the question of German demilitarisation as they had in the autumn of 1950, the Soviet Union now attacked West European rearmament in general and insisted that there could be no substantive four-power talks unless the Western powers were prepared to discuss the twin issues of NATO and American military bases in Europe. For the Western powers to accept this demand would suggest that they were the cause of world tension. The West could at least agree that this tension was the result of Soviet expansionism.[44] Soviet intransigence at the conference convinced the British that Stalin was impressed by the deterrent effect of the Atlantic alliance, and Attlee concluded that the West should 'continue to resist encroachment', while Strang regarded the sixteen weeks of futile argument at the conference as a 'failure for the Russians'.[45]

The end of the preliminary four-power talks, which followed both the French elections of 17 June and the conclusion of the Bonn talks on 4 June, suggested to the Western allies that they should now make more serious efforts to break the stalemate over the question of a German defence contribution.

4. The US decision to support the European army project

The United States, while broadly agreeing with Britain, even before the Brussels meeting, that the German problem should be approached circumspectly, had not by the beginning of February 1951, fully appreciated the extent of their failure to obtain West German Support for the Spofford plan.[46] The lack of any sense of urgency on Britain's part, which was reflected in 'Attlee's Four Conditions', irritated Washington, since the Truman administration needed to demonstrate that progress was being made on the question of a West German military contribution in order to persuade the Senate to vote for military aid to Europe.[47] Yet Washington had no clear idea how to achieve this. Acheson, in a telegram to Bruce on 28 June 1951 admitted that:

> it was not possible [to] create Ger[German] units on this interim basis [the Spofford plan] and a complete plan for a Eur[European] Army under Fr[the French] concept has not been completed. We therefore still seem to face [the] same dilemma as before[the Brussels conference].[48]

American civilian and military leaders now began to express a growing interest in the cause of a European army, which at least promised closer European cooperation and a self-contained continental military organisation.[49] It would fulfil long-term US security purposes in Europe and, despite being sceptical about the feasibility of the French project, Washington was disposed to see a European army as a long-term solution of the West German military problem.[50] As a result of these considerations Acheson accepted a French request that the forthcoming tripartite meeting of Foreign Ministers in Washington in

September should discuss the German military question on the basis not only of the Bonn talks, which had been all that the United States wanted, but also in the light of the discussions at the Paris conference. To this end, the Paris conference was now attempting to finalise an interim report on a European army as a counter to the Bonn report.[51]

Thus, Washington's main concern was to find a practical method of promoting the ultimate creation of a European army. The problem of resources had become less of an obstacle by July, since the US had become more confident that it could provide sufficient arms for German training purposes.[52] However, there still remained the divergence between the French demand for the creation of a European army first and the West German insistence on a political settlement first. It was not easy to find a way of reconciling these differences to meet immediate US interests. Acheson therefore came round to the British position of seeking the simultaneous resolution of both the military and political issues.[53]

However, he went even further than this by trying to find a faster method of raising West German armed forces for later integration into a European army without upsetting the French. He suggested that, pending the completion of the French plan and the coming into full operation of the European army, German armed units might be incorporated into the national forces of those NATO countries who were full participants at the Paris conference, under the newly appointed commander of the allied ground forces in the central sector, General Alphonse Juin. Acheson's efforts to link German rearmament with NATO in some form also reflected his apprehension that, while a European army would be a convenient body in which to assimilate German contingents in the long run, it was also a French device to attain the leadership of Western Europe which, if successful, might threaten American interests in the future.[54] His distrust of this aspect of the French plan for a European army was shared by the Pentagon.[55] Thus direct American supervision of the German contingents at the outset was in his view essential in order to ensure that the matter should not be left solely in French hands. Any solution to this problem must serve American interests, which was probably the underlying reason for Washington's attachment to an interim NATO solution.

Bonn's train of thought was similar, although for different reasons. German public opinion was now becoming more favourable to the idea of a defence contribution, mainly because of the belief that it would lead to an improvement in West Germany's political status. As a result Adenauer began to take a more forthright stance on the prospects for the early realisation of German rearmament.[56] The Chancellor supported European integration and appreciated that a European army might be a possible means of achieving this while, at the same time, leading to a reconciliation between France and West Germany.[57] On the other hand, the NATO concept remained attractive to Bonn because of its military efficiency and simplicity, and it would also help West Germany to maintain close links with the United States.[58]

Was there then a chance of a joint approach towards an interim NATO solution by Washington and Bonn? This was unlikely since American pro-European integrationists, outside Washington, like Bruce and John McCloy, the US High Commissioner for Germany, had skillfully undermined the NATO approach – McCloy by encouraging the West German Chancellor and Speidel to believe that the US government supported a European army,[59] and Bruce by assuring Acheson that the Federal Republic preferred participation in a supranational organisation.[60] Bruce, McCloy and Eisenhower were united in the view that a piecemeal approach through NATO would be unacceptable to the French and would cause delays in setting up a European army. They were convinced that the US government must fully support the plan for a European army as the best and quickest solution to the question of a German military contribution.[61]

Washington was also impressed by the sentiments which were increasingly expressed at the Paris conference in favour of European unity, sentiments which Eisenhower actively encouraged. In his speech to the English Speaking Union in London on 3 July 1951, the General asserted that:

> Europe cannot attain the towering material stature possible to (*sic*) its people's skills and spirit so long as it is divided by patchwork territorial fences. But with unity achieved, Europe could build adequate security and, at the same time, continue the march of human betterment that has characterised Western civilization[62]

This speech was in accord with a feature of the French concept which was most attractive to European federationists, that is, the idea that a supranational European entity would be a considerable improvement on, in Schuman's words, 'outdated nationalism'.[63] While the new Supreme Commander was genuinely enthusiastic about furthering unity through team work, his exploratory trip in Europe early in 1951 reinforced his belief that European political cohesion was essential if the United States wished to see any military progress there.[64] McCloy also encouraged Eisenhower to support the European army project.[65]

Consequently, the general was converted during his six months in Europe from an attitude of contempt for the French plan to one of full support.[66] Given the wide publicity Eisenhower had received as Supreme Allied Commander during the Second World War, his new-found dedication to the cause of the European army made a most favourable impression not only on the delegates at the Paris conference but also on Washington's thinking about the French project.

During the summer, the conference in Paris agreed that there should be close liaison between the projected European army organisation and SHAPE on technical and military aspects. As a result the contentious problem of the size and composition of a basic unit would be settled on the basis of recommendations by SHAPE. During the initial build-up stage, problems of logistics, intelligence, planning, specific goals for total forces, equipment and the costs of a European army would be examined and determined in cooperation with SHAPE. Eisenhower indeed even contemplated volunteering himself as temporary European Defence Commissioner, pending a permanent appointee, in order to ensure the rapid and smooth beginning of recruiting for, and training of, the European army effectives.

The conference also agreed that, in an emergency, the NATO Supreme Commander could command individual European units of a European army and Eisenhower could break the European army into parts and deploy German forces with British or American contingents if he found it militarily necessary and effective to do so. With Washington's approval, Eisenhower also accepted a French invitation to send a SHAPE observer to the Paris conference on 19 July 1951.[67]

A second and equally important development at the Paris conference was France's agreement to the principle of equality. Under the initial French scheme, only West Germany's force would be completely absorbed into the European army, since the other five members would maintain two separate forces during the transition period (that is, the period before the European army became fully operational), their existing national forces already available to NATO and newly created forces which were to be welded into a European army. To meet German objections, the conference decided to include all the forces of potential member countries for the defence of Europe into the European army from the outset, except those assigned to overseas and internal security duties, such as police forces. For example, the French national army would cease to exist as a separate force within Europe upon the ratification of the treaty for a European army.[68]

One of the major causes for this change of atmosphere in Paris was France's fear, which was shared by the other continental Europeans, that unless the Paris conference made some progress in satisfying American and West German reservations, the outcome might be the inclusion of German soldiers directly in NATO on the basis of the Bonn talks.[69] Indeed, the Pentagon and the State Department regarded West Germany's proposals at the Bonn conference as 'reasonable'.[70] However, the significant progress made at Paris in terms of the agreement for close cooperation between SHAPE and the projected European army led Acheson and General Marshall to express their pleasure at these 'rapid' developments.[71] Once the full impact of Eisenhower's support and of Washington's backing was felt at the Paris conference at the end of July, scepticism about the value of a European army significantly diminished and thereafter the discussions advanced more constructively, especially after the completion of the interim report of 24 July 1951. By that time Adenauer had decided to support the European army project.[72]

This connection between developments at the Paris conference and the increasing American support for a European army also suggested that the whole problem of the defence of Western Europe, including the question of West German rearmament, was becoming largely a political rather than a military issue. This was partly because the Truman administration's promise of more troops and material support for NATO was now being implemented and, as a result, the United States could no longer threaten to withhold these as a means of pressurising her European NATO allies to agree to an early settlement of the West German rearmament issue. Moreover, progress was at least beginning to be made towards the formation of a NATO integrated force under SHAPE, while European public opinion had greeted with relief the opening of the Korean armistice talks in July. The long drawn out and unsuccessful conference of the four-power deputies had not resulted in any increase in Cold War tensions. Accordingly, by the summer, the earlier intense fear of a Soviet Union threat had begun to fade away in Europe. Rearmament in depth now seemed unnecessary, and its unpopularity was largely confirmed by the growing clamour for neutralism in France and West Germany in the early months of 1951.[73] On the other hand, the Europeans were fully aware of the growing isolationist tendency in Congress and they were torn between their continued interest in benefiting from US economic and military power and their reluctance to yield to American pressure to make sacrifices for rearmament.[74] For the common defence, European unity as a political goal appeared as a tempting and inexpensive alternative to rearmament, which could be used to show the Americans that the Europeans did have some positive ideas about Western collaboration. Once the importance of European unity was accepted by Washington, France would find it easier to sell the European army project to the French people and to other Continental Europeans as the logical culmination of integration. The fact that the Paris conference decided in July that the European army should be described as 'the European Defence Force' or 'the European Defence Community' reflected a conscious French effort to reinforce the political importance of the French project in the minds of the European peoples.[75]

For her part, in order to secure US interest in strengthening Western Europe without either aggravating European anti-American sentiment or necessitating a further US commitment to European defence, the United States felt that, in the wake of the failure of the Spofford plan, her only remaining option was to encourage moves towards closer European integration, founded upon a Franco-German agreement, via the European Defence Community (EDC). However, because Acheson and General Marshall remained dubious about the French project even by the end of July 1951, the change in the American attitude towards it was much slower and more uneven than the Europeans appreciated. That it took place at all was the result of the cumulative effect of a number of developments. In this process two factors carried weight in Washington: that Eisenhower himself was now convinced that a European army was a militarily practicable option and second, the realisation that the French would not adopt any solution to the problem of German military participation other than the European Defence Community.[76]

5.   The British decision to support the EDC project

Like the other European powers, Britain was suffering from the effects of rearmament on her balance of payments and on her rate of inflation, and this was obviously a threat to the survival of the Labour government at the next election. The opposition of Aneurin Bevan, who became Minister of Labour in January 1951, to the British rearmament programme (which had risen from £3,000 million for the next three years, approved in November 1950, to a new figure of £4,700 million for the same time span, in January 1951), led to his resignation in April, and he was followed by Harold Wilson (the President of the Board of Trade) and John Freeman (Under Secretary at the Ministry of Supply).[77] The Prime Minister in a minute for the Cabinet on 30 August 1951 demonstrated British disenchantment

with the fruits of rearmament by maintaining that '[t]oo much pressure to increase defensive expenditure of nations which lack resources
of economic wealth may be very dangerous, and may result in opening the way to Soviet penetration and thus defeating the very object
of containment'.[78]

Thus Britain was ready to abandon her leadership in the field of
NATO rearmament and was prepared to support continental efforts
to cooperate more closely in European defence questions. If she did
so, Britain would reap two advantages: first, like the other
Europeans, she would be required to make only a moral and not a
material commitment and second, it would temper continental criticisms that Britain was hostile or apathetic to the idea of European
federation.[79] Consequently, in parallel with the continental shift from
rearmament to unity, Britain began to emphasise the good relations
she enjoyed with France and the rest of Western Europe and, at the
same time, to point out how closely France, the United States and
Great Britain had cooperated on European questions. Britain's
renewed enthusiasm for Europe was partly the consequence of Morrison's appointment as Foreign Secretary. Despite his unpopularity in
the Foreign Office, Morrison tended to be more sympathetic than
Bevin had been towards European aspirations for a European
federation.[80]

However, this positive interest in European unity did not lead
immediately to Britain's automatic support for a European army. At
the end of July two important Cabinet meetings, attended by the
Service Chiefs, were held to try to bring about a more constructive
British policy towards the practical application of the principle of
German rearmament. The ensuing discussions were rather chaotic
and revealed considerable divisions of opinion. This probably reflected the fact that the ministers were insufficiently acquainted with
recent developments in Washington and Paris. Neither the more
favourable European attitude towards the EDC nor the change in the
US government's policy towards it were as yet clear to them. They
were only aware that Washington remained anxious for West German military forces to be raised at the cost of affecting the supply of
military equipment to the European allies. Ministers had received
indications that the United States now appeared willing to see the
NATO interim solution, modified in some way to make it more
acceptable to the West Germans than the Spofford plan, as the basis
for German rearmament. These British assumptions corresponded to
the views which were held in Washington and in Paris before July.[81]

Since this was how the British understood the situation, it was hardly surprising that it caused a stir among the anti-German rearmament section of the Labour party, represented by Hugh Dalton, Minister of Town and Country Planning, and Bevan, now outside the Cabinet, who were joined by Slim and John Strachey, the Secretary of State for War, who all wanted Britain to try to secure 'Attlee's Four Conditions' and, in particular, the Prime Minister's insistence on the strengthening of NATO before the rearming of the West Germans. However, if it was essential for Britain to make an immediate decision, this group preferred that she opt for a European army. Dalton asserted at a Cabinet meeting on 30 July 1951 that:

> we should certainly not agree to the organisation of any German units outside the European Army, where at least there would be some chance of preventing the growth of a dominant German General Staff.[82]

Conversely, there were those like Morrison, Shinwell, Attlee and the Royal Air Force and Navy Chiefs of Staff, who felt that British policy towards the nature and timing of a German contribution should be re-examined. Morrison, with the support of the Foreign Office, Patrick Gordon-Walker, the Secretary of State for Commonwealth Relations, and Shinwell, wanted West German military formations to be incorporated into the EDC.[83] Other ministers clung to a direct NATO solution, mainly because they did not regard a European army as a practical possibility. Despite this confusion, it soon became clear that the Bonn talks had had a profound impact on Britain's thinking: like France, she would not agree to the West German demand for equality within NATO and, accordingly, she could no longer be confident about pursuing the NATO solution if safeguards were not to be imposed on West Germany. This increasing lack of enthusiasm for the NATO approach suggested that Britain might now move towards supporting the EDC scheme. Indeed, by the beginning of September, these British views had crystallized into a definite policy in favour of the creation of the EDC.

The forthcoming Washington conference of the three Foreign Ministers on West Germany made it imperative for British government to come to a firm decision on the subject. Also British ministers became concerned that further delay in the final settlement of the West German question might lead to serious political difficulties in Bonn, which would result in West Germany drifting into the Soviet camp. More importantly, given that the question of West German rearmament had become interlocked with that of her sovereignty and that the West Germans were insisting on equality of status, Attlee was particularly worried that West Germany might acquire too great a degree of independence in rearmament matters. This too presented Britain with a dilemma: while it would be unfair for the Western allies to continue to shoulder the burden of defending a West Germany which had recovered much of her sovereignty, it would be dangerous to allow her to raise a national army under national control. The best solution therefore seemed to be the tight integration of West German soldiers into a European common defence force under NATO. Hence Attlee also became a convert to the idea of a supranational army, thereby adopting the views of Morrison and Shinwell.[84]

In theory, the French scheme appeared to satisfy a number of criteria. First, such a supranational military formation would lessen the danger of provoking the Soviet Union and reduce French fears of the German military threat. Secondly, it would meet German demands for equality. Thirdly, the friendly atmosphere generated between the French and Germans during the Paris conference after July, and the increasing American enthusiasm for a European army, about which the British were fully informed by the end of August, was equally important in helping to change Britain's mind on the question. In any case, it was now as clear to the British as it was to the Americans that the European Defence Community was the only means by which the French would approve a German defence partici-pation. Fourthly, from the point of view of tactics, the German ques-tion would be dealt with in the context of a political move towards European unity rather than as a purely military problem, which might make the rearmament of West Germany a little more palatable both to the Russians and to the anti-German rearmament lobbies in Paris, Bonn and London. Finally, what also encouraged British sup-port was Eisenhower's offer to act as a temporary European Defence Commissioner, thus ensuring that the European Defence Community would be subordinate to SHAPE. The importance to the British of such a close Atlantic and Continental connection requires no elaboration.[85]

Seen in this light, the advantage of accepting the French project as the most desirable solution to the question of a German contribution outweighed continuing British reservations about the possible effect of this scheme on her relations with the United States. Accordingly, Attlee was now ready 'to look very sympathetically on the European Army Plan provided it can be shown to be militarily effective', a view which was accepted by the Cabinet on 4 September 1951.[86]

Nevertheless, this decision did not overcome all Britain's reserva-tions about German rearmament. First, the British were more scepti-cal than the Americans about the progress made at the Paris conference during the summer.[87] The plan for the European Defence Community was only a skeleton one and the institutional framework – the establishment of a Council of Ministers, an Assembly and a Court of Justice – was not likely to cause the participants any great difficulty, as it was modelled broadly on the machinery of the Schuman plan.[88] However, more contentious matters would have to be settled, including the time-consuming process of resolving such issues as the common budget and common armaments. Secondly, Britain's uneasiness about agreeing to the European project was buttressed by her concern about her delicate position in the negotiations, which differed considerably from that of the United States. The latter could easily declare her full support for the EDC plan and could intervene as much as she wished in the details of the plan in order to secure its early implementation and in accordance with American interests. The Americans were not eligible for membership of the EDC, whereas the British, if they wanted to follow the American example and involve themselves in the negotiations, were bound to be asked to join the EDC. Cabinet ministers remained uncertain about how they could commit Britain to the EDC scheme without creating the impression that Britain might be willing to participate fully in the organisation.[89]

Finally, the scale and timing of Germany's defence contribution was particularly important for Britain in view of the possible financial impact of West German rearmament on Britain's economy. Since 1945 the cost of the maintenance of allied forces had been charged to the German budget on a mandatory basis as occupation costs. However, allied forces would lose this status when the occupation regime was abolished and would thereafter be regarded as part of a European common defence force stationed in a Western allied country.[90] The Federal Republic was unlikely to be willing to bear a large defence expenditure if this was to be at the cost of her social security system. Therefore, once she embarked upon remilitarisation, it would be difficult for her to continue to make her existing payments towards the cost of financing allied forces on her soil, which would amount to about 7–9 per cent of her GNP in 1951–2.[91] Accordingly, the three allied powers were likely to lose part or even the whole of what was currently being paid to them by the West German government. At the very worst Britain might have to increase her defence budget of £4,700 million by 7 per cent over the next three years.[92] Given the absolute limit imposed on her defence spending, Britain would be unable to provide for such an increase. Thus the issue of West Germany's rearmament would cause further complications resulting from what Attlee described as 'the far reaching economic and financial problems which will arise from any German defence effort.'[93]

The economic implications for West German rearmament would have the sharpest impact on Britain, since the United States possessed far more resources and France would probably be able to handle the issue satistfactorily within the context of EDC financial arrangements.[94] Britain's dilemma stemmed from the unwillingness or the inability of her European allies to increase Western Europe's military strength by their own efforts. In order to obtain West German resources to fill this gap, the allies were now faced with the possibility that they would have to spend even more money to keep their troops in West Germany. Inevitably, Britain complained about the unfairness of all this – Morrison told a tripartite meeting of Foreign Ministers during the Ottawa NATO Council conference on 17 September 1951 that he could see 'no good reason' why the West German government 'should not pay' for the defence of its country 'just as we were paying for ours' and that he could not ask 'the Chancellor of the Exchequer to impose this additional burden on the British people'.[95]

The presence of allied forces in West Germany had a two-fold purpose: as a means of deterring the revival of German militarism, and as part of the defence of West Germany's territory, which was as important to the European NATO powers as to the West Germans. In this context Morrison's case was much weaker than he thought. The ideal course for Britain, despite her decision to support the EDC, would be to delay for as long as possible an actual German defence contribution to it or, alternatively, to ensure that the process of raising a very small number of German soldiers was a slow one. In either case Britain would continue to obtain most of her occupation costs from the Federal Republic of Germany for a lengthy period.[96]

Britain's uneasiness about the European Defence Community and over what part she was to play in it, and her anxiety about the likely adverse effect of German rearmament on British finances, was concealed by the high-sounding British declaration issued at the end of the Washington meeting of the three Foreign Ministers between 10 and 14 September 1951 that 'The Government of the United Kingdom desires to establish the closest possible association with the European continental community at all stages in its development.'[97] In an effort to show that Britain was shifting from the status of a passive to an active observer at the Paris conference, this statement sought to find the most faithful translation of the words 'look very sympathetically'.[98] To this end, the British government sent Major-General Kimmins to take part in the work of the Paris conference's military committee.[99] Acheson and Schuman were, of course, pleased with Britain's more positive attitude towards the Community and neither contemplated at the moment raising the issue of British membership of the EDC formally with the British government.[100]

The Washington conference accordingly reestablished unity between the three powers on the objective of finalising a West German military commitment to the European army, while consideration of the Bonn report on the direct German inclusion in NATO was postponed *sine die*. The three parties were also in agreement on the need for completing the contractual agreements with the Federal Republic, at the same time as West Germany collaborated in the defence of Western Europe.[101] Schuman was determined to present a complete report on the EDC before the NATO Council next met in Rome, either in October or November 1951, which Acheson, as Morrison put it, 'optimistically' hoped that the contractual agreements with Bonn would be concluded by that time.[102] This tight schedule provided for the integration of West Germany into the European community militarily and politically by the end of 1951.

However, this hope was unlikely to be fulfilled. Although West Germany and Italy had formally expressed their agreement in principle to the EDC, the Belgian government was not convinced that all her forces, including those already in NATO, should participate in the EDC from the outset, since she feared that this would entail the loss of her military sovereignty.[103] On the other hand, the Dutch government, despite its decision to join the Paris conference as a full participant in October, remained sceptical about the whole nature of the supranational organisation, which she suspected was intended to revive French hegemony in Europe.[104] Furthermore, the constructive French approach at the Paris conference during the summer was made during the five weeks after the general election, when the French lacked a properly constituted government owing to a ministerial crisis. Not until 11 August was the Pleven government able to resume office. While this election had removed rigid anti-German rearmament ministers like Moch, it had resulted in an increase in the number of Gaullist and Communist deputies in the Chamber who were opposed to a supranational European army.[105] Therefore, the prospect for a rapid and successful conclusion of the EDC treaty still remained questionable.

5 THE SIGNATURE OF THE EDC TREATY IN MAY 1952

1. The impact of Churchill on European unity

At the end of October 1951, as a result of the Conservative victory, with a slender majority of 17, at the general election, Winston Churchill returned to Downing Street for the second time as Prime Minister. This change of administration was bound to raise European expectations that Britain would launch a new initiative for the closer integration of Western Europe. This assumption was by no means unreasonable, given Churchill's passionate support for the European movement when he was opposition leader – notably his call for a United States of Europe in Zurich in September 1946 and, more recently, in his Strasbourg resolution on the formation of a European army in August 1950. This contrasted markedly with the Labour government's somewhat reserved attitude on the subject. However, during his early months as Prime Minister, Churchill's interest in continental federal arrangements and the European army declined. This is already well known, but the motives for this shift have not been fully explored.[1]

Churchill's affection for the continental Europeans was more pronounced when they were facing appalling trials during the war and the depressing early post-war period. On these occasions, he was able to boost European morale. However, on his return to office in 1951, he awoke to the fact that the British Empire, to which he was greatly attached, was now in decline, with the United States in the ascendant, economically, militarily and politically. This reality aroused his strong patriotism: he informed Lord Moran, his medical adviser and close friend in January 1952 that '[t]hey [the Americans] have become so great and we are now so small. Poor England! We threw away so much in 1945',[2] Consequently, Churchill's main concern was to restore Britain's economic vitality, so badly damaged during the recent war. Indeed, the Conservatives had campaigned during the 1951 election on the slogan 'Work, Homes and Food'.[3] In the field of foreign affairs, his priorities, expressed in a memorandum he wrote for the Cabinet on 29 November 1951, were 'the unity and the consolidation of the British Commonwealth and what is left of the former British Empire', together with the 'fraternal association of the English-speaking world', which implied the recreation of a special union with the United States modelled on the war-time partnership. Europe thus came a poor third in this order of priorities – its future relationship with Britain was defined in detached and vague terms as 'a separate closely – and specially – related ally and friend'.[4]

At the back of Churchill's mind was the belief that Britain would be content with the moral leadership of Western Europe, and would not be an active participant in continental projects. In February 1930, when he published his concept of a United States of Europe in the New York *Saturday Evening Post*, he stated that: 'We have our own dream and our own task, we are with Europe but not of it. We are linked but not compromised.'[5] More than twenty years later, in November 1951, he reiterated this view in his Cabinet memorandum:

> I am not opposed to a European Federation...But I never thought that Britain or the British Commonwealths [sic] should...become an integral part of a European Federation, and have never given the slightest support to the idea. We should not, however, obstruct but rather favour the movement to closer European unity.[6]

While he can be said to have been consistent in this view over a long period, his attitude to Europe was in fact much the same as that of the Labour party, that is, the British would support a continental federation but would not participate in it.

He was equally negative towards the French concept of a European army. The substance of his opposition was based on his instinctive aversion to its supranational character. He doubted that France would really abolish her national army – 'France is not France without "L'Armée Française"' – and poured scorn on 'the military spirit of a "sludgy amalgam" of volunteers or conscripts to defend the EDC'.[7]

Churchill's ideas in late 1951 about a European army, which differed slightly from his August 1950 version, were for the pooling of part of the national forces of the European members of NATO in order to create a European army, while keeping the rest of their national forces under the NATO Supreme Commander. Thus, a European army, including West German armed units, would be paid for and equipped on a national basis, inside the NATO defence force. While Churchill contemplated attaching some special conditions to the European army, such as prohibiting it from possessing heavy weapons, he thought essentially of this army as a symbolic entity expressing European unity.[8] He told Pleven and Schuman in Paris in December 1951 that: 'the forces "dedicated" to the European Army would wear their national uniforms but would carry a special badge denoting their membership of the European Army'.[9] If this badge was intended to be the only means of distinguishing a European army from the other contingents earmarked for NATO, Britain, as the Chiefs of Staff and the Foreign Office pointed out, could certainly contemplate the possibility of participating in the European army in the same way as she was a member of NATO.[10] The Prime Minister's proposed European army was really only a coalition of national forces, that is, the application of the NATO solution to the continental area. The Pleven plan had already demonstrated French opposition to the idea of a West German defence contribution on a national basis. Nor would the West Germans accept Churchill's concept of a European army since, under it, they would still face discrimination: German troops would only exist within a European army, while the other participants would retain separate armed forces for NATO service as well. Furthermore, the West Germans would not have any say in deciding on the size and the manner of their participation in Western defence, since this would be the responsibility of 'the Victorious Powers of the late war'.[11] At the Paris meeting with the French in December 1951, he went on to say that:

> She [West Germany] must be made to realize the mortal peril in which she would stand if she declined to join in the defence of Western Europe. If, by her action, the other countries of Europe were forced to hold the line of the Rhine, she would become a no man's land subject to Communist disintegration from within and atomic attack from without.[12]

The Prime Minister's statement was in part influenced by his friendly feelings towards France and by his concern about her continued military weakness. He was mindful about West Germany's latent potential and of the likelihood that she would overtake Britain economically and France militarily in the future.[13] He believed that if the West accepted Germany's demand for equality, the West European powers, and especially France, would be placed at a serious disadvantage. While Churchill's reasoning was not unsound, it did not accord with political reality. A series of negotiations with the Germans had already shown that the introduction of safeguards against a possible German military threat under a NATO solution would not work, which was the main reason why Attlee had eventually approved the French scheme for a European army.

Churchill's concept of a European army was by now out of date.

It must also be borne in mind that Churchill was 77 years old in November 1951 and that he had become slower, more critical, less energetic and more dogmatic than during the war years.[14] Moreover he did not regard the EDC question as a stimulating and dynamic project especially when compared with his ambition to settle the Cold War with the Soviet Union. Accordingly, the Conservative government's policy on European unity was left primarily to the Foreign Secretary, Anthony Eden, who, at 54, was Churchill's heir apparent to the post of Prime Minister.[15]

2. The Conservatives' affirmation of the Washington declaration

Unlike Churchill, Eden had never felt any strong emotional attachment to Europe. In July 1944 the Anglophile Paul-Henri Spaak of Belgium, for whom Eden professed great admiration, came to London to discover Britain's intended role in the future of Europe. He asked Eden whether the British people fully realised 'how much all the countries of Western Europe looked to them'.[16] In reply Eden was not very forthcoming, mainly because he feared that British involvement in a purely European organisation might lose Britain the chance of maintaining her war-time friendship with the Soviet Union. Instead he put forward the vague idea that Britain might be willing to conclude 'some closer arrangement with France, Holland, Belgium and Norway within the framework of any new world order which may be established and in support of the Anglo-Soviet Alliance which with US collaboration is [the] basis of our policy'.[17]

Although his hope of maintaining the alliance with the Soviet Union became academic in the light of the subsequent development of the Cold War, he had never associated himself with Churchill's pro-European activities at the Council of Europe at Strasbourg.[18] Eden admitted that he favoured Bevin's European policy, that is, the reconstruction and strengthening of Western Europe in the context of the Atlantic community, which would be based on the concept of the three pillars of the United States, Britain (including the Commonwealth) and Continental Europe.[19] However, unlike Bevin, Eden did not seem to grasp fully the implications of the French concept of a European federation. When the Pleven plan was put forward in autumn 1950, he asked in the House of Commons 'why there should not be this small nucleus European army if it suits the French and

Germans better that way, within the wider concept of the Atlantic Force?' During Parliamentary debates in February 1951, he suggested that Britain should be included in the European army: 'there is here unique opportunity for which we may never forgive ourselves if we miss it'.[20] Of course this was a pretence: he minuted to Churchill on 1 December 1951 that he had never thought 'it possible that we could join such an army'.[21]

Having returned to the Foreign Office, Eden came more to appreciate the distinction between the French European army scheme and the NATO solution in that the main attraction of the former was the abolition of national armies and the prohibition of a West German one, which would be less provocative to the Russians than a NATO which included a separate West German army. A more important consideration was that the EDC programme was the only one acceptable to both the French and the Germans, and it had Eisenhower's support.[22] In his memoirs Eden wrote that he liked 'the idea' for 'I have never thought that my country need have any apprehension on account of a closer union between the nations of continental Europe. We have suffered too much from the lack of it.' However, his liking for the plan's imaginative supra-national idea paradoxically led him to doubt both its practicability and feasibility.[23] He told Acheson in Paris on 5 November 1951 that his 'personal' anxiety was that 'the EDF [European Defence Force] was not advantageous to France, as in a limited arrangement such as that, in contrast to a broader arrangement of a NATO army, Germany would be in a position to play a more major role'.[24]

These were about the only ideas Eden had about the European issue at that time, since he was more concerned about the uneasy situation in Iran and in Egypt and with the negotiations on the Korean cease fire. Indeed, extra-European problems appeared to be more urgent than those of Europe: he once said to his private secretary, Shuckburgh, that:

> if you were to open the personal mail arriving from overseas in any post office in England you would find that 90 percent of it came from beyond Europe...where British soldiers and adminstrators had served or British families settled. How could we ignore all that?[25]

The Foreign Secretary was convinced that Britain must see herself 'as an active and enlightened European nation with a world role and not as a limbo of Europe'. Equally important for Eden was the creation of a viable Anglo-American working relationship as a basis for dealing with international problems.[26]

Accordingly his first move on the European question was based partly on political considerations: in the face of continental expectations that Britain might take a more active role in Europe, he thought that 'it would be a pity if they got the impression that we were less forthcoming than our predecessors'.[27] Hence the Conservative government reaffirmed twice in the House of Commons on 12 and 19 November that it would abide by the Washington declaration of September 1951 in which the Labour government promised Britain's 'closest possible association with the European continental community at all stages in its development'.[28] This was as far as Eden was prepared to commit Britain on the EDC question during the first month of the government's term in office.

3. 'The Battle of Strasbourg' and 'The Rome Coup'

This British attitude was in due course challenged by the Strasbourg Assembly of the Council of Europe, a 'talking shop' for the enthusiasts of European federation, which met for nearly a month from 19 November 1951. Anthony Nutting, the Parliamentary Under-Secretary for Foreign Affairs, described the ensuing debate as 'The Battle of Strasbourg'.[29] The proceedings were marked by considerable rancour against the British Conservatives, a rancour which was occasioned by the inner workings of Conservative party politics. Prior to the Strasbourg meetings, the Conservative pro-European group, which included Duncan Sandys, the Minister of Supply, Sir David Maxwell-Fyfe, the Home Secretary, Harold Macmillan, the Minister of Housing and Local Government, Peter Thorneycroft, the President of the Board of Trade and, from the back benches, Julian Amery and Robert Boothby, had become uneasy about Eden's lacklustre approach to European unity.[30]

Eden and the Foreign Office on the other hand feared that Britain might be drawn into a European federation if she became too closely involved in the negotiations in Paris. Furthermore, British public opinion remained opposed to Britain's involvement in such continental arrangements.[31] Eden, before flying out to Paris for talks on Germany on 21 and 22 November, was rather off-handed when Maxwell-Fyfe, who was the chief British delegate to the forthcoming Strasbourg Assembly, wanted to consult him about his speech to that body:

> If the Home Secretary & Mr Nutting are happy on our agreed line [i.e., endorsement of the Washington statement] that would spare me. And I really have no time before I leave Wed [Wednesday]. But I cannot refuse if Sir David requires to see me.[32]

Nutting arranged for Maxwell-Fyfe to meet Lord Hood, the head of the Western Organisations Department at the Foreign Office, on 21 November, although the latter did not diverge from the 'agreed line'. On the 22nd the Home Secretary brought the subject up in the Cabinet, with Churchill, Macmillan and Thorneycroft present but, despite Eden's absence, the advice subsequently given to Maxwell-Fyfe contained nothing more than what Eden had told the House of Commons earlier.[33]

While on 29 November Maxwell-Fyfe delivered his statement at Strasbourg in accordance with the Cabinet's instructions, he also included his personal ideas on the subject. He stated that 'I cannot promise you that our eventual association with the European Defence Community will amount to full and unconditional participation', adding, at a subsequent press conference, that:

> It is quite wrong to suggest that what I said was any closing of the door by Britain...I made it plain that there is no refusal on the part of Britain.[34]

Later on the same day, in Rome, Eden felt bound to make a statement, which he had not planned to do, as a result of the great interest the press were showing in the question of British participation in the EDC. His speech was an exact copy of the Washington declaration, but he had to expand on this in response to a question as to whether 'the use of the word "Association" in the September Washington declaration ruled out any participation of British units?' Eden's answer to this was 'yes', although he added, 'but there might be some other form of association',[35]

Consequently two interpretations of these almost simultaneous announcements emerged since, while Maxwell-Fyfe's speech initially raised the hopes of the Europeans, Eden then shattered them by suddenly refusing a British contribution to the EDC.[36] The Home Secretary accused the Foreign Secretary of having 'destroyed our name on the Continent', while Nutting simply pointed out that 'Eden was in every sense a NATO man'.[37] To counter this Eden asked whether it was true that 'all was well until my comments to the press in Rome?'[38]Indeed, Paul Reynaud, a prominent French Conservative politician, who followed the Home Secretary's presentation and who spoke before Eden's press conference in Rome, did not welcome Maxwell-Fyfe's message and bitterly criticised the British refusal to merge their forces with those of the rest of Western Europe.[39] Nor did Benjamin Hulley, the First Secretary at the American Embassy in

London, mention Eden at all in a telegram about the Assembly meeting to the State Department on 7 December, although he stated that '[a] political duststorm was raised over Sir David Maxwell Fyfe's exposition of the British attitude in the Assembly on November 28'.[40] It was also debatable whether these two statements were, as Maxwell-Fyfe argued, 'totally contradictory'. At first glance, Eden had apparently tried to clarify the Home Secretary's vague if friendly reservations about the possibility of full British membership of the EDC. Maxwell-Fyfe's additional remark about 'no refusal on the part of Britain' seemed to be nothing more than an attempt to gloss over the negative impact of his earlier speech to the Assembly.[41]

What made this 'Rome Coup' (Eden's words)[42] so alarming was that it revealed two apparently irreconcilable problems at once. First, it brought the divergence between Eden and the pro-European faction into the open. This was partly a result of Eden's failure to explain to the pro-Europeans what Britain was prepared to do in the context of the 'closest possible association with the European continental community' as defined under the Washington declaration. Consequently pro-European Conservatives were confused and dismayed by Eden's outright rejection of British participation in the European military federation.

A letter to Churchill on 3 December signed by seven Conservative participants in the Strasbourg Assembly pointed out that:

> There are doubtless formidable reasons against our participation in a European Army at this juncture; but we do not know them. All we are aware of is the impression, given by the Rome Communiqué, that we are not prepared to play any part...we feel sure you will appreciate that...we must have some guidance.[43]

This plaintive appeal to Churchill, together with a separate letter from Robert Boothby in the same vein, and approaches by Macmillan to Churchill in February and March 1952, demonstrated the naivety of the pro-Europeans in believing that Churchill, by being reminded of his earlier proposal for a European army in August 1950, would do anything to revise Eden's policy on the European issue.[44] As has been pointed out, the Prime Minister was in broad agreement with Eden's opposition to Britain's participation in any European federal organisation. Although in a minute to Eden on 13 December 1951 he did not conceal his emotional reaction: 'I am naturally distressed at the way things have gone at Strasbourg. We seem in fact to have succeeded to the Socialist Party hostility to United Europe', he was not prepared to challenge Eden on this issue.[45]

A further weakness in the pro-Europeans' argument was that they were by no means clear as to the course they preferred. While Max-well-Fyfe wanted British agreement to 'the principle of joining a European Army', the other Strasbourg delegates, in their collective letter to Churchill, urged that the Conservative government agree that the British should 'play their part in the military defence...of a united Europe'.[46] What did the words 'the principle' or 'their part' actually mean?

Interestingly, none of them, even Macmillan, was willing to assert that Britain should unconditionally participate in the EDC project. This indecisiveness was partly the result of the complexity and ambiguity surrounding the negotiations on the European army. It was doubtful whether any of these ministers, preoccupied as they were with their own departments, could hope to become fully acquainted with the complex details of the structure of the EDC, such as the common procurement of armaments and common defence expenditure – even Eden and Acheson complained about their inability to grasp exactly what was going on in Paris.[47] The Conservative anti-Eden faction was concerned to advocate British leadership in this matter, but had no concrete ideas about how to achieve this. Nevertheless, to Eden's chagrin, their criticisms about his 'anti-European' posture lingered on and, as a result, he suffered from the effects of the 'Rome coup' for the rest of his life.[48]

Equally important was the fact that the two speeches by Maxwell-Fyfe and Eden dealt, in Boothby's words, 'a shattering blow' to the morale of Continental Europe.[49] It was clumsy tactics to restate the Labour government's Washington declaration in public, with its phrase about Britain's 'closest possible association' with the EDC, which could have meant anything, and thereby obscure the Conservative attitude towards the subject. Furthermore, it was tactless of Eden to reject so emphatically the participation of any British military formations in the EDC, and his hints about some other form of association seemed too abstract to do much to relieve the general feeling that he had renounced British membership of the Community. Hence, the bitterness about being betrayed by the Conservatives resulted in Spaak's resignation as president of the Council of Europe, and also led to much conjecture about the imminent fall of the French and West German governments and the collapse of all continental federal arrangements.[50]

4. The Paris conference for a European army (October–December 1951)

The military representatives at the EDC conference had made significant progress by the end of November 1951, on the basis of consultations with SHAPE and the Temporary Council Committee (TCC), or 'wise men'.[51] The latter was a new NATO body, comprising twelve representatives from each member country, which had been set up at the last NATO Council meeting in Ottawa in September 1951 in response to European protests about the defence burdens imposed on them by the NATO medium-term plan. The task of the TCC was to examine the optimum level of the rearmament efforts of each member country, together with West Germany, in the light of its economic and social problems.[52]

The EDC conference agreed that the basic size of a national land unit should be called a 'groupement', with armoured, mechanised and infantry 'groupements' forming a small 'division' of between 12,600 and 13,000 men. Two such basic units of different nationalities would be integrated into an army corps capable of carrying out an independent mission. Thus the French yielded to the original German request about the basic size of a unit and the level of integration. The total size of the land forces of a European army would be about 43⅔ *groupements*, comprising 14 units from France, 12 units each from Italy and West Germany, and 5⅔ units from the Benelux countries. These targets for each participating member of the EDC were to be met by 1 July 1954 (the first 6 German units were to be recruited on 1 July 1952), based on the assumption that the process of ratification of the EDC treaty would be completed by 1 April 1952. In the case of the air force, a basic unit would be called a 'demi-brigade', comparable to an American wing, with 75 combat aircraft with an average of 1,200 air men in each 'demi-brigade'. The overall size of a European air force had not been decided on by 27 November, although a German contribution of 1,158 front-line aircraft had been agreed to by the French and by SHAPE, but the Germans insisted on a higher figure of 1,746 (which was lower than their original demand at the Bonn talks for 1,900 aircraft), on the grounds that this was necessary to support the agreed size of the land forces of German origin. West Germany was also expected to contribute to the naval coastal defence forces of the EDC, although the details were still being studied.[53] It was now clear that West German land forces would provide nearly one-third of the total strength of the European army, which was higher than the agreed ratio of one-fifth under the Spofford plan, while the French were to be allowed only two additional *groupements*.

The settlement of this major outstanding Franco-German disagreement on the minimum level of national integration encouraged France, West Germany and Italy to approach the other issues at the Paris talks with a greater degree of confidence. However the Benelux countries continued to voice their reservations about the derogation of so much of their sovereignty by the European Defence Community. They objected to the setting up of a centralised High Authority endowed with large executive powers over the Community, regardless of whether it was to consist of a single Commissioner, as the French had initially proposed, or was to be composed of a three-member board, as Italy and West Germany were now proposing. The Benelux countries preferred a Commission of six members, each representing one of the member states, which would be subordinate to the Council of Ministers. Moreover, Belgium wanted a loosely knit coalition of national forces analogous to the NATO structure, with these forces equipped and paid for by each member nation. The Dutch followed the Belgian line, although they proposed that it should operate only for the transitional period before the date on which the EDC became fully functional.[54]

These Benelux complaints reflected the natural apprehensions of the weaker powers about being dominated by the stronger powers in a tightly meshed organisation like the EDC. Belgium would have to give up her bilingual territorial army, an important symbol of the unity of the Flemish and Walloon communities, for the sake of a Franco-German agreement on the principle of equality of rights, i.e., that no national forces, apart from the police, would exist within Europe outside the EDC. Moreover, the Benelux leadership, especially the Dutch, were concerned about the willingness of the French, Italians and West Germans to contemplate the creation of an entity which was to be co-equal with NATO, since this would reduce Benelux influence in NATO, while at the same time giving them only a minor role in the EDC. The fear of losing their national identities was coupled with their anxieties about the creation of an independent and rearmed Germany, even if she was to become a member of the EDC.[55] Finally, the Benelux powers also disliked the prospect of French leadership of the European army, although they were even more concerned, given the weakness of France, about possible German domination of the Community.[56]

Hence, while the Paris negotiations were making progress, mostly in Germany's favour, the EDC did not appear, in the eyes of other Continental Europeans, to solve the problem of how West Germany could be rearmed without her once more becoming a threat to Europe and this led to a growing clamour for the close association of Britain in the project. Although the French government had reluctantly acquiesced in Britain's refusal to join the European army, the Deputy Foreign Minister, Maurice Schumann, could not conceal his disappointment with Eden's announcement in Rome. He informed Harvey that '[t]he fact remained that our [Britain's] attitude might have the effect of causing the French parliament to refuse its support to the project'.[57] The Benelux powers were equally anxious for active British participation in the scheme; for instance, the Belgians were 'accustomed to rely on Great Britain for protection coupled with [the] knowledge that behind [the] UK' was '[the] US'.[58]

5. The development of British policy towards the EDC

As a result of the Strasbourg incident, Eden now felt unable completely to ignore European demands for Britain to play a part in the EDC. The Foreign Office and the Chiefs of Staff were well aware that the EDC project might collapse because of Benelux hesitations and the lack of support for the scheme in the French National Assembly. This led them to contemplate alternative plans for an EDC which comprised only France, Italy and West Germany, or for a loosely federated European army, without the EDC political structure, in order to conform to Benelux wishes.[59] The former approach would of course undermine the entire concept of European unity and as such, as Adenauer pointed out, might not be acceptable to the Parliaments of West Germany, France and Italy.[60] On the other hand, if Britain suggested her alternative scheme of creating a European army without the EDC, strong pressures would build up for Britain to join such an organisation. Both the Foreign Office and the Chiefs of Staff were reluctant to participate even in such a modified European army, which would entail a derogation of Britain's sovereignty.[61]

In parallel with these ideas, British civilian and military officials formulated, in the middle of December, several methods by which Britain might be associated with the EDC once it was established. These included the setting up of a consultative machinery to examine political and military interests shared by both the EDC and Britain, and the provision of British training assistance, logistical support and military supplies to the Community. Furthermore the British proposed to give SACEUR the authority to second British formations to the EDC in the event of war and to place them under the command of

91

an EDC Commander if necessary, while promising that in peacetime, temporary British secondment to the EDC could be authorised for joint training programmes under the overall command of NATO. Finally as a psychological gesture to her European allies, Britain would make it clear that she intended to maintain her armed forces in West Germany for as long as was necessary for EDC purposes, and because of her special responsibilities in Germany.[62] Although these schemes were provisional in nature, they were approved by Eden, and they did reveal a new-found British willingness to cooperate as far as possible with the EDC, short of their full participation in the organisation. Such gestures would also enable Britain to maintain her influence in Europe.[63]

However Eden's immediate concern was how to disarm the growing anti-British feelings which were now spreading from Western Europe to the United States.[64] His officials therefore consulted American and French politicians and officials about future possible developments in British policy towards Europe. From these soundings it became clear that, while France and the United States hoped that Britain would move towards a close military and technical association with the European Defence Community once it had been set up, they did not think it desirable at the moment that Britain should intervene actively in the negotiations at Paris, although they wanted Britain to support the EDC from the outside as a means of raising European morale. The French were, of course, afraid that Britain's proposed amendments to the existing plan were intended to wreck the whole concept of a European army. At the same time, if Britain now put forward concrete proposals for her future association with the EDC, the Benelux powers might be encouraged to follow Britain's example and reject full membership of the Community.[65] From the American point of view, such a British initiative would complicate the discussions and delay West Germany's future rearmament. In view of the imminence of the presidential elections in November 1952, Acheson felt that there was no time left to consider alternative proposals or, indeed, to contemplate any major revision of the current EDC project.[66]

On the basis of this advice, Eden and the Foreign Office decided against initiating new proposals or detailed suggestions about the form of any future British relationship with the Community, whose only result might be the collapse of the present French project. They thought that this would be most 'unfortunate' for Britain, because 'the failure of the Paris Conference would be blamed on us and we should incur, however unjustly, much odium...We thus have a strong interest in bringing the Paris Conference to a rapid and successful conclusion.'[67] Certainly this was the line the promoters of the EDC wanted Britain to follow, and it was first employed during the Churchill–Eden visit to Paris on 17 and 18 December 1951. The resulting communiqué merely stated that Britain genuinely desired to cooperate with the EDC, while suggesting that she would be willing to become involved in 'a technical association with the future European Defence Forces' but without going into detail about the forms of this association.[68] When Eisenhower expressed his satisfaction with the communiqué to Eden (although Churchill complained that it went too far), the Foreign Secretary replied: 'I knew you wld [would] think so since it was written chiefly from your point of view.'[69] Indeed, the statement marked a shift away from Eden's refusal in Rome to agree to any participation of British armed units in the EDC, towards accepting this possibility through a technical linkage.

6. The London talks, 13–19 February 1952

The United States continued to hope that Britain might one day be included in European federations like the EDC, but she remained hesitant about pressing her ally on this subject, since this might undermine their close relations. Indeed, in private communications with Eden, Eisenhower and Acheson both insisted that they had never dreamt that Britain would become a full member of the EDC.[70] However, on other occasions, the United States did imply that she would like Britain eventually to become a part of the Community once it was set up. Eisenhower made a subtle but significant qualification to his earlier private views in a public statement in January: any 'attempt to include Britain *immediately*' in the EDC would be 'a stumbling block rather than a help'.[71] He also wrote to Eden on 8 December 1951 that, 'Sometimes I wonder whether all of you, on that side of the Channel, realise how hungrily many Europeans look to Britain for political guidance.'[72] These American reminders of the importance of Britain's influence on continental politics were successful in their intention of cultivating a British sense of responsibility towards the European Defence Community, while leaving the question of Britain's eventual membership of the Community in abeyance.

Due in part to Britain's encouragement of the Paris negotiations, Eisenhower and Acheson were able to moderate Benelux antipathy towards the European army project by repeated warnings to Belgium and Holland that failure to achieve the EDC would so disappoint the US Congress that continued US defence assistance to Europe might be seriously threatened. They also pointed out that persistent Benelux intransigence would result in either a direct German national contribution to NATO, which would be unacceptable to the French, or in the modification of the character of the EDC in the direction desired by Benelux but which might not satisfy German demands for equality in the Community.[73]

As a result of this pressure, the Paris conference began to make substantial progress by the end of January 1952. The participants agreed on the establishment of a Board of Commissioners composed of nine members, of whom there were to be not more than two nationals of the same state, chosen by unanimous agreement of the six governments. By this arrangement, the small powers were assured of a fair representation in the High Authority, which would deal directly with the common budget. Secondly, France, Italy and West Germany accepted the principle of unanimity in the Council of Ministers when such important issues as the common budget and the scale of national troop contributions were being discussed. This would enhance the powers of the Council *vis-à-vis* the High Authority. Finally, a compromise was reached on the thorny question of the common budget which, while it would take effect from the first day after the ratification of the EDC treaty, would, during the initial stage, be based on the NATO procedure for fixing the national contributions.[74]

Overall, the original French concept of supranationality was somewhat watered down in order to obtain Benelux cooperation and also by the need to complete the final report on the EDC in time for the forthcoming Lisbon conference of the NATO Council between 21 and 25 February 1951. France, West Germany and Italy were at the same time able to postpone several controversial questions: the six agreed that the EDC Assembly would study the problem of a future political federation, which would preside over the European Coal and Steel Community and the European Defence Community, at a later stage (Article 38 of the EDC treaty),[75] and they decided to set up an Interim Committee immediately after the signature of the treaty which would deal with the complex technical question of how to raise the European Defence Force during the initial period in which the EDC structure was still incomplete.[76] Thus, the EDC treaty was mainly a set of voluminous agreements in principle with the details left to be filled in after its signature.

94

However, the enhanced momentum of the negotiations was hampered by a deterioration in Franco-German relations as a result of two apparently different issues. First, the West German delegation at Paris raised the question of Germany's future relationship with NATO, with which the EDC was to be associated institutionally, but in which West Germany, unlike the other participants in the Community, had no formal voice. Secondly France reopened the issue of the Saar by her abrupt decision at the end of January to appoint an ambassador to that territory.[77] The Saar was a symbol of the long-standing hostility between the two countries. Its status in 1951 was one of political autonomy, but in economic union with the French, who were also responsible for the Saar's defence and foreign relations. The French appointment was regarded by the Germans as prejudging the political future of the Saar.[78] Similarly, the German query about their relationship with NATO irritated the French, who remained suspicious of German intentions.[79]

This growing Franco-German antagonism led to renewed anxiety in Washington and London about the prospects for the successful conclusion of the Paris negotiations. Accordingly Eden arranged to hold talks in London with Acheson and Schuman, and Adenauer was invited to attend the latter part of the meeting.[80] These conversations, which took place between 13 and 19 February 1952, during the funeral of King George VI, were designed to settle the outstanding West German political and military questions in the hope of laying sound foundations for the success of the Lisbon NATO conference.

At the London talks Eden was presented with a French request for an Anglo-American guarantee against the unilateral secession from the EDC of any of its members. When the idea was originally put forward by the French at the beginning of December 1951, Eden rejected it on the grounds that 'such a declaration would cast doubt from the outset upon the validity of the European Defence Community'.[81] However, in London in February, Eden felt it essential to take some further step towards reinforcing his December mission to Paris and he decided to accept Schuman's proposal. Consequently Eden obtained both Acheson's agreement and, subsequently, Cabinet approval for such a declaration before Schuman renewed his request for it on the evening of 14 February at the first tripartite meeting of the Foreign Ministers.[82] The three appreciated the importance of not suggesting in any way that this guarantee was directed solely against West Germany, and they believed that Adenauer would approve the idea provided the guarantee was applied to all the member governments of the Community.[83] Schuman wanted this guarantee to be combined with a pledge that the two powers would retain their armed forces in Europe. Acheson was reluctant to agree to these French requests before he had obtained the President's approval. Conversely, Eden asserted that even if the US was unable to make an identical statement now, Britain was prepared to make a unilateral public declaration immediately.[84]

Eden claimed at a Cabinet meeting on 18 February that this 'might help to remove any remaining misapprehension that the United Kingdom Government had been lukewarm in their support of the conception of a European Defence Community'. The Cabinet was divided: some ministers supported Eden, believing that positive action would assert Britain's leadership in Europe, while others expressed misgivings about acting in advance of any assurance that the United States would follow suit. However, no formal decision was made by the Cabinet: Eden was asked only to note the various opinions that had been expressed, which effectively gave him a free hand on the issue.[85]

Hence, at the end of the London talks, agreement was reached by the three Foreign Ministers that the Anglo-American guarantee to the EDC would be included in a tripartite declaration to be issued at the time of the signature of the EDC treaty. Meanwhile the three powers issued a communiqué on 19 February declaring 'their abiding interest in the establishment and integrity of the European Defence Community', while 'recalling' the decision of their governments 'to maintain armed forces in Europe...in association with the European Defence Forces'.[86] This avoided any clear-cut Anglo-American pledge about the duration and extent of their commitment towards the EDC. Moreover, the word 'recalling' would add nothing to their existing responsibilities for the defence of Western Europe under the NATO treaty. Acheson was particularly insistent on the need for caution in this matter and Eden's strategy of turning the London meeting to the advantage of Britain was frustrated.[87]

Britain, France and the United States were as far apart as ever in their attitude towards the EDC. The United States hoped that the EDC project would provide them with an opportunity to reduce their obligations towards the defence of Western Europe. They also hoped to avoid becoming irrevocably committed to the EDC. On the other hand, France, faced with increasing opposition towards the EDC in the Chamber of Deputies, sought more substantial Anglo-American commitments towards the proposed Community as a means of securing more support for the project in the Chamber.[88] For her part Britain was anxious to lessen anti-British sentiments in Europe and the

United States by making gestures towards the EDC which would not, however, involve her joining the organisation as a full member. Eden therefore clung to the idea of making a unilateral declaration against any secession from the EDC on the grounds that 'what they [the British] did with the US was not as important as what they did alone'.[89] However the French government pressed the British to abandon their plan to issue a unilateral declaration, implying that this would not, in itself, be sufficient to rally the French Parliament in support of the EDC.[90]

Nevertheless, the London talks did help to improve the prospects both of finalising the contractual agreement with West Germany and of drafting the EDC treaty. One of the most vexatious questions was how to retain some controls over Germany's armaments after the abolition of the occupation regime, without including this obligation in the contractual agreement. The quadripartite meetings of the three occupying powers and West Germany finally agreed that the EDC treaty should contain a provision to the effect that a number of listed items, such as atomic, biological and chemical weapons, long-range and guided missiles, military aircraft and naval vessels (except for minor defensive craft) should not be produced 'in strategically exposed areas', i.e., by implication West Germany, unless it was unanimously agreed to by the Council of Ministers of the Community.[91] As a further assurance to the Western allies, Adenauer was willing to pledge that the Federal Republic would not regard this provision as discriminatory against her and to promise Britain and the United States, who were not members of the EDC, that West Germany would abide by this treaty obligation.[92]

The disquiet engendered in London about the future of the Saar and West Germany's eventual status within NATO was relieved to some extent when the conference agreed that the former question should be discussed between France and West Germany after the signature of the EDC treaty, while, as for the latter question, Adenauer accepted the substance of the terms set out for the NATO–EDC relationship, which had been prepared by the NATO Council of Deputies. This provided, *inter alia*, for a combined joint meeting of the two organisations when requested by a member of either body. This was designed to give West Germany a voice in NATO in the absence of her full membership.[93] Finally, the NATO Lisbon conference on 22 February adopted reciprocal security undertakings between the EDC and NATO that any armed attack on the former would be regarded as an armed attack on the latter and vice versa.

At the same time Schuman was able to present the final report on the EDC to the conference, declaring triumphantly that the project was 'so near completion'.[94]

7. Britain's treaty relations with the European Defence Community

By the middle of March, however, the Paris conference once again deadlocked over a West German proposal for including a provision for an automatic defence guarantee in the proposed EDC Treaty. This envisaged the imposition on the EDC members of the same obligations as were defined under article IV of the Brussels Treaty of 1948, that is, that all members of the EDC would automatically fight to repel an attack upon any member of the Community. Conversely, the NATO treaty allowed each of its members to take 'such action as it deems necessary, including the use of armed force, to restore and maintain the security of the North Atlantic area'. The Dutch were unwilling to enter into a more binding guarantee than that provided by NATO, for the sake of West Germany, unless the British followed suit. The Dutch attitude reflected a general reluctance by the West Europeans to use their armed forces to defend West Germany in all circumstances, and the latter's awareness of this led the Federal Republic to insist on the adoption by the EDC of a compulsory military undertaking, otherwise she could never feel secure that the Community would come to her defence.[95] In the words of James Dunn, the American ambassador to Paris, West Germany's case was 'so unshakable' that the European army conference could not resolve the impasse between the Dutch and the Germans without asking Britain to form a treaty relationship with the EDC.[96]

Accordingly, the Paris conference proposed that if Britain signed a treaty with the EDC it would only involve her in extending to Italy and West Germany the same reciprocal military undertakings she had already given to the Brussels treaty powers: France, Belgium, Luxembourg and the Netherlands.[97] By the end of March it became clear to Eden that: 'the EDC is not likely to be established unless we respond to this latest proposal'.[98] The French government warned London that British rejection of this proposal would lead to even stronger French Parliamentary clamour for British membership in the EDC, while the Dutch would abandon the EDC project, resulting in the withdrawal of the two other Benelux powers.[99]

The request from the Paris conference would mean the establishment of a common *casus foederis* for both the Brussels pact and the

EDC. The former was to last for fifty years after its inception in 1948 and it was intended that the latter should continue for the same length of time. Conversely, each member state of NATO could denounce the treaty twenty years after 1949 by giving one year's notice. Britain's acceptance of the request from the Paris conference meant involving Britain in automatic guarantees to Italy and West Germany for 50 years, while the United States could refuse to act in an emergency since she was bound only to fulfil the weaker obligations of the NATO treaty. If the United States, where isolationist tendencies seemed to the British to remain influential, was to leave NATO after the twenty years' compulsory membership period, Britain would be left alone to bear onerous commitments to the European Defence Community.[100]

Despite these drawbacks, Eden was willing to enter some form of treaty arrangement with the EDC in order to 'demonstrate' to the Europeans and the Americans that, 'though not a part of the Continent, we are linked with its fortunes'.[101] Hence, Eden persuaded the Cabinet to approve a new formula for a British treaty relationship with the Community on 4 April 1952: essentially Britain would accept an obligation to provide military assistance in the event of an attack on any party to the EDC or the European Defence Forces, by virtue of the innocuous and broad concept of 'the inherent right of individual or collective self-defence' under Article 51 of the UN Charter, which would enable Britain to avoid being committed directly to the Brussels formula. Furthermore this commitment would be limited to the duration of the NATO treaty and not to that of the Brussels pact. Thus Britain's proposed treaty obligations to the Community would amount to little more that what she had already accepted under the NATO treaty in terms of its length and its legal requirements.[102] Nevertheless, European responses to this formula, which was put forward at the Paris conference on 9 April, were generally favourable. Van Vredenburch of the Dutch delegation went so far as to say that Britain 'had broken [a] serious Conf[erence] deadlock', while Alphand, the French chairman, commented that 'without this answer from [the] UK there wld [would] have been no EDC'.[103]

8. *The economic factors behind Britain's cooperation with the EDC*

During the final stages of the negotiations on Germany's future political and military arrangements with the West, Britain became increasingly concerned about the economic dimension of the German rearmament question. The problem of how to extract the local costs of the allied forces stationed in West Germany from the Federal government, and for as long as possible, continued to torment leading British diplomats, soldiers and financial experts. A fundamental reason for Britain's frustrating experiences in this area was that while Britain could not assume any additional financial burdens for the defence of Western Europe, the three occupying powers would not be able to impose on West German taxpayers the entire costs incurred by allied troops stationed in West Germany after the occupation regime was replaced by the new contractual arrangements. The question of these costs would have to be determined by negotiations between West Germany and the three allied powers.

By the end of February 1952 it was agreed that West Germany should pay a financial contribution to the West on the basis of figures recommended by the Temporary Council Committee of NATO to the European Defence Community, which would distribute her payments to cover both German support for the local expenditures of the allied forces and German rearmament for the EDC. Accordingly, West Germany was to make available DM 850 million monthly (i.e., an annual rate of DM 10.2 thousand million nearly equivalent to £867 million in November 1951 – which was roughly 10 per cent of the GNP of each NATO member state), from the date of entry into force of both the new contractual agreement and the EDC treaty until 30 June 1953, on the assumption that the treaty would be ratified before the autumn of 1952.[104] The three allied powers hoped that during this initial period of less than a year the cost of maintaining her contingents would be met in full if the Federal government agreed to devote two-thirds of the DM 850 million a month to this purpose, as it was expected that the scale of German rearmament for the EDC would at first be fairly low. However, allied expectations were only partially fulfilled when after tough negotiations with the West Germans on the eve of the signature of the EDC treaty, it was agreed that the Federal Republic would cover the support costs fully for the first six months, but that thereafter they would be drastically reduced.[105]

Britain could solve this financial problem if the United States agreed to pay for the difference between the average annual cost of the British forces of £130 millions (a figure which had been reduced from the previous one of £164 millions as a result of economies imposed on the British Army of the Rhine by the British government since October 1951) and the amount that the Germans would cover. It remained uncertain whether the US would provide such aid: any new authorisation of funds could not take effect until after 1953 when a more strict Congressional definition for such American assistance would apply.[106] Furthermore, Britain's dependence on US financial help would hardly assist her purpose of reasserting the special relationship, a consideration of which Eden was well aware as he embarked for the Washington talks in January 1952.[107]

Nevertheless, without any additional financial support from the US or elsewhere, Britain might well have to withdraw her four divisions (an additional division had been sent to West Germany in the autumn of 1950) from West Germany in a few years' time. This possibility was considered at a joint meeting of officials of the Ministry of Defence, the Treasury, the Foreign Office and the Chiefs of Staff on 28 April 1952. This meeting concluded that the reduction and redeployment of Britain's overseas garrisons elsewhere to provide the savings to pay for the maintenance of British troops in Germany would be impossible to achieve at short notice and would in any case be undesirable on military and political grounds.[108]

More significantly, British willingness to contemplate pulling her troops out of West Germany reflected a move away from relying for her defence on conventional weapons towards a future strategy based on deterrence by nuclear weapons. In view of the recent reduction in East–West tension in Europe and Britain's economic difficulties, the Chiefs of Staff began to examine Britain's long-term strategic requirements in the spring of 1952, which culminated in a report on 'Defence Policy and Global Strategy', which was approved by the Cabinet in July 1952.[109] The new strategic thinking was inspired by Air Chief Marshal Slessor, the Chief of the Air Staff, who argued that Britain should develop her strategic air offensive power, in terms of long-range bombers rather than the Canberra light bombers on which she relied in 1952, in order both to counter effectively a Soviet atomic threat and to enable Britain to establish a nuclear partnership with the US in Europe.[110] One of the virtues of this strategy was that it would enable Britain to reduce considerably the number of troops she maintained in Trieste and Austria, and possibly even in West Germany.[111]

On the other hand, the Foreign Office was conscious of the likely repercussions of a British decision to withdraw her armed forces from West Germany, i.e., Britain's main defence contribution to NATO, on European aspirations for closer integration and on her political and diplomatic relations with both the continental powers and the United States. Furthermore, this policy would run directly counter to NATO's strategy for the deployment of sufficient conventional forces, which had only recently been affirmed at Lisbon in February.[112] It was ironical that, while Britain was making solemn promises to maintain her forces in Europe as a means of sustaining the EDC, she was privately agonising about the heavy financial costs of such a decision. As Strang noted gloomily on 29 April 1952: 'The financial consequences of German rearmament, not clearly foreseen when the original decisions were taken, are now looming up with increasing menace'.[113]

9. Last minute doubts about the signature of the EDC treaty

Almost at the last minute two setbacks occurred which threatened the final conclusion and signature of the EDC treaty. First the Dutch threatened not to sign the treaty unless the fifty-year duration was reduced to seventeen years (which applied to the NATO treaty) or unless the Netherlands was allowed to withdraw from the Community should the British and American guarantees be terminated. This was another manifestation of the Netherlands' fear of becoming entangled in the EDC without concrete assurances of Anglo-American support.[114] The United States and Britain would be committed to their guarantees to the EDC only for so long as they remained members of NATO, and if they decided to leave that organisation their EDC guarantees would automatically lapse. However, this crisis was soon resolved when, after the Anglo-Americans had assured the Netherlands that they regarded their membership of NATO as permanent, the Dutch agreed to the insertion of a compromise Article (i.e., 128) into the EDC treaty, which stipulated that: 'If...the North Atlantic Treaty should cease to be in force or there should be an essential modification of the membership of the North Atlantic Treaty Organisation, the High Contracting Parties shall examine together the new situation thus created.' Furthermore, when the EDC treaty was signed on 27 May 1952, the six Foreign Ministers stated that they intended to examine the issue of making the NATO treaty co-terminate with that of the EDC.[115]

This problem was no sooner settled than France also began to make difficulties about the guarantee. It will be recalled that it had been decided in London that this would be issued in the form of a tripartite declaration at the time of the signature of the EDC treaty. Britain, the United States and France were to affirm their interest in the continued existence of the EDC, and this would involve an Anglo-American resolution to retain their armed forces in Europe 'as they deem necessary and appropriate'. This implied that the two countries would be empowered to decide when they should withdraw their troops from Europe. The French now demanded that the phrase 'as they *deem* necessary and appropriate' be replaced by 'as they *are* necessary and appropriate to contribute to the joint defence of the North Atlantic Treaty area', thus reducing Anglo-American freedom in the matter. Furthermore, the French tried to persuade the two powers to agree that they would provide additional military forces to substitute for those of any member of the EDC who decided to secede from the Community.[116]

Britain and the United States refused to extend their obligations to the EDC beyond what they had accepted under the NATO treaty, and they accordingly rejected the two French proposals. Nevertheless, they agreed to modify part of the final text of their joint guarantee in order to satisfy the French:

> Accordingly, if any action from whatever quarter threatens the integrity or unity of the community, the two Governments will regard this as a threat to their own security. They will *act* in accordance with Article 4 of the North Atlantic Treaty.[117]

By replacing the word 'consider' with 'act' and also by omitting the reference to 'consultation' in the previous text, the statement appeared now to be both more straightforward and more positive.[118]

The resolution of these last-minute difficulties enabled the powers concerned to sign the EDC treaty and its related documents, which included the protocol on the relations between the EDC and NATO, together with a treaty between Britain and the EDC on an internal defence commitment. The ceremony took place in Paris on 27 May 1952, one day after the signature of the contractual agreements between the three occupying powers and West Germany in Bonn.

This signature of the EDC treaty did not mark the end of the six powers' efforts to create a European army. On the contrary, the negotiations since the autumn of 1951 had revealed that the prospective member countries of the Community were becoming increasingly worried about how much they would have to pay in order to achieve the supposed political advantage of furthering European unity via the European army. Many deputies in the French Parliament and the leaders of the Benelux countries now recognised that the EDC would not prevent the resurgence of West Germany, whose economic strength was growing steadily and, indeed, even faster than the allies had anticipated, in marked contrast with that of France, distracted and weakened as she was by her overseas commitments.[119] In order to fill the gap between French weakness and burgeoning German strength, the continental powers began to insist that Britain become more closely involved in Western Europe, not as a mere balancer in the traditional sense, but as an active participant, preferably by joining the Community as a full member.

Britain's policy on the EDC also signified a shift from Eden's earlier reluctance to become involved in the organisation to a decision to bind Britain more closely to it. First, Britain agreed to enter into a technical association with the Community, secondly, she offered a security guarantee to the EDC, and finally in March 1951 she decided to establish a treaty relationship with the European Defence Community. These steps, although they were carefully designed not to exceed British defence commitments under the NATO treaty, were taken mainly to disarm those critics who claimed she was lukewarm towards the European army, to prevent her from being made the scapegoat in the event of the failure of the EDC, which would have a serious effect on her relationships with her European allies and particularly with the USA. Eden commented sarcastically in his 15 December 1951 minute to Churchill that '[i]t would indeed be fantastic if the test for American military assistance was not our defence effort but our readiness to merge in a European Federation'.[120]

Consequently, Britain contributed to the negative aspects of the EDC treaty in her anxiety to encourage its successful conclusion. Of course, failure to reach agreement would have had dire consequences, with no solution to the problem of a German military contribution, which would have meant that the contractual agreement with West Germany could not have been finalised, while Adenauer's policy of securing West German integration into the West on equal terms would have been frustrated. The Truman administration was impatient for the conclusion of the negotiations before the Presidential elections in November 1952. A setback in Europe at this stage would have caused Congress to lose faith in the strength of purpose of the Western Europeans and would have resulted in the reduction of American military aid to them. At the same time, American opinion would have blamed British lack of support for the premature death of the EDC. On the other hand the alternative of reverting to a NATO solution would have been even more unacceptable to the Europeans, especially to the French. The combined effect of these considerations persuaded the six Western European powers to take the risk of signing the EDC treaty.

6 THE FATE OF THE EDC PROJECT

1. *The aftermath of the signature of the EDC treaty*

The tortuous negotiations leading to the signature of the EDC treaty were the precursor of the frustrating process of ratifying the treaty. Inevitably, democratic societies with highly developed bureaucracies were to find ratification a time-consuming process. Their legislatures would have to examine the voluminous treaty of 132 Articles, together with several protocols (in contrast to the fourteen Articles of the NATO treaty), before voting on the bill to approve it.

The signatories had to produce draft provisions covering the initial period when the West German elements within the European framework would be recruited and trained. Under protocol 8 of the EDC treaty this task was assigned to the EDC Interim Committee under its President, Alphand. The Interim Committee could not authorise or execute any measures, but was to act as a coordinating and planning body during the period between the signature of the treaty and its full ratification by the participants. All this was supposed to be completed within the six months prior to 1 January 1953, the date on which it was anticipated that the EDC would come into force. By the end of July 1952, however, it had become clear that these discussions were faced with the same conflicts of national interests which had delayed the previous negotiations in Paris. The West Germans continued to demand absolute equality in the Community, the French remained fearful of West Germany's future military resurgence, while the Benelux countries were still doubtful about the wisdom of participating in such an organisation.[1]

The West German Chancellor could not, in any case, take any further action on the treaty in the *Bundestag* until the Federal Court had ruled whether or not remilitarisation was constitutionally compatible with the Basic Law of 1949. Consequently, Adenauer was forced to postpone the third reading of the bill to ratify the treaty (the Lower House had passed the first and second readings by a simple majority) until the end of January 1953, thereby destroying Anglo-American hopes that West Germany would ratify the treaty by the end of 1952.[2]

Alcide de Gasperi, the Italian Prime Minister, a leading partisan of the EDC, also found himself involved in internal political complications. Despite British and American pressure, he was reluctant to put the EDC bill to the Italian Parliament while the problem of Trieste remained unsettled. Eventually he decided not to go ahead with the ratification process until after the general elections which would probably not take place before the spring of 1953. The Benelux countries were naturally unwilling to take the lead in ratifying the treaty before the West Germans and the French had done so.[3]

France was already behind the other five in that she was in no mood even to consider placing the treaty before the National Assembly for approval. There remained the usual stumbling blocks which had hindered the negotiating stages of the EDC treaty: the question of the Saar, French involvement in Indochina and her consequent military weakness in Europe, the refusal of Britain to join the Community, and France's anxiety to find out how the Soviet Union regarded the project. French hostility towards the EDC was demonstrated by favourable press responses to anti-EDC speeches by Edouard Herriot and Edouard Daladier at the otherwise pro-European Radical party's congress in the autumn of 1952.[4]

Geoffrey Harrison, the Assistant Under-Secretary in charge of Western European affairs at the Foreign Office, minuted, on 12 November 1952, that: 'It would be easy but unhelpful to say that the rot is in France itself. The moral sickness is a permanent factor in the situation.' Robert Scott, another Assistant Under-Secretary of State, criticised the French on similar lines:

> Everyone recognises that Indo-China is a frightful drain on France. Yet in a sense it is a symptom rather than a cause of French impotence. Since Turkey recovered twenty years ago France has taken her place as the sick man of Europe. She exploits her feebleness and the debt which others owe to her to secure palliatives from abroad.

Eden agreed with these sentiments – he commented 'Very Good' on Scott's minute.[5]

Nevertheless, if Britain did not respond sympathetically to France's grievances, there would be continued impasse over the ratification of the EDC treaty. The Foreign Office interpreted French fears about

German predominance in terms of the imbalance of French military strength *vis-à-vis* the military potential of West Germany. The Federal Republic was now to contribute more troops than France to the EDC– West Germany had promised an initial contribution of twelve *groupements* – because in February 1952 France was forced to reduce her original target of fourteen *groupements* to ten as a result of the increasing demands of the Indochina war. At the same time she was also forced to cut the size of the air force she had earmarked for the EDC. Ironically, the West Germans had never applied their demand for equality to the scale of the participating forces, and France could easily have found more troops for Europe if she had extended the period of military service to two years as she had promised in 1950. Thus, Eden and the Foreign Office were inclined to blame France's political incompetence for the predicament in which she found herself.[6]

France's fear of a rearmed West Germany was not based solely on the disparity in Franco-German force strengths in the European army. The original concept of the Pleven plan was that France would be able to supervise and contain West German rearmament. However, during the Paris negotiations France had been compelled to agree to the collective leadership of the Board of Commissioners over the European army – in which body West Germany was to be represented – instead of the overall command being vested in a French general as she had originally intended. She had also been forced to accede to the German view that the most practical minimum size of a national unit should be about 13,000 men, the size of a small division, in preference to her initial idea of merging German forces in the European army at battalion level. Moreover, France had had to swallow West Germany's demand for a fifty-year automatic security guarantee in the EDC treaty. Thus it gradually became evident to her that West Germany, by virtue of her military expertise and her steadily growing economic power, would eventually dominate the European Defence Community.[7]

Indeed, a number of British politicians and military leaders, who were anxious to perpetuate Britain's influence on the Continent, also regarded such an outcome as detrimental to British interests in Europe. Slessor minuted on 20 October 1952 that:

> If we joined the EDC, we could probably make it a reality and we could assume the leadership. If we do not it is more than possible either that the whole thing will collapse and probably carry NATO with it, or if it survives, it will only be a matter of time before the Germans lead it.[8]

Montgomery, who had reversed his previous opposition to British membership in the EDC, upset Churchill by insisting, on 10 December 1952, that:

> Unless the British will...join in the European Army, the European Army ship will crash on the rocks...I can see no justification why the British should not come in. They can make any reservations they like, e.g. the Navy is not to be included, the bulk of the British Air Forces in the UK are not included, a reservation about the maximum strength of land forces to be kept in peacetime on the Continent, etc. etc.[9]

Slessor and Montgomery pointed to one method of overcoming Britain's reluctance to be subjected to any control over her armed forces by entering a federal organisation and this demonstrated that there could be no purely supranational army in Europe: if the French did not dominate it, Britain would have to do so before the West Germans did.

Denis Healey, who led the pro-European section in the Labour party, recommended to his party colleagues in the spring of 1953 that Britain should offer to put the BAOR in the EDC, with the Americans contributing part of their forces to it, if, in return, France agreed to West Germany's membership of NATO. The idea was to reduce the danger of West Germany's predominance in Europe since, even if Germany could swamp the EDC despite an Anglo-American contribution, she could not swamp NATO.[10] Macmillan, who shared Healey's concern, minuted on 19 March 1953 that, if the EDC collapsed, Britain should seize the opportunity to recommend a fresh approach to the question, possibly along the lines of Churchill's idea of forming a coalition army in Europe, modelled largely on NATO, in which each government would be responsible for its forces in that army.[11]

However, the Conservative government's policy towards the EDC had remained virtually unchanged since December 1951, when Eden and the Foreign Office had first outlined their basic attitude to the EDC – that Britain would support the consummation of the Community from the outside, but would refuse to become a full member. Since then Eden had agreed to make a few concessions to ensure the success of the EDC, but he would go no further unless he was assured that the United States would follow suit. Nor would he encourage the French to make any major modifications in the EDC treaty or to adopt an alternative approach to the question of West German rearmament since these would create further delays in establishing the Community. Britain was willing to explore further the means of strengthening her links with the EDC, for instance through British force collaboration with the European Defence Force, but that was all. Why did Britain continue to support the setting up of the EDC after anti-British feelings in Europe and the United States had subsided and in the face of increasing French reservations about the project? The answer to this question lies in an examination of the extremely narrow course which remained open to Britain if she was to settle the problem of West Germany's rearmament in her favour.

When the question was first mooted in 1950 Britain had felt more confident that she could solve it within the framework of NATO. However, as has been discussed, the NATO solution became less attractive to Britain after the West Germans made known their conditions for their participation in NATO during the Bonn talks of 1951. Furthermore Eden and his officials were not convinced of the reliability of the West German people or the stability of German democracy, at least to the extent of supporting her full membership of NATO.[12] As Liddell Hart noted in July 1952:

> For in Germany even more than in other countries the maxim 'attack is the best defence' has been dogma. The persistence of this dogma can lead to what is paradoxically called 'preventive war'.[13]

Of course the French were even more obsessed by this fear, but British politicians pretended not to take seriously French anxiety about a possible German provocation to the USSR once they had rearmed. For instance, Eden told President Vincent Auriol on 16 December 1952 that:

> In any event Germans were not in the habit of embarking on wars unless they had formidable military superiority. The day when Western Germany would be in such a position *vis-à-vis* Soviet Russia was surely some way off.[14]

However, within the Foreign Office this was regarded as a 'very real problem' should Germany be admitted to NATO. A Foreign Office paper, approved by Eden on 19 December 1952, suggested that the Western allies obtain a written agreement from the Federal Republic that she would not attempt to fulfil her ambition to reunify the country or to recover her former territories beyond the Oder-Neisse line other than by peaceful means.[15] Tactically it was better not to agree with the French about the danger of a rearmed West Germany, for, if Britain did so, it would be more difficult for her to encourage France to ratify the EDC treaty without being forced to offer her further British concessions to strengthen her position in the

Community. In fact in 1952 Britain's concern about a possible German military resurgence was felt more strongly than it had been two years earlier. This was probably influenced by recent developments culminating in West Germany's signature of both the Bonn Conventions (the contractual agreements) and the EDC treaty. If the French were now unable to ratify the latter, there could be no going back on the question of German rearmament. In view of this possibility, the Foreign Office, at the beginning of December, began to prepare an alternative to the EDC through the revision of the existing NATO framework.

The thorny problem with which Eden's officials were confronted was whether the West Germans could be included in NATO without either prejudicing their demand for equality or preventing the West from securing controls over West Germany's military establishment. The solution seemed to be to provide NATO with a more integrated structure. To this end, the British plan, although it was no more than an outline, proposed the adoption of some common arrangements concerning the infrastruture, equipment, armaments and supplies, and a common budget which would be administered by a Defence Commissioner who would be separate from SACEUR.

This British scheme for a remodelled NATO bore some resemblance to Bevin's abortive proposal for an Atlantic confederate force which he had put forward as a counter proposal to the Pleven plan in the autumn of 1950. Indeed, the present plan suffered from the same problems as had Bevin's in respect to its acceptability to the United States and to the British Chiefs of Staff. In an effort to overcome this drawback, the new Foreign Office proposal concentrated on the concepts of 'standardisation' and 'specialisation'. Continental NATO powers would be expected to promote the same degree of standardisation as provided for under the EDC treaty, but West Germany would require special treatment in terms of her armaments production and, for this purpose, as was defined in the EDC treaty, she would be regarded as 'a strategically exposed area'. Conversely, in view of their heavy non-NATO responsibilities, the United States and Britain would not be subject to the same provisions as the European NATO countries, but in return they would be required to accept special responsibilities – for instance, in providing the entire strategic air force for NATO. This was now less militarily impracticable than when the COS had adopted the idea in their global strategy paper, as Britain had since acquired her own means of producing atomic bombs. Moreover, such 'specialisation' would justify a reduction of British troops in West Germany, thus alleviating the financial strain of maintaining the BAOR when the West Germans began their own rearmament.[16]

Overall, this alternative proposal for a reformed NATO envisaged the creation of a continental federation inside NATO. Under this scheme Norway, Denmark, Portugal, together with the five signatories of the EDC treaty, were to be deprived of their independent voices in NATO, but they would be on the same level as West Germany, in contrast to the United States and Britain, who were to enjoy a special status as extra-European great powers. No mention was made in the paper about the roles of Canada and Iceland.

Clearly the other allies would be most unlikely to accept this British vision of a revised NATO. The fact that the Foreign office's plan provided for a common defence budget and a Defence Minister in NATO directly challenged one of the main reasons for Britain not joining the EDC – that it embraced the federalist principle. Indeed, President Auriol had suggested to Eden in Paris on 16 December 1952 that Britain could join a looser confederated defence community 'without sacrifice or [of] sovereignty within the State of Europe by means of a joint Council of Ministers at the top'.[17]

In the end Britain decided not to put forward this Foreign Office plan for developing a confederate NATO army since it would only raise France's expectations that Britain might agree to participate in a European military organisation after all. Instead, Britain tried to per-suade the French to ratify the existing EDC treaty by making it clear that the only alternative to this would be the outright admission of West Germany into NATO – a form of blackmail designed to convince the French that the EDC was the lesser of the two evils, despite the fact that the British were themselves apprehensive about the NATO solution.[18]

Of course, Britain's political and economic position ruled out her participation in a European federation, and this was further rein-forced by strategic and military considerations inherent in the West German rearmament question: Britain would not join in European military arrangements to include a rearmed West Germany without the close involvement of the United States. Thus Eden's policy was essentially that of Bevin's in that he too wanted to solve the problem of West Germany's rearmament only in the context of the Atlantic community. However, given the profound difficulties involved in making the NATO solution acceptable to all the powers concerned, and also given that the Americans were encouraging the EDC project, there was no point in Britain trying to break the EDC stalemate by putting forward vague ideas for a remodelled NATO, which might endanger whatever prospect there remained of securing the ratification of the EDC treaty. Therefore Britain's only recourse was the limited and frustrating one of continuing to press France to ratify the EDC treaty even if this meant that Britain had to make further concessions to the French and move even closer to the EDC than she had intended.

2. The Eisenhower administration and the EDC

The inauguration of a Republican President in January 1953 for the first time in twenty years did not result in any dramatic departure from Truman's policy towards Europe. Eisenhower was more concerned about the strains imposed on the United States by her role as a global power and intended to perform this role in future less intrusively and more indirectly by seeking to avoid Truman's tendency to undertake onerous commitments as a 'world policeman', of which, in Eisenhower's eyes, American intervention in the Korean war was the most glaring example.[19] A major priority for the new Republican administration was to end the war on the Korean peninsula, and it was relatively sanguine about the European theatre, clearly anticipating that the EDC treaty would be ratified in the near future.[20]

The new President's enthusiastic support for the EDC project was shared by his Secretary of State, John Foster Dulles. Dulles was as attracted by the supranational concept of the European army as a means of rejuvenating Europe and of ending the historical Franco-German discord as he was by the vision of the United States liberating the enslaved peoples of Communist-dominated Eastern Europe.[21]

The EDC fitted in as satisfactorily with Eisenhower's policy for Europe as it had with that of the Truman administration; the project was a European innovation and its success depended upon the efforts of the Europeans themselves. Moreover, the finalisation of the EDC project would ensure a German military contribution to Western defence and, as a result, the need for a large American military presence in the central strategic area of Europe would decrease. The US government regarded the EDC, in the words of William Draper, the US special representative to NATO, as 'the most pressing current problem in Europe', for the security of the United States.[22]

However, how could the US attain this goal in view of the diminishing likelihood of the EDC treaty being ratified? Dulles's first major policy announcement of 27 January 1953 was designed to revitalise the EDC project which, in his eyes, appeared 'to be somewhat stalled'.

> if it appeared there were no chance of getting effective unity, and in particular France, Germany and England should go their separate ways, then certainly it would be necessary to give a little re-thinking to America's own foreign policy in relation to Western Europe.[23]

In reality, the United States was unlikely to achieve much by any such 'little re-thinking'. From the American perspective there were three ways in which a new momentum could be injected into the EDC project: by an American threat to retreat to the peripheral defence of Europe, by instigating an alternative approach to the problem of West Germany's rearmament, or by applying strenuous pressure on France to ratify the treaty.

Dulles suggested the first option of adopting a peripheral approach to the defence of Western Europe to the Joint Chiefs of Staff on 28 January. However, Bradley exposed this as wishful thinking by countering that:

> If one looks at the alternative [i.e., peripheral defence] and contemplates going back on to the continent after having lost it, all the people we now know would be gone...If we were to give up the concept of defending Germany, the Iron Curtain might move to the Rhine which would give us a very serious military problem.[24]

Joseph J. Wolf, in charge of European regional affairs at the State Department, was equally negative, commenting that the idea of peripheral defence was 'such strong and unwholesome medicine that it would probably hurt us more than help us'.[25]

As for the second suggestion for American policy in the event of the non-ratification of the EDC, the Joint Chiefs of Staff were prepared to accept West Germany's membership of NATO, without imposing 'undue restrictions on the build-up of her military force or on her output of military equipment'.[26] However, on account of its unacceptability to the French (Dulles suspected that the French 'would' and 'could' veto such a NATO solution), Admiral William Fechteler, the Chief of Naval Operations, suggested an Anglo-German–US alliance. A similar proposal for the conclusion of a separate US–West German security pact had already been considered by Draper in a minute of 26 January 1953, but it was obvious that the exclusion of the French from the defence of Western Europe would create even more serious complications for American defence planners and it was a risk that the US was not prepared to take. Nor was Wolf's idea of a revised NATO modelled on the EDC (broadly similar to the Foreign Office's concept of a remodelled NATO) taken up seriously as a promising alternative by Eisenhower or Dulles, who were both inclined to cling to the theoretical virtues of the EDC.[27]

The last possibility was to inform the French that they would not receive any more aid from the US until 'they do something about ratifying the EDC'. However this also involved appalling consequences for the security of South-east Asia if it caused the French to withdraw from Indochina. Bradley, who had proposed this 'aid' only in return 'for the EDC' policy, admitted that the loss of Indochina might lead to the loss of all South-east Asia while Dulles added that this would probably lead to 'the loss of Japan' as well.[28] Conversely, the US might adopt a generous attitude towards French requests for American financial and diplomatic support in return for a French promise to ratify the treaty. Leon Fuller (the Deputy Director of the Office of German Political Affairs in the State Department) and James Dunn both supported a generous aid policy in order 'to salvage a dangerous situation', as the US believed that the EDC was, in Draper's words, 'Hobson's choice'.[29]

Just as Britain was both unwilling and unable to make any positive contribution to the resolution of the EDC problem, the United States, despite resounding pledges of her support for the project, was equally incapable of finding a constructive approach towards its fulfilment. But, with a view to exercising the maximum psychological pressure on the Europeans, Dulles visited Europe between 30 January and 8 February, and on 18 February Bruce was appointed head of the US observer delegation to the Paris Interim Committee.[30]

4. France's demand for further British cooperation with the EDC project, January–May 1953

George Bidault, who was appointed French Foreign Minister in January 1953, was less enthusiastic than Schuman towards the cause of European unity. René Mayer's coalition government tried to dispel the mood of indecisiveness generated by the previous administration by emphasising the continuity in France's policy in Europe since Schuman. The Mayer government's evident determination to see the EDC project through could not alter the fact that the French had become disenchanted with the European army plan and were now opposed to France surrendering her military sovereignty for the sake of it. This opposition to the EDC was reinforced by the fact that the Gaullists continued to attack the EDC on the grounds that it would entail the disappearance of the French national army and because of Britain's continued refusal to participate in the Community.[31]

As a result of these factors the new French government decided to attach three conditions for France's ratification of the treaty: first, that the future status of the Saar be clearly defined; second, that Britain become more closely associated with the EDC and third, consideration by the six of additional protocols to the EDC treaty which the French now insisted on putting forward. While the Mayer government did not attempt to clarify its first and second conditions during its first month in office, the additional protocols, which had evidently been prepared by the previous government, soon became public knowledge.[32]

These protocols were intended to guarantee the French greater freedom and flexibility within the Community in order to maintain the integrity of the French national army. First, France wanted the right to transfer part of her EDC contingents to the French Union, should an emergency arise there, without having to obtain both the prior approval of the EDC Board of Commissioners and the agreements in advance of SACEUR, as provided for under Article 13 of the EDC treaty. Second, the French wished to acquire more control over the nomination of French officers serving in the Community, and to exchange them with other French personnel if their services were required for non-EDC purposes – under Articles 10 and 31 of the treaty, the EDC administration had the right to determine personnel questions. A third demand was for her unequivocal right to manufacture, import and export armaments for use in conjunction with France's military commitments outside Europe in place of the restrictions to this process imposed under Article 107 of the treaty. Fourth, although Article 43-bis laid down a system of weighting the votes in the Council of Ministers, largely in proportion to the size of forces allocated to the EDC by each of the six member states, during the transitional period France was given the same voting scale of three (as opposed to one for Luxembourg) as that of West Germany. The French now wanted to freeze that scale for an indefinite period and thereby maintain a voice in the Council at least equal to that of West Germany regardless of the actual size of France's contribution to the EDC. The remainder of the French demands were concerned with the continuation of national plans for mobilisation until the EDC had worked out detailed formulae for these; the right to use the EDC military school by French forces for non-EDC purposes; the definition of a special status for French occupation troops stationed in West Germany for the first two years of the transitional period; and prior

115

agreement on the arrangements for the distribution of aid from the United States destined for the EDC contingents.[33]

Not surprisingly, the other five designated states of the EDC were irritated by France's attempt to insert these additional protocols into the treaty and, when they were first discussed on 11 February at a meeting of the Steering Committee, their delegations insisted that they were incompatible with both the spirit and the language of the EDC treaty. Adenauer bitterly criticised the French initiative for 'destroying much of its [the treaty's] European character' and for discriminating against Germany. The French action encouraged the SPD to launch a strong anti-EDC and anti-French campaign.[34] Conversely, the Benelux powers and Italy, partly as a result of Dulles's efforts during his visit to Europe in early February, were generally agreeable to his suggestion that their four governments should proceed with the process of ratification without waiting for the completion of the negotiations on the additional French protocols. This agreement was also important in helping Adenauer to overcome his increasing political difficulties.[35]

In mid-March, at a meeting of the Steering Committee on this issue, the French delegation made significant concessions to the views of the other delegations, thus opening the way for a revision of the French protocols. The most important feature of this was agreement on a formula in which the most controversial French protocols – such as the demand for the withdrawal of French troops from the EDC as of right, and her absolute freedom to manufacture arms, etc. for her troops overseas – would be treated as 'interpretive instructions' to be issued by the Council of Ministers of the EDC after the treaty was ratified. However, the delegations accepted the French demands for the right to exchange French personnel for the EDC for those for non-European service, and the indefinite continuation of the interim weighting of votes, which would be covered by additional protocols to the EDC treaty as the French had requested.[36]

The agreed text was ready for approval by the six governments by 24 March 1953 and, four days later, a communiqué issued after Franco-American talks in Washington effectively brought to an end the controversy over the much publicised protocols.[37] Although the original French demands had been moderated, the French had managed to secure significant concessions from the other five powers. Now the French turned to Britain in an effort to extract further concessions from her.

France approached Britain on 12 February with a proposal to establish 'a relationship of organic co-operation going further than mere association' between the EDC and Britain. The essence of the French proposal was that Britain should agree to maintain her armed forces in Europe at their existing strength and, in return, Britain would be entitled to participate in EDC institutions. However, after consultation with SACEUR, Britain could withdraw her forces in the event of emergencies elsewhere.[38]

This was a far-reaching proposal in the sense that it went much further than Britain's NATO obligation, under which the size and nature of her force contribution was determined, for the following year, by the NATO annual review. Moreover, under it Britain would face greater restrictions than France, a signatory of the EDC, who was seeking the right to withdraw her forces from the EDC without consulting SACEUR in advance. In any event, as has been shown earlier, Britain could not accept such a restriction. In addition, Britain's difficulties about the support costs of her troops in West Germany were already forcing the Joint Planning Staff to plan for the reduction of one armoured division out of the present strength of four divisions (one infantry and three armoured) of the BAOR. Eden had already written to Churchill on 7 January 1953 that he did not 'feel like being blackmailed by the new French Government into any more concessions'.[39] However, in the face of this persistent French pressure, he was now prepared to go a little further towards meeting French requirements by promising to consult the EDC institution about the level of British forces on the Continent if, as he told the Cabinet on 24 February, 'that would help the French to secure ratification of the Treaty'.[40]

A second facet of the French proposal was the way Britain's military undertaking was tied to her 'political right' to attend the EDC institution. Although Eden disliked this linkage, Britain was willing to establish close political and military contacts with the EDC.[41] To this end, Britain had already suggested some form of British military association with the EDC forces to the EDC Interim Military Committee on 24 January 1953.[42] Thus, it appeared to the British that the most satisfactory method of meeting the latest French request was to propose a programme of close political cooperation, while at the same time attempting to reach a compromise over the question of future British troop deployments. The British counter proposals were approved by Cabinet ministers on 26 February, and handed to Bidault in the form of a unilateral British declaration on 2 March, while a similar declaration was subsequently submitted to the EDC Interim Committee.[43]

After pointing out that Britain had already entered into a number of commitments to the EDC before the signature of the treaty, the British declaration suggested that the most effective way of increasing political links between the EDC and Britain would be for Britain to send a mission to the Board of Commissioners of the Community in order to keep in day to day contact with that body, and for a British minister to attend meetings of the Council of Ministers when matters of mutual concern were to be discussed, 'including the level of United Kingdom and EDC forces to be maintained on the Continent at any given time'. Finally, Britain expressed her willingness to join the EDC signatories in making 'a proposal to the other NATO countries' for the extension of the NATO treaty for a further thirty years in order to make it 'co-terminus' with the EDC treaty.[44]

Although the extension of the initial compulsory membership of the NATO from twenty to fifty years entailed the prolongation both of her treaty relationship with the EDC and the period of her guarantee to that institution, Britain felt that she could compromise on this issue because it would force the United States to follow her example: this had, of course, been Britain's original formula for settling the German rearmament question. This was, of course, contrary to the American interest in reducing their commitment to the defence of Western Europe, although they were only too willing to encourage Britain to move closer to the EDC so long as this did not affect the existing US undertaking to the Continent.[45]

While Shuckburgh described the relations between Eden and Dulles as 'like two lute strings whose vibrations never coincide',[46] the British Foreign Secretary, firmly convinced of the 'cardinal importance' of developing the closest possible cooperation with the US, was now trying to help the American Secretary of State to reach agreement with the EDC. However, during Anglo-American talks in Washington on 5 March 1953, Dulles insisted that 'it should be understood that the US and UK would take corresponding action, not concerted action'.[47] His attitude reflected in part the Eisenhower administration's anxiety not to be seen as too ostentatiously threatening towards the Continental Europeans, but also suggested Dulles's wish to keep Britain (in his view 'a rapidly declining power' in contrast to the US, 'the greatest power in the world') at arm's length.[48] At the Washington conversations, Dulles at first took a noncommittal attitude towards the question of the extension of the NATO treaty for a further thirty years but he later expressed his reluctance to cooperate with Britain on the grounds that such a modification of the NATO treaty would require a two-thirds majority in the Senate before it could be accepted by the US government.[49]

By May 1953 the French government had accepted the substance of the British counter proposals, although they would have preferred Britain to enter into a formal agreement on her future political and military association with the EDC, rather than by the unilateral declaration which Britain favoured.[50] However, after prolonged Cabinet discussions in May and July, Britain decided to accede to the French request for a formal agreement in order, as Selwyn Lloyd, the Minister of State, expressed it, to 'help to maintain the gathering momentum towards the creation' of the European Defence Community. The terms of British military and political association then became the subject of negotiations with officials of the EDC governments in Paris, and it was not until April 1954 that the draft agreement was ready for signature.[51]

In the light of these Anglo-French exchanges, Theodore Achilles, the Chief of Mission of the American Embassy in France, remarked on 6 March that:

> [The] comments of British officials in Paris indicate [that] they are particularly irritated by any presentation which creates [the] impression [that] United Kingdom is paying for [the] right to 'participate in' [the] EDC institutions. However [the] British are in a sense responsible for giving [the] French this negotiating position.[52]

To be more precise, the outcome was the result of a parallel approach towards the issue of a German military contribution by France and Britain. The French appreciated the dilemma when they informed Britain on 12 March 1953 that: 'the British reply is animated by a very different spirit from that which inspired the [French] memorandum of 12 February'.[53] While Britain continued to try to limit her commitments under NATO by a single-minded approach towards easing the French passage of the EDC treaty, and France tried hard to entangle Britain in the EDC and separate her from the US, Britain was bound to be exploited by France, especially as the US did not intend to try to match the ever-increasing British commitment to the projected Community. Nor did she have any reason to do so.

However, the Americans also had little success in dealing with the French. Mayer, during a visit to Washington at the end of March, made it abundantly clear that the settlement of the Saar was a precondition for France's ratification of the EDC.[54] Since Dulles was in the habit of frequently reminding the Europeans about the importance of Franco-German reconciliation as a means of emphasising the virtues of the EDC, he found himself compelled to support France on this issue. Hence, Eisenhower and Dulles in turn pressed Adenauer, who was invited to Washington after the French Prime Minister, to make a move towards the settlement of the Saar question. The Chancellor was opposed to the linking of the Saar with the EDC, but he was forced to agree to a brief reference to the Saar in a communiqué issued after the talks, similar to that contained in the Franco-American communiqué. The French, who also obtained American assurances that military assistance to French forces in Indochina would continue, again lost nothing by adopting a demanding attitude.[55]

Meanwhile, in March and April 1953, Dulles instructed American diplomats in Europe to concentrate on persuading the leaders of the other five governments, and in particular Belgium and Holland, to complete their ratifications of the EDC treaty in the hope that if they did so, the French government would stand out as the sole impediment to the setting up of the EDC. By the end of May, however, these efforts had achieved no tangible results.[56]

The Luxembourg government, which was to contribute one brigade to the EDC, was faced with no obstacles to the ratification of the treaty in its Parliament, where the subject was being examined, but Luxembourg refused to press Parliament to act until Belgium and France had made substantial progress towards ratification. The Belgian Lower House was likely to pass the bill smoothly, but that body also would not take any action until France had moved more positively towards ratification. The Netherlands were generally susceptible to US pressure. By May 1953 the necessary amendments to the Dutch constitution, which would enable the Netherlands to participate in a supranational military organisation, was completed and this paved the way for the EDC's ratification by the Lower House on 23 January 1953.[57]

The EDC treaty was approved by a majority in the Italian Foreign Affairs Committee of the Chamber of Deputies on 24 March 1953. Nevertheless, this did not cause Gasperi to change his mind about the need to delay Italian ratification of the treaty until after the dissolution of the Italian Parliament. He too wanted France to be the first to ratify the treaty. In West Germany, the Federal government had not yet obtained a judgement from the Federal Court on the compatibility of the EDC treaty with the constitution. Furthermore, at the beginning of May the Chancellor decided that he could not seriously consider a settlement of the Saar question before the German general elections in the early autumn.[58] This meant that there could be no French ratification until later in 1953, but in any case the matter was further delayed by the fall of the Mayer government on 21 May, when the Fourth Republic entered into its longest political crisis so far. The confusion did not end until Joseph Laniel formed a new government on 28 June 1953.

Neither Dulles's diplomatic pressure nor Eden's willingness to respond favourably to French requests for further British concessions created a more hopeful climate for a successful conclusion of the EDC question. To complicate the situation even further, a thaw in Cold war tension after Stalin's death on 5 March 1953 threatened the very foundations upon which the EDC had been constructed.

5. Before and after the death of Stalin, 1952–1953

During the last phase of Joseph V. Stalin's life, that is, from the breakdown of the four power deputies talks in June 1951 until March 1953, Western Europe had not allowed itself to be influenced by Soviet moves designed to frustrate allied efforts to promote European unity. One of these approaches was the so-called 'Stalin Note' of 10 March 1952 calling for the creation of a united, independent and neutralised Germany with her own armed forces for defensive purposes only.[59] The timing of this note coincided with the delicate period when the Europeans were moving towards the signature of the EDC treaty and reflected Stalin's intense anxiety about the imminent prospect of West Germany becoming formally associated with NATO as a result of the Lisbon conference in February 1952. Under the Lisbon goals, West Germany would contribute six divisions by 1953 and twelve divisions by 1954 to the defence of Western Europe via a European army.[60]

Western leaders were not taken completely by surprise by Stalin's initiative – Acheson had anticipated 'some move of this sort as a last ditch effort to prevent Germany integrating with the West'. Eden thought that it was 'an astute manoeuvre' designed to appeal to the public opinion of West Germany, while Slessor dismissed it as 'pure propaganda'. As the COS argued, if the Soviet Union succeeded in its design, the West would lose its 'strongest bargaining counter', that is, the realisation of a West German contribution to the EDC. Washington,[61] London[62] and Bonn[63] shared Slessor's apprehensions and they all tacitly gave priority to the consummation of the EDC project over Germany's reunification. The Quai d'Orsay also condemned the note as nothing more than a device to undermine current Western policy.[64] However, Western leaders were still officially committed to the ultimate goal of a peace treaty with Germany. They feared that if the West ignored legitimate German aspirations for unity, Germany would remain, as the Foreign Office suggested in September 1953, 'an ulcer' in the middle of Europe. They were willing to test Stalin's readiness to achieve German unity, although they of course insisted that such unity was only possible if it accorded with Western interests.[65] The Soviet note of 10 March was followed for the next six months by what Eden described as 'the battle of Notes'.[66]

The Stalin note was, and continues to be, a subject of contention among historians – particularly whether Stalin was genuinely willing to support German reunification even if this was at the cost of Soviet control over East Germany.[67] In the absence of evidence from Kremlin archives, it is impossible to come to a definite conclusion about this, but even if the West and Adenauer did miss a promising opportunity of achieving a reunified Germany at that time, it remains arguable whether a reunited, rearmed and neutralised Germany would have been, under any circumstances, an attractive proposition from the Western point of view.[68] The State Department and the Foreign Office were both dubious about the kind of 'neutrality' Stalin envisaged when he referred to this subject in his note.

A neutralised and rearmed united Germany would not only be in perpetual danger of falling into the Soviet orbit, but might also be a potential menace to the West in its own right. At best the Western powers would have been uneasy about the opportunities presented to a rearmed Germany to play off the East against the West. Moreover, a neutralised or neutral Germany would have meant the loss to the West of both German territory and German troops, and the end of all Western hopes of employing a forward strategy in the event of a war with the Soviet Union.[69]

By the winter of 1952–3, after Stalin had broken off the exchange of notes in August, Eden and the Foreign Office became convinced that the Soviet Union, while accepting the consolidation of West Germany into Western Europe, had decided to rest content with her control over Eastern Germany. There was no need for the West to try to disturb this satisfactory balance of power.[70] Following the death of Stalin on 5 March 1953, the new Soviet administration under a collective leadership, with Georgy Malenkov as the new chairman of the Council of Ministers, tried to create a partial détente, characterised by the holding of four-power talks on air safety in Berlin, a slight easing of Soviet restrictions on the movement of traffic between Berlin and West Germany and a readiness to use their good offices with the North Korean government over the vexed question of the repatriation of prisoners of war from Korea. Western leaders did not believe that the Kremlin's 'new look' implied any profound change in Soviet

policy which, in their view, was designed to gain time for the consolidation of the new regime at home and for the settling of future
Soviet relations with the satellites.[71]This Western approach towards
post-Stalin Moscow was summarised in a Foreign Office paper in
early April, which was in broad agreement with the views of the
French Foreign Office and the American State Department:

> But this change of tactic offers an opportunity to the Western
> powers, who should meet Soviet conciliatory moves halfway with a
> view to reaching agreement on specific outstanding questions. We
> must avoid being lulled into a sense of false security and must
> continue with the essential measures still required to complete the
> defensive strength of the non-Soviet World.[72]

These 'specific outstanding questions' were the early settlement of
the Korean War armistice and the Austrian treaty.[73] but not such
controversial issues as the future of Germany or of NATO. Although
the West anticipated a fresh Soviet initiative about Germany, in the
event none was forthcoming.[74]

   That Stalin's death had so little impact on the minds of Western
policy makers was the result of the world having entered into what
Montgomery described as 'a generation of "Cold" War', marked by
an evidently tenacious and lasting threat from the East. Its main
feature was that the West could no longer predict any specific year of
maximum danger from the Soviet Union, a view which the British
Chiefs of Staff had held at the end of 1951[75] and which was now
accepted by Eisenhower and Dulles but not by the American Joint
Chiefs of Staff.[76] British strategists did not think that the Soviet Union
would deliberately start a general war until 1955, but there remained
the danger of two other kinds of war breaking out: 'unintentional
war' in which limited and local aggression, such as had taken place in
Korea and could possibly arise in Berlin, might develop into a global
conflict and, secondly, 'a preventive war' in which the Soviet Union
might be tempted to launch a first strike against the West in the belief
that the West was about to attack her. For the West, the best hope of
avoiding a general war with the Communist bloc rested in 'combining
strength and unity with resolution and restraint' – a COS conclusion
of January 1953 to which they adhered throughout 1953, although
they now assumed that the new Soviet leaders would adopt a more
cautious line in the conduct of Soviet foreign policy.[77]

6. Churchill's call for summit talks, 11 May 1953

Churchill's statement to the House of Commons on 11 May 1953 marked a departure from the West's previous conviction that no real advantage was to be gained from negotiating with Moscow on the issue of German reunification. In his speech, Churchill described Germany as a 'dominating problem' in Europe, and he fully endorsed the need to set up the EDC as soon as possible. The Prime Minister also welcomed the West's 'remarkable relationship' with West Germany and expressed his unqualified admiration for Adenauer's foreign policy. But he also suggested the vague idea of applying the 'Locarno' principle to the problem of a reunited Germany and to Soviet relations with her as a possible means of securing a peace settlement with Germany. He then appealed to the new Soviet leaders to agree to the holding of high-level talks. Although he made it clear that these should be of an informal and explanatory character, his speech was sufficiently misleading to confuse European public opinion and as a result he deflected attention from the EDC project. Certainly, if there was to be a reunited Germany, the association of West Germany with the EDC would become redundant.[78]

Adenauer was very apprehensive about the possible adverse effects of Churchill's speech on progress towards European unity. According to Dr Herbert Blankenhorn, Assistant Secretary of West German foreign affairs, the Chancellor was 'scared stiff' by the Prime Minister's 11 May initiative and since then he 'had not known nor had he really decided...whether he was now standing on his head or on his heels'.[79]

Eisenhower, who had expressed an interest in meeting Stalin early in 1953, took a more cautious line than Churchill about the possibility of a summit meeting. In a speech on 16 April 1953, dealing with the prospects for world peace, the President demanded that Moscow demonstrate its willingness to make concrete concessions rather than merely indulge in rhetorical flourishes.[80] When, on 22 April 1953, Churchill sounded out the President on the possibility of a summit meeting with Malenkov, Eisenhower replied a few days later that he was now opposed to the idea and asked the Prime Minister for 'as much advance notice as you could possibly give us...if you should find it necessary for some special and local reason to seek a personal contact'.[81] However this warning did not affect the Prime Minister's determination to push ahead with his plan for a summit – and he was in a better position to achieve his ambition as he was now in charge of Britain's foreign affairs owing to Eden's illness early in April.[82] The

Foreign Secretary was later critical of Churchill's 11 May statement, which was made without consultation with him or with Lord Salisbury. Eden complained that '[w]orst of all it probably cost us [the] EDC in France'.[83]

Churchill's Cabinet colleagues were not only alarmed by his sudden and unexpected appeal for top-level talks in May 1953, they were also puzzled as to what his broad concept for German reunification in that speech actually entailed. In fact Churchill contemplated the creation of a united and 'independent' Germany, although he avoided using the words 'neutral' and 'non-aligned'. He was, of course, well aware of the threat that an independent Germany might pose to the rest of Europe. When, on 30 May 1953, Strang warned the Prime Minister that, 'If we reverse our German policy, we may bring the whole structure tumbling about our ears and advance the frontiers of the Soviet bloc to the Rhine', Churchill replied: 'Odd as it may seem, many of these points have long been in [my] mind.'[84] Nevertheless, he remained confident that his initiative would ultimately be successful, a confidence which was based on an assumption which he put forward in a minute of 6 July 1953 that an independent Germany would never ally with the Soviet Union against the West, since Germany would never tolerate 'the servile conditions of the Communist world' or 'the horrors of Communist rule' but would prefer to maintain 'her moral association' with the free Western world.[85]

His reference to the 'Locarno' principle remained obscure. If this was intended literally as a multilateral security guarantee embracing Germany and the Soviet Union, it would presumably follow the recommendation made by Slessor on 19 November 1953 for an air Locarno, which was to be guaranteed by Anglo-American atomic air power and that 'if any of the three powers, Russia, Germany or France, committed aggression against another...aggressor would instantly be subjected to the full weight of atomic and hydrogen attack'. Slessor even went on to suggest that 'a strong, rearmed Germany between Russia and the West would be a massive safeguard against the threat which called NATO into being'.[86]

Slessor and Montgomery,[87] who supported and encouraged the Prime Minister's proposal, shared Churchill's optimism that a united Germany would look to the West culturally and economically. This conclusion was influenced by their recognition of the intense fear in the Soviet Union of a future reunited Germany closely aligned with the West. When faced with this nightmare, Moscow might agree to the creation of a reunited and neutral Germany on terms acceptable to the West. This line of thinking resulted of course from their belief that

German reunification was essential in the near future. Soviet agreement to this hinged upon how much she felt committed to a reunited
Germany. Furthermore, Churchill, Montgomery and Slessor believed
that Germany's natural militancy once she had rearmed would not be
containable within the EDC or NATO structures. She might prefer to
recover her complete military sovereignty, apart perhaps from a few
limitations in the atomic field imposed by the peace treaty, and the
West might even find that Germany was less troublesome as friendly
neighbour than as a close military ally. Should an independent Germany join the Soviet bloc, such a Germany, in Churchill's words,
would 'only form part of a wider no-man's land, communications
across which could be dealt with by the Atomic Bomb'.[88]

While Churchill and his military advisers distrusted Germany to
the extent that they had grave reservations about entering into any
commitment with her, they ignored West Germany's fear of being
involved in a confrontation with the Eastern camp without Western
military protection – this was one of the main motives for Adenauer's
anxiety for West Germany to be integrated into Western Europe.
Even more to the point, how could the French possibly accept
Churchill's proposed independent, reunified and rearmed Germany
on their border?

After Churchill's statement on 11 May 1953, France's European
policy became virtually paralysed. According to the French, German
reunification should be achieved as part of a general European settlement, which should be coupled with an agreement on disarmament
with the Soviet Union. The French felt that if Germany were to be
reunited, there would be no need for the EDC. Alternatively, if the
Western allies began to negotiate the reunification issue with the
Soviet Union and ignored Cold War considerations, there could be no
question of France's ratifying the EDC treaty until she knew the
outcome of such negotiations. Nor were the French certain as to
whether their country would be invited to participate in the summit
talks which Churchill was now proposing.[89]

The increasingly confused allied policy towards Germany caused
the Mayer government to demand that Eisenhower agree to an early
meeting of the three heads of state and, as a result, the President
obtained Churchill's support for this on 20 May. The Anglo-American
leaders also agreed that the proposed big-three conference should
take place in the middle of June in Bermuda, a venue chosen by
Churchill. However, owing to the prolonged governmental crisis in
France, and after Churchill's stroke on the eve of his departure for
Bermuda, the conference had to be postponed. Instead, a meeting of

the three Foreign Ministers (Eisenhower insisted on the inclusion of France) was arranged in Washington in July.[90]

7. The tripartite Washington talks, 10–14 July 1953

The efforts of the acting Foreign Secretary, Lord Salisbury, to readjust Britain's policy in Europe in the light of Churchill's speech in the House of Commons were not made easier by the fact that he completely disagreed with the Prime Minister's approach.[91] The Foreign Office fully supported Nutting's fervent wish that 'the idea of a 4-power meeting' had 'never been mooted'.[92] In the event, Salisbury adopted a dual policy by which Britain would continue to encourage the earliest possible ratification of the EDC treaty, while at the same time exploring the possibility of holding a four-power meeting of heads of government with no fixed agenda. Churchill accepted – and the Cabinet agreed on 6 July 1953 – that the ratification of the EDC treaty was to be the prerequisite for holding a summit conference.[93]

The Washington talks between 10 and 14 July 1953[94] were dominated by France's insistence on the re-opening of four-power discussions on Germany as a condition for her ratification of the EDC treaty. This French demand was shared by the Federal Republic: the Chancellor, who had initially opposed the resumption of the four-power talks, was forced to change his policy as a result of a *Bundestag* resolution of 10 June 1953 which called for an early four-power meeting and which reflected mounting criticism within Germany of Adenauer's evident enthusiasm for the EDC at the expense of the reunification of Germany.[95] In the middle of the Washington talks, the Chancellor, in the letter which he gave Blankenhorn to take to the American capital, appealed to the three Foreign Ministers to begin negotiations with the Soviet Union on Germany only after voting in the German general election had taken place.[96]

While Adenauer's direct intervention in the talks irritated the three Foreign Ministers, Dulles was soon persuaded to endorse the Franco-German demands for early four-power talks on Germany and he even took a sympathetic attitude towards Bidault's parliamentary difficulties. Salisbury, isolated on this issue, fought hard to convince Dulles and Bidault of the serious risks involved in taking such a Western initiative before the resolution of the EDC issue. However, he was acutely embarrassed by Bidault's counter arguments that:

> it was not the fault of the French that the idea of a four-power meeting had entered European thinking...if a certain country took

certain action which it had so far refused, the French government would ratify EDC within a month.[97]

Although it was now doubtful whether even British membership of the EDC would make any significant difference to France's growing hostility towards it, Britain had after all been responsible for distracting French attention from the EDC treaty. Salisbury, with the support of the Cabinet on 13 July 1953, had no option but to accept the Bidault–Dulles agreement to the holding of a four-power meeting of Foreign Ministers after the German elections, with the agenda confined to Germany and Austria.[98] This meant the rejection of Churchill's original proposal for a high-level conference which was not confined to the discussion of any specific issues.

On the basis of the Washington agreement, the three Western allies reopened 'the battle of notes' with the Soviet Union on 15 July with an appeal for a quadripartite discussion on 'the organisation of free elections and conditions for the establishment of a free all-German Government'. Hence the Washington talks had resulted in the Western powers once again testing Russian willingness to discuss the German problem, while at the same time continuing their existing policy of seeking the ratification of the EDC treaty.

This unexpected overture to the USSR was nothing more than a manoeuvre designed to paper over the cracks in the Western alliance which arose from Churchill's intervention. The Western proponents of the EDC – Adenauer, Dulles, Eisenhower and most of Eden's officials in the Foreign Office – did not really believe that the Soviet Union was ready to give up East Germany and considered that, even if she did agree to hold talks with the West, her sole purpose would be to undermine the solidarity of the Western allies and hold up the EDC project.[99] The recent unrest in East Germany and the resultant Soviet military intervention there confirmed them in their view that the fundamental nature of Soviet policy remained basically unchanged even with the death of Stalin.[100] Moreover, whatever assurances to the contrary they made in public, Western leaders were convinced that even a reunified Germany established on Western terms would not necessarily lead to a more stable Europe than the existing *status quo*, that is, a divided Germany. Selwyn Lloyd reminded Churchill of this unpalatable fact on 22 June 1953:

> Germany is the key to the peace of Europe. A divided Europe has meant a divided Germany. To unite Germany while Europe is divided, if practicable, is fraught with danger for all. Therefore everyone – Dr Adenauer, the Russians, the Americans, the French and ourselves – feel in our hearts that a divided Germany is safer for

the time being. But none of us dare say so openly because of the effect upon German public opinion. Therefore we all publicly support a united Germany, each on his own terms.[101]

In any event the Soviets were still free to abandon reunification if this was to be on the basis of Western *desiderata*, that is a reunified Germany within the EDC, and concentrate instead on their existing policy of tightening their grip on East Germany. Indeed, the disappearance of any lingering Soviet support for German reunification was clearly demonstrated to the West when the new Kremlin leaders, in their reply to the allied note of 15 July calling for the resumption of four-power talks, did not express any enthusiasm.[102] Accordingly, the possibility that a four-power meeting would he held at all remained problematic during the autumn of 1953 and this, in turn, created continuing uncertainty about French intentions towards the EDC.

Meanwhile, Adenauer's triumph in the West German general election temporarily raised American hopes for an early French ratification of the EDC, while Eden, who returned to the Foreign Office on 5 October 1953, continued to insist that the EDC was still 'our best bet'.[103] By the middle of December, the Chancellor, who now commanded two-thirds majorities in both the Upper and Lower Houses, decided to amend the Constitution without waiting any longer for the Federal Court to rule on the question of the compatibility of the EDC with the Basic Law. The Belgian Lower House ratified the EDC bill on 26 November and the treaty was now before the Upper House. The situation was the same in the Netherlands. On the other hand, Italy continued to delay their ratification process until the French had ratified the EDC.[104]

The French National Assembly debates in November provided further evidence of the decline of France's interest in the EDC project, which was now interlocked with the outcome of the four-power conference. If these talks failed to achieve what was clearly now the remote prospect of agreement on German reunification, France would be faced with the familiar dilemma – fundamentally averse to German remilitarisation in any form, and fearing West German domination of the EDC, both of which fostered French nationalism, she would try to bind Britain even more closely to the EDC. However, at the same time, the French clung to the hope that successful negotiations with the Soviet Union might lead to the easing of tensions and pave the way for an eventual reunited Germany, which would be neutralised and disarmed under four-power supervision. The latter was, of course, a more attractive prospect for the French. Thus, the fact that the Soviet Union, in a note of 26 November, finally agreed to discuss the German question with the other three occupying powers (thereby abandoning her original demand for the inclusion of Communist China in the talks) loomed large in the minds of French deputies.[105]

8. The revived Bermuda conference, December 1953

The principle motive for Churchill's public overture to Moscow on 11 May 1953 was his ambition for a summit meeting between the leaders of great powers, an ambition which was all-important to him. He told his personal physician, Dr Moran, in April 1954 that: 'I shall not relinquish office until I meet Malenkov.'[106] With the fall of Beria becoming public knowledge by August 1953, Churchill admitted that '[t]here has been no change of heart in Russia', but he added that 'she wants peace'.[107] While the Washington talks were held at the level of Foreign Ministers, the Prime Minister hoped that these would presage later summit talks with the USSR.[108] However, Soviet procrastination over agreeing even to conversations between the Foreign Ministers until the end of November strained Churchill's patience to the limit. On 5 November 1953 he suggested to Eisenhower that the big-three meeting at Bermuda, which had been postponed in June, should now take place. The American President reluctantly agreed, while France accepted an invitation to attend on 10 November.[109]

The Bermuda conference of 4 to 8 December 1953,[110] the first tripartite summit since the end of the Second World War, between the President, the two Prime Ministers and their three Foreign Ministers, failed to adopt a constructive approach towards the Soviet Union and the EDC. Churchill tried to persuade Eisenhower that the West should be ready to 'look for any hope of an improved state of mind [in Moscow], even if it were necessary to run a slight mental risk'.[111] It was uncertain whether 'a slight mental risk' would involve the danger of further reducing France's already wavering support for the EDC as a result of negotiating with the Soviet Union about the future of Germany or whether it entailed the 'risk' of creating intense public disappointment in the West if the Soviets proved to be as unyielding during the negotiations as they had been in the past. Eisenhower, lamenting Churchill's anxiety to 'relive the days of World War II' with his continuing belief in personal diplomacy,[112] countered that the Soviet 'new look' amounted to 'the same old girl' in 'an old patched dress', despite her 'bath, perfume or lace', an opinion shared by

Eden, Dulles and Bidault. Churchill was isolated on this issue.[113] Nor were they impressed with Churchill's suggestion for the application of the 'Locarno' principle to Germany and were equally sceptical about the possibility of a Western guarantee of Soviet security. Accordingly, a Western note to Moscow on 8 December was confined to a short statement in which the three governments noted with pleasure the Soviet agreement to a four-power conference and proposed that this should meet at Berlin in January 1954.[114]

The discussion of the EDC at Bermuda merely confirmed how divided the three powers were over this issue. Eisenhower and Dulles repeated their views on the importance of Franco-German reconciliation through the EDC, and expressed their hope for firm French leadership on this issue – failing which, they pointed out, their difficulties with the US Congress (who had passed the Richard Amendment in early July which provided for the withholding of 50 per cent of aid appropriations to the signatories of EDC if they failed to ratify the treaty) would become insurmountable.[115] The French Prime Minister, Josef Laniel (who was absent from most of the discussions having been taken ill after arriving in Bermuda), and Bidault countered this pressure by raising the question of the Saar and the need for closer British association with the EDC.[116] Churchill insisted that the EDC was a French innovation and Eden argued that it was unfair to blame Britain for what she 'did or did not do in the light of what had already been done'. The Prime Minister complained that the West had wasted three years in futile negotiations as a result of French inaction. Indeed, in private talks with Eisenhower, he suggested that the EDC should be finalised without the French and that the West should return to the idea of including West Germany in NATO. Nor did he feel that the West should become involved in arguments about 'a few fields in the Saar valley'.[117]

In the light of these disputes, the final communiqué, which was issued on 8 December, and which stated that the Bermuda conference 'symbolized and confirmed the unity of purpose of our three countries', sounded very hollow. Dulles's famous speech prior to the NATO Council meeting in Paris on 14 December was more truthful in expressing in eloquent terms US disappointment with the results of the Bermuda conference: 'If however, the EDC should not become effective, if France and Germany remained apart…That would compel an agonizing reappraisal of basic United States policy.'[118]

Although French politicians, including Bidault, were upset by the tone of this speech, Dulles's threat had little effect on them. Its impact had already been reduced, not only by the Secretary's reference to 'a little re-thinking' in January 1953, but also by his use of similar expressions during the tripartite Foreign Ministers' meeting in London on 16 October 1953, during a private meeting between Dillon and Laniel on 21 October 1953, and more forcefully when Dulles threatened 'a complete re-evaluation of our whole foreign policy' during Franco-US talks at Bermuda on 5 December 1953.[119] Furthermore, during 1953 it became increasingly unclear whether the US was genuinely angered by French hesitations about the EDC or whether she was really sympathetic to France's difficulties. The 'agonising reappraisal' threat was ironic in view of the contradictions involved in the US policy of pursuing the goal of the early establishment of the EDC, while at the same time giving the French a plausible excuse to delay action on this by agreeing, however reluctantly, to the invitation to the Soviet Union. In any case, the French now insisted that, owing to the forthcoming French Presidential elections, which involved the formal resignation of the Laniel government, it would be impossible for the National Assembly to take up the subject of the EDC again before the spring of 1954.

7 EDEN'S SUCCESSFUL ALTERNATIVE

For nearly two years after the signature of the EDC treaty in May 1952, the prospects for its successful ratification remained doubtful. This was hardly surprising given that there were no startling changes in the European balance or serious threats to that balance which would encourage its prospective members either to dismiss the project as irrelevant or to regard its fulfilment as urgent. The Soviet Union did not respond with threats of counter-measures when the EDC treaty was signed and failed to reply to Churchill's call for summit talks with any new proposals. Cold War tensions subsided in the immediate aftermath of the death of Stalin, but they were unlikely to disappear altogether in the foreseeable future. Nor could the Europeans and British overcome their fears of a rearmed West Germany. All this meant that West Germany's integration into the West through the European Defence Community was still regarded as essential in order to frustrate future Russian intrigues and to avert the revival of West German revanchism once the country had been re-militarised. However, continued Anglo-American support for the EDC project seemed to have become both unrealistic and irrational in the light of France's hesitations over the EDC. Neither of these powers attempted any new initiatives designed to rekindle the stalled negotiations: the Eisenhower administration tended to revert to a traditional form of American diplomacy which sought to avoid too close an involvement in European quarrels. In contrast, Britain's interests seemed to be best served by refraining from active intervention which might lead to the premature demise of the treaty while at the same time grudgingly accepting increased commitments towards the project, if France and the other co-signatories of the treaty requested her to do so, in order to keep it alive. Thus, by the beginning of 1954, the European defence issue had become stalemated and this situation was unlikely to change until France had finally made up her mind whether or not to ratify the treaty.

1. Agreement on Britain's military association with the EDC

The failure of the four-power conference (25 January–18 February 1954) in Berlin to resolve the German question meant that Britain and the United States were still faced with the problem of the EDC. After the Berlin conference they renewed their pressure on the French to ratify the EDC treaty and this in turn presented the French with the opportunity to press for additional assurances both from London and from Washington about their future security.

While the issue of Britain's political participation in the EDC institutions on questions of mutual concern has already been discussed, the problem of defining how the armed forces of the EDC and Britain were to collaborate led Britain to make her last and most controversial offer to the EDC.

When the Chiefs of Staff first introduced into the Cabinet a broad outline of their recommendations on this subject in December 1951, they proposed that, at least for training purposes, there should be close cooperation between the British armed services and the European army in peace time, while in the event of war they suggested the actual inclusion of British formations in the European army.[1] However, in the process of translating this into a concrete programme Britain's military planners tended to interpret 'association' in terms of providing British military experts to help organise, train and develop a European army. To this end Britain wanted to integrate some EDC groupements into her formations, but not vice versa. Unlike the Foreign Office, the Chiefs of Staff were particularly nervous about using the word 'integration', which might connote 'a more hard and fast association than was really acceptable'.[2] Nevertheless, Britain's political interest in facilitating the early establishment of the European Defence Community had to be weighed against these military considerations. Consequently, by the end of November 1953, the Chiefs of Staff accepted an improved version of a military agreement between the EDC and Britain, which had been drawn up by the Military Committee of the EDC Interim Committee in Paris at which Air Vice Marshal Merer represented Britain.

According to this November draft agreement,[3] the military authorities in Britain and the EDC were to seek 'a common military outlook' in harmonising tactical doctrine and logistics, and in standardising equipment and methods of training. While the second part of the document was concerned with the measures to be taken by each of the three armed services to ensure practical collaboration, the Royal Air Force was in a better position to contribute in that it was to participate not only in the establishment, and, later, in the operation, of the integrated headquarters of the air defence force of the EDC, but also in the 'acceptance' of EDC air squadrons within Royal Air Force formations and vice versa, 'when military considerations make this desirable and logistic considerations make it possible'. Moreover, the word 'acceptance' was modified twice – first when the word 'placing' was substituted for it and later, in March 1954, by the word 'inclusion', thereby deepening both the degree and sense of commitment.[4]

Conversely, the naval forces of the different NATO member countries, although they were assigned to the Allied Commander-in-Chief Channel, remained 'strictly national'. The Royal Navy would thus cooperate, rather than associate, in 'the organisation, working and function of the European Admiralty of the EDC'. Britain's underlying intention, however, was to prevent the EDC naval authorities from interfering with the existing range of British naval operations.[5]

The British army was originally reluctant to be fully associated with EDC land formations, owing to the difficulties of overcoming differences in tactical doctrine, logistics and equipment between the two armies. No significant progress had been made in solving these basic problems by November 1953. Apart from assisting in the formation of the European army, BAOR was also to organise exchanges of staff and officers and joint military exercises on the lines of similar arrangements which had already been made with the forces of other NATO countries. On the training level, British divisions would be incorporated into the EDC army and vice versa. Earl Alexander of Tunis, the Minister of Defence, warned Eden on 23 December 1953 that the Chiefs of Staff, in accepting this document, had 'gone to the limit...short of joining the EDC'.[6] The French did not agree.

France's renewed pressure for more definite Anglo-American military commitments to the Continent demonstrated her unwillingness to contemplate the consequences of her possible failure to ratify the EDC treaty. It also reflected her increasing misgivings about recent moves in London and Washington to substitute atomic fire power for manpower in Europe.[7] Conventional warfare appeared to play a reduced role in American strategy in 1954, when Washington enunciated the so-called 'New Look' whereby in future Communist aggression was to be contained more effectively by the threat of nuclear retaliation.[8] However, a guarantee against a future German menace was now regarded as crucial by the French, especially given the reduction of the Soviet military threat to Europe. That was the main purpose behind Bidault's request at Bermuda in December 1953 for 'an arithmetical ratio' between Anglo-American and other continental forces in order to prevent the two great powers from withdrawing troops from the Continent. France also hoped to arrange special consultations with the United States and Britain in order to uphold France's great power status. While Britain and the United States were willing to repeat their pledge to respect France's status as a great power, neither was prepared to accept the establishment of a 'ratio' of their troops on the Continent to other forces.[9]

Nevertheless, the Foreign Office was 'anxious' to give further assurances to France in order to influence the French Parliament, which was expected to begin debating the EDC treaty early in April.[10] Accordingly, the Foreign Secretary put forward three proposals to the Cabinet on 9 March. First, Britain would be prepared to declare that she had 'no intention of withdrawing' her troops 'from the Continent so long as the threat exists to the security of Western Europe and of the EDC'. Although this declaration avoided specifying the size of Britain's contribution, this proposal, which the Cabinet endorsed, was seen as a major improvement on her previous agreement to consult with the EDC if Britain felt unable to maintain the existing level of her forces on the Continent.[11]

The second proposal was more straightforward, and was one which the EDC powers wanted. Eden persuaded the Cabinet on 10 March to agree to 'the inclusion' of British army formations within European army formations, and vice versa, if SACEUR so requested. By following the course the Royal Air Force had taken in November 1953, Britain's armed forces in Europe, apart from the Navy, were now prepared to operate jointly with other units of the EDC forces, 'where military considerations make this desirable, and logistic considerations make it practicable'. These two additional steps led on 13 April 1954 to the signature of a formal agreement between the EDC powers and Britain on Britain's future association with the EDC.[12]

The third proposal was announced in the House of Commons by the Foreign Secretary on the following day. Britain, as a gesture towards implementing the terms of her association with the EDC, would place an armoured division into the European army when it was established.[13] While Eden's statement obtained wide support in Parliament, especially from many Labour MPs, the motives behind this support were by no means similar. In general, Labour MPs were reluctant to agree to the rearming of the West Germans unless Attlee's four conditions of February 1951 were satisfied. Accordingly, compared with the alternative methods of securing a German defence contribution, the EDC scheme seemed to be the safest way to regulate West German rearmament. The Labour leadership was more apprehensive than their Conservative counterparts about the possibility of West Germany becoming a predominant power in the Community. Mainly because of this fear they welcomed the decision to include a division permanently within the EDC as a means of demonstrating British solidarity in the defence of Western Europe.[14]

Conversely Eden sought to use this offer, which had originally been inspired by Bidault at Bermuda, as a means of influencing the hesitating French deputies. However, he did not intend it to be regarded as an irrevocable commitment by Britain to remain permanently on the Continent. He probably reasoned that, as the EDC became operational, with the full mobilisation of West German manpower and resources, the need for Britain's armoured division to remain in that organisation would be correspondingly reduced.[15]

While Britain's military planners continued to regard Europe as the most vital strategic area in terms of Britain's security and they were compelled to implement this Europe-first strategy by establishing an organic link with the EDC, they never liked the idea of placing limitations on the exercise of British military sovereignty, except during an emergency.[16] Moreover, the Chiefs of Staff, conscious of 'national prestige', did not want a close association with the EDC unless British military formations could be organised and deployed as efficiently as possible in order to impress the continental armed units with the British example.[17] These considerations suggested that more money, more highly skilled soldiers and better quality weapons would have to be provided for the European theatre. As R. A. Butler, the Chancellor of the Exchequer, commented at a Cabinet meeting on 10 March: 'Britain's forces on the Continent...would have to be considered as a first charge on the defence budget', at the cost of reducing military commitments elsewhere.[18]

Britain's military leaders were at first vehemently opposed to Eden's idea of transferring an armoured division to the EDC command. This would force them to split BAOR into two, with three divisions remaining under national control and one being placed under supranational authority. The latter would also involve at least some British participation in the common budget and in common logistics. The Chiefs of Staff were, in addition, concerned that France would be tempted to press for the inclusion of all the British land units stationed on the mainland of Europe in the EDC. Thus Eden's gesture would lead gradually to Britain's full membership of the Community. Consequently, they accepted Eden's proposal 'extremely reluctantly' for the sake of the diplomatic advantages that might accrue from it.[19]

Although the leading British officials differed in their interpretation of the political and military advantages which they thought might flow from this concession, Eden had made an important decision in that for the first time he had entered into a commitment to the EDC without having ascertained whether the United States would follow Britain's lead. In the spring of 1954 it dawned on the Foreign Secretary that Britain had become more closely committed to the EDC than the United States. Indeed, Eden now began to stress the differences between the two powers regarding the extent of their commitments to the EDC in Britain's favour in order to give her more leverage in dealing with Europe.[20]

2. Eisenhower's statement in support of the EDC in April 1954

Dulles was irritated by the lead Britain was not taking on the EDC issue,[21] but Washington was even more divided than London on how to respond to French pressure for a firmer commitment on the deployment of American troops on the Continent. This flew in the face of Eisenhower's determination to reduce the size of American conventional forces stationed overseas. The President's patience with the seemingly endless EDC imbroglio was now exhausted. He asked the National Security Council on 4 March 1954:

> Must we go on for ever coddling the French? We have stationed forces in Western Europe, we have constructed bases, and lots of other things. How much more must we do?[22]

However, given the crucial importance of her European allies to the successful implementation of America's global Cold War policy, Eisenhower was compelled to control his patience and endorse a new State Department draft proposal which included further compromises towards the EDC.[23]

This draft declaration, apart from repeating the terms of the US resolution of May 1952 about the retention of her troops in Europe, included two new and important provisions. First, the US agreed to consult on her level of forces on the Continent with the Community, thus following Britain's example – although Britain, unlike the United States, would consult the EDC through her representatives on Community institutions, as stipulated in the recent convention on Britain's association with the Community. Secondly, the US would regard NATO 'as of indefinite duration rather than for any definite number of years', thus compromising on the vexed question of extending the duration of the initial membership of NATO so that it was coterminate with that of the EDC. These American efforts to reinforce her commitment to the defence of Western Europe were intended to dispel continental doubts about US intentions, which had been increased by the introduction of the 'New Look' policy.[24]

However, in view of the deep gulf between what Britain and the US were prepared to offer the French, and what the French wanted from them in order to make the EDC more acceptable to the French Parliament, it was hardly surprising that these further Anglo-American assurances had little impact on France's lukewarm attitude toward the EDC. Meanwhile, the EDC treaty had been ratified by the Netherlands (20 January), Belgium (11 March), West Germany (29 March) and Luxembourg (7 April), while the Italian Parliament had almost completed its procedural work on the treaty so that all that remained was the final vote to put it into effect. Thus further progress on the EDC now depended entirely on France. To complicate the situation, the surrender of French forces at Dien Bien Phu in Indochina in May made it impossible for the Laniel government to concentrate on European issues.[25]

3. The death of the EDC on 30 August 1954

As a result of the Geneva agreement on Indochina on 21 July 1954, France, now headed by Pierre Mendès-France, made a final effort to secure further changes to the EDC treaty in France's favour.[26] At Brussels, the other five member countries of the EDC were presented with another set of French demands, seeking to remove some of the supranational features from the treaty, while at the same time adding to or abandoning certain provisions which would help to reduce France's fear of a future rearmed Germany.[27] Understandably, the other participants could not agree to modifications of the magnitude proposed by France and the Brussels conference between 19 and 22 August ended with a public acknowledgement of its failure to 'reach an agreement' on the question of France's proposed amendments.[28]

After the conference, Mendès-France, convinced of the crucial importance of Britain's close cooperation with France over the German rearmament question, arranged to visit Churchill at Chartwell on 23 August.[29] The Chartwell talks might well have had a decisive effect on France's attitude towards the EDC if the Brussels conference had agreed that alternative approaches to the EDC should now be considered or if Britain had reacted positively to a brief reference by Mendès-France to a possible British association with the six EDC powers in a European grouping within NATO. Churchill and Eden refused to budge from their existing policy towards the EDC, insisting that France should immediately place the EDC treaty before the French National Assembly. The French Prime Minister was told that if the EDC collapsed, France would be faced with two alternatives: either with being forced to accept West Germany's direct entry into NATO or with being excluded from the Western alliance altogether – the so-called policy of 'the empty chair'.[30]

On 30 August 1954, France finally solved the problem of the future of the EDC, when the treaty was defeated by a vote of 319 to 264, with 12 abstentions, in the French Parliament.[31]

4. Crisis management in September 1954

In view of the increasingly slim prospects of a French ratification of the EDC treaty and the correspondingly embarrassing position in which this placed the West German Chancellor,[32] the British and Americans had, during the summer, already undertaken a joint examination of the options open to them if France remained indecisive or she finally rejected the treaty at the end of August. An Anglo-American Study Group was set up in London for this purpose and spent the week of 5–12 July working out proposals based on guide lines which had been agreed upon by Churchill and Eisenhower during their talks in Washington at the end of June. The group concentrated on the questions of the timing and method of divorcing the Bonn Conventions from the EDC treaty with a view to restoring the political sovereignty of West Germany at once, while deferring the question of German rearmament until an alternative approach had been worked out. This step was designed to meet West Germany's growing pressure for the early termination of the occupation regime, the realisation of which had been delayed because of France's continued difficulties over the ratification of the EDC.[33]

However, the success of this procedure required French agreement as a signatory of the Bonn Conventions although, even without her consent, the West Germans might still recover a limited number of sovereign rights. Nevertheless the legal complexities involved in trying to avoid infringing the tripartite agreements would be daunting.[34] Moreover, there was a serious flaw in the idea of disassociating the Bonn Conventions from the EDC treaty which was to furnish the

French with a further opportunity to postpone consideration of the German rearmament question.

When France abandoned the EDC treaty, the American and the British High Commissioners approached Adenauer on 1 September with the proposals put forward by the Anglo-American Study Group for solving the problem of West Germany's sovereignty. The Anglo-American Commissioners were taken by surprise when Adenauer rejected these proposals, partly because he no longer believed that the Bonn Conventions of 1952 would be acceptable to the West German Parliament since some of the provisions were either outdated or needed reconsideration. Adenauer, although shocked by France's abandonment of the EDC project, continued to believe in the wisdom of furthering European integration, and now demanded a simultaneous solution of the military as well as the political problems of Germany.[35]

This outright West German rejection of the Anglo-American initiative left Britain and the United States with no agreed strategy for dealing with post-EDC Europe. This outcome could have been avoided if the two powers had turned their attention to the consideration of alternatives to the EDC at an earlier stage: this however had not been possible because of the reluctance of West Germany and the Benelux countries to agree to any consultations with or between Britain and the United States before France had made up her mind about the EDC.[36] In any case, the Americans, who were more optimistic than the British about the ultimate success of the EDC, declined to discuss post-EDC questions with London.[37]

After Dulles's 'terrifying' experience over the collapse of the EDC project, he could only bring himself, on Bruce's recommendation, to suggest, in a statement on 31 August, the calling of an emergency meeting of the NATO Council,[38] but he had then immediately flown to the Manila conference to establish the Organisation of the South-East Asia Collective Defence Treaty (SEATO). He also visited Tokyo and, on his way back to the United States, took a short holiday in Hawaii.[39] Nevertheless the American government was now ready to consider alternatives to replace the abortive EDC project: in a personal note to Churchill on 10 September Eisenhower promised that Britain 'would be kept informed' when American ideas became 'a little more clear on the planning level'.[40] By mid-September, however, no clear cut policies had been formulated in Washington, while even more crucially the administration remained undecided as to when and to what extent the United States should take the initiative on this question.[41] Washington's indecision was reinforced by the

141

State Department's increasing preoccupation with the situation in the Far East – 'a constantly boiling kettle of possible trouble' in Eisenhower's words – where the Chinese communists began to shell the Nationalist-held off-shore islands in the Formosa Strait early in September.[42]

While the US was hesitating about her next move, Eden came to the conclusion that it was imperative for him to act swiftly at 'a very grave moment in European history'. With the failure of the EDC, Britain's leaders were now confronted with the danger that a weakened and divided Europe would provide the Soviet Union with greater leverage to settle the German question in her favour, with the result that West Germany might become neutralised or succumb to Communism and, at the same time, with the possibility that the United States might retreat into peripheral defence.[43] Dulles's apparent loss of interest in Europe caused Eden great concern: he sent a message to Dulles in Manila urging the Secretary of State to return from the Far East as soon as possible as Eden needed his 'invaluable help in unravelling the tangle'. However, the two men did not finally meet until mid-September.[44] The Foreign Secretary was convinced of the importance of Britain taking the lead in resolving the issue, even in the absence of American support, while his diplomatic skills were widely recognised in the autumn of 1954 as a result of his success in negotiating an agreement over Indochina at Geneva, and in handling Britain's disputes with Egypt and Iran. Achieving short-term goals and settling problems as quickly as possible, rather than evaluating long-term objectives, were Eden's main strengths.

With the demise of the EDC, Britain was uncertain whether the NATO solution, which she still preferred, would be acceptable to both France and West Germany. The German Chancellor was apprehensive about the effect on the other European powers of Germany becoming a full member of NATO. He was therefore willing to cooperate with Britain on the NATO solution and ready to accept Churchill's suggestion that Germany's armed strength could be limited through an act of 'self-abnegation'.[45] France, on the other hand, would have no confidence in a voluntary German declaration.[46] In the light of these difficulties and given the overriding need for 'a rapid solution' which would utilise existing organisations, the Cabinet agreed, on 8 September, that the Brussels Treaty Organisation should be modified to include West Germany and Italy, while the NATO solution should be put into effect at the same time.[47] The Foreign Secretary proposed to convene a nine-power conference in London (the six EDC nations plus Britain, the US and Canada) to discuss the British plan, rather than to rush into NATO ministerial talks in Paris as Dulles had proposed on 31 August. It seemed more sensible to engage in such complex negotiations in a forum limited to a compact group of powers who were directly concerned with the German problem.[48]

While Eden had obtained United States agreement to his proposals,[49] the Foreign Secretary was anxious to take further steps to ensure the success of the conference, especially as Dulles and Adenauer feared a repetition of the failure of the Brussels conference in August.[50] To this end, Eden in mid-September embarked on a hurried tour of Brussels, Bonn, Rome and Paris to sound out their views on his proposal for West Germany's simultaneous entry into the Brussels treaty and NATO. All except the French welcomed Eden's plan.[51] Another worrying factor for the Foreign Secretary was Dulles's negative response: during the course of a three-hour meeting with him on 17 September, the American Secretary of State expressed grave doubts as to whether Congress would agree to provide the Brussels pact with the same guarantees which had been extended to the EDC, since the pact possessed no supranational features and would not be regarded in Washington as a step towards European integration. However, to Eden's relief, the American Secretary finally confessed that he could not propose 'a better way' or 'at any rate he had not thought of it'.[52]

These French and American reservations did not discourage Eden, who thought, correctly as it turned out, that the time was ripe for establishing a new post-war Western European relationship with the Federal Republic of Germany at the forthcoming London conference.[53]

5. *The final resolution on Germany: from the London conference (28 September – 3 October 1954) to the ratification of the Paris Agreements on 5 May 1955*

As a result of Eden's effective chairmanship the London conference proved to be the most productive conference on Western European defence since the end of the Second World War. New arrangements with West Germany on her rearmament and on her sovereignty were sketched out during the London meetings and left to the legal experts for fuller definition. The ensuing conference in Paris between 20 and 23 October, which included a meeting of the NATO Council, was assembled mainly for final adjustments to be made before the signature of the documents – the so-called 'Paris Agreements'.[54]

The dominant problem for London was how to control West Germany's rearmament by means of a combination of the Brussels Treaty Organisation (BTO) and NATO. The main purpose of the BTO – renamed the Western European Union (WEU) under the Paris Agreements – was to provide for the minimum defence of Western Europe by regulating the level of forces each member country should assign to NATO so that they did not exceed the agreed maxima which had been laid down in a special unpublished annex to the EDC treaty. Accordingly, the initial West German force contribution would be no less than twelve divisions and 1,300 aircraft, while its naval force was to consist of formations for defensive missions only and whose size would be determined by the NATO Annual Review.[55]

Another important question was how to control armaments production. The West German Chancellor offered to make a voluntary German declaration to the effect that West Germany would not manufacture atomic, biological or chemical weapons (ABC weapons), nor produce long-range missiles, guided missiles, or warships of more than 3,000 tons without the approval of the Brussels Council of Ministers by a two-thirds majority and on the recommendation of the NATO Supreme Commander. While the French would have liked to discuss their proposal for the pooling and standardisation of armaments production, designed to keep West German weapons production as low as possible, they were persuaded to accept Adenauer's offer, which was later recorded as annex I to protocol III of the modified Brussels Treaty.[56]

The majority at London decided to take a broader approach to the problem of German armaments production than that favoured by the French by establishing an agency for controlling armaments on the mainland of Europe by the continental members of the Western European Union, thereby exempting Britain from this restriction. Compared to Article 107 of the EDC treaty, which covered entire categories of weapons, including sporting guns of more than 7 mm, which were to have been restricted by the Board of Commissioners, the Brussels treaty's armament agency was to control purely offensive and destructive weapons (ranging from the ABC weapons to all guided missiles and warships of over 1,500 tons) by means of on-site inspections or test checks.[57]

Finally, the question of restrictions on the size of future German military effectives was resolved in London by the recommendation that NATO SACEUR should have greater authority in the integration and deployment of the forces under his command. All NATO forces on the mainland of Europe were to be anchored firmly to SACEUR, except those intended for overseas purposes, while the functions and size of the internal defence and police forces on the mainland of Europe would be determined by the members of the WEU and notified to the NATO Council. Unless military effectiveness was likely to be severely impaired, the maximum possible integration of forces would be exercised by SACEUR, who would be empowered to inspect and supervise the forces placed under him, in terms of logistics, equipment, armaments and training. The results of such inspections would be reported regularly to the Council of the Brussels pact by 'a high-ranking officer' appointed by the SACEUR.[58] Although these measures involved greatly increased responsibilities on the part of General Gruenther, the Allied Supreme Commander in Europe, he was confident that they would 'effectively' abolish 'the danger...of a revived German General Staff going off on its own'.[59]

The London conference thus transformed the complexities of the European army project into a much simpler association of West Germany with the West through NATO and the WEU. As for the problem of West Germany's future sovereignty, the Bonn conventions were updated so that the provision for special allied emergency powers was abolished, while those sections dealing with German debts had been rendered superfluous by a recent Debt Agreement. West Germany was now to enjoy full sovereignty except that decisions over West Berlin, the reunification of Germany and a future peace settlement remained the prerogative of the three allied powers.[60]

The London agreements opened the way for the establishment of West Germany as an independent sovereign state and to her acceptance by the West as an equal. In return for the acceptance by the other Western European powers of what Eden described as these 'unpleasant realities', he decided that Britain must offer them 'some striking *quid pro quo*'.[61] At the fourth plenary meeting of the nine-power conference on 29 September, Dulles promised that the US would renew the assurances they had offered to the EDC to the Western European Union. Then Eden declared Britain's intention of maintaining in Europe her existing level of armed forces under SACEUR, that is, four divisions and the Second Tactical Air Force of about 780 aircraft, and which would not be withdrawn against the wishes of the majority of the Brussels powers. Such a British pledge had been sought by France since 1952.[62]

The Foreign Secretary's declaration was a major factor in the success of the London conference, which ended with the signature of the Paris Agreements on 23 October 1954. These contained four protocols modifying and completing the Brussels treaty of 1948, a protocol to the NATO treaty providing for the admission to the organisation of the Federal Republic of Germany, a protocol and related conventions on the termination of the occupation regime in West Germany, and finally a Franco-German agreement on the future of the Saar. The latter, which had been a notorious sticking point during the EDC debates, was one which Eden wanted to disassociate completely from the general settlement of the West German question. The French, however, insisted on including the Saar question in the Paris Agreements and agreed that the Saar should be given a 'European statute' within the framework of the Western European Union.[63]

Thereafter the Paris Agreements were ratified fairly smoothly by each national parliament, although France once again proved troublesome by raising familiar questions such as the future of the Saar, another meeting with the Soviet Union, a firm US troop commitment on the lines of Eden's pledge and the setting up of an armaments pool. The process of depositing the instruments of the Paris Agreements was completed on 5 May 1955, and as a result the occupation regime in the Federal Republic of Germany terminated at 12.00 noon on that day while, at the same time, the Western European Union was established. Four days later, West Germany became the fifteenth member country of the North Atlantic Treaty Organisation.

6. The implications of Britain's leadership

What were Britain's motives behind her sudden decision to play an active role in resolving the issue of West Germany's military association with the West? There was nothing new in the idea of using the Brussels organisation as a vehicle for West Germany's entry into NATO. Although Eden claimed in his memoirs that the idea 'suddenly occurred' to him when he was having a bath at his Wiltshire cottage on the morning of Sunday 5 September, Macmillan had already suggested the Brussels solution at a Cabinet meeting of 27 August, on the eve of France's rejection of the EDC treaty, a meeting which the Foreign Secretary attended.[64] Indeed, Van Zeeland, the Belgian Foreign minister, had considered this possibility in October 1952, while, in December 1952, Eden had mentioned it briefly in his Cabinet minute.[65] A similar French scheme was also considered during the summer of 1954 under the title 'a little NATO'.[66] Although the

Americans had not apparently explored this possibility, it was hardly surprising that European leaders in Paris, Bonn, London and elsewhere had thought of it as an alternative to the EDC, especially during the period from 1952 to 1954 when they were becoming increasingly impatient with France's continual hesitations over the EDC.

Secondly, it remains questionable whether Britain, in proposing the Brussels formula, had really overcome her reluctance to become involved in a European military alliance which included both West German and Italy, but excluded the United States. Avoiding this outcome had been an important consideration for Britain during the EDC negotiations. The Foreign Secretary regarded an enlarged BTO purely as a means of making the idea of West Germany's formal adherence to NATO more 'palatable' to French opinion.[67] However NATO, not BTO, would provide the necessary controls over West German rearmament. In theory Britain's commitment to Italy and West Germany through a modified Brussels Treaty entailed her in guaranteeing their future security for fifty years, a commitment which Britain had rejected when it had been requested in March 1952. Under Eden's new scheme, NATO was to develop into a more centralised organisation in which West Germany would participate as a full member. In this context, if any major military threat developed over West Berlin or along the border between East and West Germany, which required allied mobilisation to protect West Germany's territory, it was debatable whether this would present Britain with much to choose between the automatic security provision of Article 4 of the Brussels pact and the loose security provision of Article 5 of the North Atlantic Treaty. In reality, such emergencies were likely to be handled by the Americans, whose general was the SACEUR and who possessed powerful nuclear weapons. Viewed in these terms, Eden's plan involved no major transformations either of Britain's policy toward Europe or of her attitude towards a German defence contribution.

Finally, how far did Eden's pledge to commit British troops to remain in Europe on a permanent basis depart from Britain's traditional policy towards Europe? Was this, as Dulles described it, 'an historical decision', or, as Blankenhorn thought, a 'revolutionary' step?[68] Eden's announcement would indeed have marked a dramatic move by Britain if it had been made out of the blue at the beginning of the EDC negotiations and without any strings attached. In retrospect, the numerous undertakings which Britain had given her allies in order to fulfil her promise of Britain's 'closest possible association' with the EDC, would have required British soldiers to perform a large number of complex tasks, such as advising the European army on

147

training and logistics matters, participating in the headquarters of the EDC air defence force and integrating her air and army units into the EDC forces. When the EDC collapsed in August 1954 the Chiefs of Staff were probably relieved that the British armed services would no longer have to become involved in these activities. Moreover, there were a number of escape clauses in his declaration, which were later recorded in the final act of the nine-power conference.

First, Britain would maintain on the mainland of Europe 'four divisions and the Tactical Air Force or *whatever SACEUR regarded as equivalent fighting capacity*', thereby leaving open the possibility of reducing manpower if tactical nuclear weapons became available. Secondly, there was a clause under which Britain could withdraw her forces from the Continent without consulting the Western European Union in advance if she was faced with an acute overseas crisis. Thirdly, future balance of payments difficulties might make it impossible for Britain to maintain the current level of her military formations in Europe.[69] Indeed, during the 1957–8 cuts in service estimates, the Macmillan government decided to reduce BAOR by nearly 22,000 men, which was equivalent to one division. Similarly, the Second Tactical Air Force of 35 squadrons in 1955 was cut by one half in 1957.[70]

Eden's declaration in September 1954 did not, therefore, represent such an unprecedented reversal of Britain's European military policy as many believed it to have been at that time. In fact, Britain's troop commitment was designed as an alternative to her refusal to meet the French demand that Britain should take the lead in securing the rearmament of West Germany within a European framework. In any event, Britain's military presence on the mainland of Europe was now an accomplished fact – Eden's declaration was calmly accepted by the Chiefs of Staff, by the Cabinet and by the House of Commons.[71]

Seen in this light, it is clear that Britain's Brussels solution, followed by her pledge to maintain her troops in Europe, did not spring from a new policy based on imaginative leadership or a willingness to make sacrifices for the sake of Europe.[72] The success of Britain's initiative was assisted by a unique combination of circumstances: Western European, and particularly West German, statesmen were anxious for the long-standing problem of defining West Germany's status in the European community to be resolved as quickly as possible after the EDC fiasco, while the Americans refused to contemplate any new initiative of their own which might upset their European allies, who might then make difficulties about the introduction of the 'New Look' into NATO's strategy.[73] France, after the trauma of the EDC debacle, became receptive to Britain's emergence as an arbitrator. Although

Britain's proposed Brussels solution contained the bitter pill of West Germany's entry into NATO, the French managed at least to secure a comprehensive European guarantee system, which now included Britain, and, without which, the French feared, there might be close collaboration between the United States and West Germany. Such an outcome would increase Cold War tensions in Europe while at the same time it would undermine France's status as a European great power.[74] All these developments encouraged Britain to seize the leadership of Europe at a critical moment when she had become seriously concerned about the prospects for the future stability of the Continent in the aftermath of the collapse of the EDC.

Furthermore, it was Britain who had organised and chaired the London conference, at which Eden made his pledge to retain British forces indefinitely on the Continent. Thus, if the French again made difficulties, Britain would be able to counter her either by threatening to cancel this pledge or by proposing that the plan should go forward without France – the policy of 'the empty chair'. The British leaders fully intended to use this threat if necessary and in this they were supported by the Brussels countries, who were equally determined to go ahead with Britain's 'empty chair' policy if necessary.[75]

The Foreign Secretary played this card after the French Parliament rejected a bill for the creation of the Western European Union on Christmas Eve 1954, although it postponed a final vote on the complete Paris Agreements until after the Christmas break. Eden believed that, as a result of France's action, Europe was once more on the brink of a serious crisis. With Churchill's full support, the Foreign Office immediately issued a public statement during the evening of 24 December that:

> The rejection of the Paris Agreements would not mean that German rearmament would not take place. The issue is not whether the German Federal Republic will rearm, but how.
>
> The United Kingdom commitment, offered at the London Conference, to maintain British forces on the Continent of Europe, depends on the ratification of the Paris Agreements by all parties.[76]

This warning led the French National Assemble to approve the Paris Agreements on 30 December 1954 by a vote of 287 to 260.[77]

However, in attempting to assess the value of Britain's initiative over the Brussels solution, it has to be borne in mind that Britain had persevered with the EDC project for four years before she could bring herself to make such a proposal: during that period both the Labour and Conservative governments had been forced reluctantly to become embroiled in the question of West Germany's rearmament in order to preserve the strength and cohesiveness of the Atlantic alliance. Britain's leaders had never liked either the American proposal of September 1950, which they dismissed as immature, or the French European army plan, which they regarded as unworkable. Nonetheless, what she achieved in 1954 was the consequence of a new strategic relationship with Europe which had evolved over the previous four years. The Western European Union did not become a thriving European organisation and it was soon to prove difficult to formulate a specific European strategy given the continuing worldwide tensions between the Eastern and Western blocs and with the close involvement of the Europeans with America's NATO nuclear strategy – indeed at a meeting of the NATO Council on 10 May 1955, five days after the birth of the WEU, Spaak insisted that 'there was no such thing as "European" defense'. The Council therefore agreed that important political and military decisions must be made through NATO rather than through the WEU.[78]

Equally significant was that Eden's solution implied the separation of the question of West Germany's rearmament from the ideal of European integration. The Brussels treaty and NATO became the means of assimilating West German effectives into the Western alliance. Consequently, even before the Paris Agreements were finalised in May, European federalists like Spaak, Monnet, and Adenauer had decided to make a fresh start toward European unity in their own way. Their initiative led to the Messina conference in June 1955, which established a framework for the integration of European transportation, trade and atomic energy and which culminated in the treaty of Rome in March 1957, signed by the six European members of the ECSC.[79]

These developments did not reflect on the success of Eden's diplomacy in 1954, which had not necessarily been intended to assert Britain's leadership in advancing European unity in the future. His aim was simply to end the vexed German rearmament question and to enable the Federal Republic of Germany to emerge as a sovereign power. He succeeded in both these objectives in September 1954 and thereby demonstrated that Britain, whose status as a global power was questioned by many observers after the Second World War, could rise to the occasion and exercise firm diplomatic leadership when the opportunity occurred.

CONCLUSION

The process of West Germany's association with the defence of Western Europe was an evolutionary, continuous, fragile and controversial one.

In terms of its evolution, the West's rationale for its policy of rearming the West Germans developed in four stages. Initially, Anglo-American leaders regarded eventual remilitarisation as a necessary part of the gradual and comprehensive assimilation of West Germany into the Western community. Before 1950, however, the question of West Germany's remilitarisation remained an academic one. The second stage was spurred by military considerations resulting from the outbreak of the Korean War, when the allies were faced with the immediate need to rearm West Germany in order to improve Europe's defences. To this end they sought a military contribution from West Germany without giving much consideration to the future role of West Germany in the defence of the West. For example Britain suggested that a Federal police force capable of acting as a defence force should be set up under the occupation regime. Alternatively, the United States proposed, in September 1950, the immediate recruitment of a few West German divisions for service with NATO, but at the same time the related question of West Germany's political sovereignty was ignored.

The third stage was dominated by France's anxiety to ensure that West Germany's future military establishment was brought under tight supranational control by means of the European Defence Community. Thus, the Pleven plan was designed to conceal from the French people the unpopular idea of German rearmament by extolling the popular idea of European unity[1] and thereafter the subject became the highly contentious political one of establishing a post-war European community in which West Germany was to become a founder member.

Finally, while the collapse of the EDC project put an end to this French initiative, the Western allies were saddled with a moral

151

obligation arising from the lengthy negotiations about the EDC treaty both to restore West Germany's sovereignty and to meet the latter's demand for equality of rights in a Western defence system. Hence, the rearming of West Germany now became for the first time identified with allied acceptance of the Federal Republic as an equal partner in the Atlantic alliance through an enlarged Brussels treaty and through NATO.

A second feature of the German rearmament question was its continuity. The question preoccupied statesmen and military leaders for nearly five years – between 1950 and 1955 – and their persistence in pursuing it reflected their uneasiness about the dangers of either postponing or abandoning altogether the idea of integrating West Germany into the West. Indeed they were even more concerned about the serious consequences which might result from the emergence of a fully independent and united Germany given the strained relations which existed between the West and the East. The failure of the West to discuss the rearming of West Germany, at a time when the political and economic integration of that country into Western Europe was making steady progress, would create an atmosphere of discontent and insecurity not only in the Federal Republic but in the other West European countries as well. Accordingly, even if there had been no Korean War, the West would have been faced with the eventual problem of the military integration of West Germany into the Western defence system.

Reluctant, and in the case of France almost non-existent, support for West German rearmament was only sustained by Adenauer's steady and enthusiastic backing and by relentless American pressure for its realisation. However ultimately self-defeating were American efforts to force the French to end their procrastination over the issue, the French and, indeed, the other European allies, were reluctant to antagonise the Americans unduly and for too long, given their dependence upon the US economically and militarily. Moreover, if West Germany's territory was to be incorporated into the Western defensive system, it would be unreasonable to expect the West Europeans, but not the West Germans, to shoulder the burden of defending West Germany indefinitely.

Paradoxically, however, a third feature of the West German question was its fragility. The West's consensus on this hinged upon West Germany's willingness to participate in Western defence. Conversely, if the West Germans had insisted on a settlement of the reunification rpoblem *before* agreement was reached on their rearmament, the Western powers might have found it difficult to suppress

West Germany's legitimate aspirations for unity with East Germany. This would preclude the possibility that West Germany, if she was later forced to participate in NATO, would become a reliable or a contented partner.

Furthermore, the allies were uncertain about the possible repercussions of their initiative in proposing the rearmament of West Germany on the Soviet Union. If the USSR had established the Warsaw pact at this time, and made it clear to the West that she was planning to include East Germany in that organisation unless the West cancelled their programme for West German military integration into NATO, the three occupying powers might have been faced with an awkward situation. If they ignored the Soviet warning by continuing their policy for West German military alignment with the West, they would virtually have acknowledged that they were the aggressors in the Cold War.

Indeed, British leaders had anticipated more strenuous Soviet resistance to West German rearmament than the long series of futile protest notes which was issued by Moscow after November 1950. This relatively mild response might have been the result of belated Soviet recognition that Stalin's early occupation policy for Germany and his attempt to wreck the allied scheme for the unification of the three Western zones through the Berlin Blockade of 1948–9 had only contributed to increasing American determination to participate in the North Atlantic alliance and to set up a separate West German state. Consequently, the Soviet leaders might have been more cautious after 1953 about resorting to military force as a means of preventing West Germany's rearmament.

Alternatively, Soviet inaction might have been due, in Sir Michael Howard's words, to 'the astonishing stupidity of Soviet policy'.[2] Certainly, the Soviet Union might have offered Germany a generous settlement of the Polish–German territorial question at the expense of her satellite state of Poland, rather than merely opposing the West's conditions for the holding of free elections for the whole of Germany as a preliminary to the formation of a reunified Germany. It could also be argued that even if a more imaginative Soviet diplomacy had enabled the USSR to frustrate the allied plan to rearm West Germany, it is hard to believe that the Soviets could have succeeded in negotiating a reunified Germany on her own terms after 1949. If this was the case, the Soviet Union might have decided that it was better to accept the realities of the existing situation rather than losing her zone in East Germany and upsetting the European *status quo*.

The fragile allied consensus on the West German rearmament

question was also undermined by European fears that they would be unable to contain a rearmed West Germany by themselves. The Benelux countries became increasingly suspicious about the ability of an EDC which did not include Britain or the United States to control West German military effectives satisfactorily. Nor were they enthusiastic about the prospect of either French or West German hegemony in the Community. France was, of course, a major contributor to the prevailing uncertainty about the fate of Western schemes for West Germany's military integration into the West. It was true that the Europeans decided to tackle the West German rearmament question as a European community problem via the EDC, but this did not necessarily mean that the Europeans felt able to ensure the security of Europe by themselves. The problem became progressively more complicated as the Europeans became more conscious of the growing American military preoccupation with utilising nuclear weapons in the defence of Western Europe, which not only made the projected European conventional army superfluous in many respects but would also make Europe more dependent on American leadership in future.

The uncomfortable mixture of continuity and fragility underlying the West German rearmament issue was inherent in its fourth characteristic, the controversy which it generated. From the onset, the allies faced a dilemma. They had agreed in 1945 to the demilitarisation and disarmament of Germany since they were then as convinced as the Soviet Union that the Germans would again become a menace to world peace unless they were deprived of the means of rearming themselves. While this fear in Europe of a revival of German militarism did not lessen significantly during the intervening years, the decision of the Western allies to abandon the policy of demilitarisation and to embark on the rearming of the West Germans stemmed from the impact of the Cold War on Europe, and as such was irrelevant to the degree of European antagonism towards their former enemy, Germany.

This dilemma was less painful to the US than to her European allies. While the former tended to define the German rearmament question in terms of countering the actual threat from the Soviet Union, the Europeans were now confronted with a possible dual threat – not only from the USSR but also from within the Western community if a rearmed West Germany was to be incorporated into the EDC or directly into NATO.

However, the allied dilemma was made worse by West Germany's refusal to accept any allied restrictions on her armed forces unless they were also imposed equally on the other allies. Consequently, the allies sought to discover a mechanism which would provide the West with sufficient safeguards against a possible resurgence of West German military power on the Continent, without making these safeguards appear too discriminating against the West Germans.

If a NATO formula could be used for this purpose, this raised the vexed question of how to apply this to those extra-European powers, and especially to the United States and Britain, who would not abandon their military sovereignties unless they were given supreme powers over NATO decision-making or a special status in that body. The US State Department had already hinted at this possibility in its August 1950 proposal. The idea of introducing more centralisation into NATO was also employed by Bevin in his plan for an Atlantic confederate force in November 1950, which became the basis of a Foreign Office draft proposal in December 1952 and eventually led to Eden's proposal in September 1954. In view of this sequence of events, if the State Department's proposal of August 1950, which had not called for the immediate remilitarisation of West Germany, had been presented to the NATO Council at New York in September, thus over-ruling the Pentagon's objections, the whole account of the German rearmament question might well have had to be rewritten.

In the absence of these two extra-European powers, it was possible, at least in theory, that integration could have been more easily developed within a compact supranational European grouping as was suggested by the Pleven plan, and which would have allowed for the close regulation of Germany's armed elements. Nevertheless, even when the European army project became more satisfactory to the West Germans as a result of their acquiring an equal voice in the EDC, the French in turn became frustrated by the fact that their original intention of assuming the leadership of the European Defence Community was unlikely to materialise.

The controversy must be further examined in the context of the intricate power politics involved in the West German rearmament question. West Germany vividly recalled the Nazi regime which had brought needless tragedy to Germany and Europe alike, and her recognition that she could not stand on her own against the Soviet Union gave her the incentive to seek integration into the West as a means both of restoring her national status and of protecting her security. West Germany did not entertain any illusions about her autonomous national army nor was she willing to rearm herself merely to help overcome the manpower shortage within the Western alliance. Knowing that the allied occupying forces would not withdraw from West Germany or West Berlin while relations between West and East remained strained, West Germany could afford to wait until the West was ready to offer them more generous terms which would protect her national interests within a Western defence arrangement.

Consequently, the issue presented the Federal Republic with a delicate political, as well as military, problem. Her policy was to secure a significant role in the Western community, without appearing to be too threatening to her European neighbours and especially to France, and this required flexible and also assertive diplomacy by Adenauer on the question of a West German military contribution. As has been shown, West Germany agreed to a number of compromises on the issue during the negotiations in London and Paris, although she persisted in her demand for equality of status within the alliance.

France shared these West German assumptions to some extent, since it was essential for France to recruit West Germany to the cause of the EDC and thus avoid pushing her towards alternatives such as her direct participation in NATO, or a unilateral agreement on her rearmament with the United States. That was why it was possible for France to cooperate with West Germany for a brief period during the EDC negotiations, but the two were bound to clash eventually, as France was not prepared under any circumstances to allow West Germany to use the EDC as a means of reasserting herself in Europe.

How far were the Americans and the British in conflict with each other behind the façade of a common policy in support of the EDC? The United States genuinely hoped that the EDC negotiations would succeed and that Britain would become fully committed to the plan so that eventually American soldiers could be withdrawn from Western Europe. This was the outcome that Britain feared most. This Anglo-American disagreement did not come to the surface, however, for no political or military circumstances arose under which the United States could justify her disengagement from the continent of Europe, and in any case London and Washington shared the same basic attitude towards Western Europe during the early post-war period. They both regarded themselves as being merely temporary guarantors of European security until a balance of power was restored there which met their respective strategic requirements.

Nonetheless, Britain's awareness that the United States was as anxious as she was to reduce her troop levels on the Continent led her to try to avoid the departure of American armed forces from Central Europe by herself becoming more committed to the cause of Western

European defence and thus encourage the US to maintain her close interest in the European theatre. This British dilemma could not be resolved, given that she was less invulnerable than the US to any disruption of Europe's strategic stability because of her geographical proximity to the Continent and her economic and military weakness in the face of the Soviet threat.

Compared to their disagreements in other parts of the world, such as over China and in their policies towards the Middle East, and British irritation at being excluded from the American security pact with Australia and New Zealand (ANZUS) in September 1951, the European security question was one area where the Americans and British could have minimised their differences and developed an authentic 'special relationship'. The EDC issue did not draw the two powers closer together in the way in which British decision-makers – Attlee, Bevin, Churchill and Eden etc – might have wished. There were personal and ideological incompatibilities between President Truman and Attlee while the friendship between Eisenhower and Churchill was not sufficient to restore the wartime intimacy between the two governments. Eden did not get on well either with Acheson or with Dulles, although his relations with Dulles were not as bad as many contemporaries assumed.[3]

It should also be borne in mind that the Americans had their own difficulties with post-war Europe, which neither the British nor the Europeans could share. The United States was forced to assume the responsibility for maintaining world peace, because of her economic and military wealth, which had burgeoned during the Second World War, because of a deep-rooted idealism which had been enshrined in Woodrow Wilson's Fourteen points and because of the inability on the part of the former European great powers, Britain and France, to uphold their former pre-eminence in areas such as Greece and Indochina. Those Americans who were generally sympathetic towards the Europeans were at times bound to feel that Britain and France in particular had eagerly taken generous American economic assistance as a means of bolstering their flagging great power statuses without offering in return any gesture of appreciation or doing much to assist the United States in her efforts to contain Soviet expansionism. In a letter to Gruenther on 23 November 1953, Eisenhower wrote that 'I get weary of the European habit of taking our money, resenting any hint what *they* should do.'[4] The dilemma the United States faced between their cultural and historical attachment to Europe and their resentment at the uphill task of trying to cooperate with Europe to resolve European problems, was a recurrent theme in American policy during the early twentieth century. This dilemma significantly contributed to Eisenhower's decision to adopt a cautious policy towards the issue of West German defence participation.

One of the major problems which Britain faced in dealing with the German rearmament question was how to reconcile her conflicting interests during the negotiations about rearming the West Germans. The outbreak of the Korean War intensified British fears of the Soviet threat and, as a result, increased the importance of her maintaining a close relationship with the US in the defence of Western Europe. Although the Pleven plan led to a renewed Franco-British confrontation over the future reconstruction of post-war Europe, it was again Britain's dominant concern for her connection with the US that determined Britain's initial response to the French project.

However, the protracted EDC debates allowed Britain to formulate her priorities in Europe more carefully. Instead of complying with the pressure of the potential EDC members to participate in the Community, Britain concentrated on ensuring that the collapse of the EDC should not occur in such a way that her lukewarm attitude could be singled out as the cause. It soon became clear that she was reluctant to become entangled with a rearmed West Germany. In spite of the pretence by the British leaders that French sensibilities stood in the way of recovering West Germany's military power, they feared and distrusted the Germans almost as much as the French. The difference was subtle but significant: the British were prepared to face a possible threat arising from a rearmed and sovereign West Germany, while the French were aiming at nullifying the threat at all costs.

It seemed that the long debate over German rearmament resulted in Britain promising a permanent troop commitment to the defence of Europe in peace time. In fact, Eden's 'historical' declaration represented nothing more than the culmination of Britain's step by step moves towards the EDC. Britain fulfilled European hopes that she would commit herself militarily to Europe mainly because she could hardly pretend to be a world power if she demonstrated that she was incapable even of rescuing Western Europe from disaster. The diplomacy of Bevin and Eden and the Chiefs of Staff's 'Europe-first' strategy between 1950 and 1955 resulted in Britain, perhaps unconsciously, becoming a European power as a means of protecting her own security.

The European status quo, which was legitimised in 1955, remained stable for the next three decades largely because Western Europe, with a continuing American military presence, has contained both the Eastern threat as well as that of a rearmed West Germany. At the time of writing, however, Europe seems to be moving in a new direction, encouraged by Moscow's apparently serious intention of reducing East–West tensions elsewhere. Whether this might result in either a unified Europe or a unified Germany remains to be seen, but Britain's insistence in the 1950s upon the NATO solution in order to entangle the United States in the West German rearmament question, which suggested that the German question was no longer exclusively a German or a European problem, might be re-examined with renewed interest.

NOTES

Introduction

1. Maj.-Gen. E. Fursdon, *The European Defence Community – History* (London: 1980) is an interesting account of the EDC negotiations, based upon interviews and extensive correspondence with major policy makers. R. McGeehan's *The German Rearmament Question: American Diplomacy and European Defense after World War II* (Urbana: 1971) is well argued, although he had to rely on secondary sources, such as press reports and published official statements, for his information. Geoffrey Warner 'The British Labour Government and the Atlantic Alliance, 1949–1951' in O. Riste (ed.), *Western Security: The Formative Years* (Oslo: 1985), pp. 247–65 and J. Young, 'German Rearmament and the European Defence Community' in Young (ed.) *The Foreign Policy of Churchill's Peacetime Administration, 1951–1955* (Leicester: 1988) are the most recent works on the subject, but they cover the German rearmament question only for a limited period.
2. Michael Howard, *War in European History* (Oxford and NY: 1987) new edn p. 55; see also *idem*, *The Continental Commitment – The Dilemma of British Defence Policy in the Era of Two World Wars* (Middlesex: 1974); Paul Kennedy, *The Realities Behind Diplomacy – Background Influences on British External Policy, 1865–1980* (London: 1981); Brian Bond, *British Military Policy between the Two World Wars* (Oxford: 1980).
3. For instance, see G. C. Peden, 'The Burden of Imperial Defence and the Continental Commitment Reconsidered', *The Historical Journal* 27:2 (1984), pp. 405–23.
4. For instance, see John L. Gaddis, in 'AHR Forum: The American Conception of National Security and the Beginning of the Cold War, 1945–48', *The American Historical Review* 89:1 (February, 1984) p. 384; Geir Lundestad, *America, Scandinavia, and the Cold War 1945–1949* (NY: 1980), pp. 332–5; Michael J. Hogan, *The Marshall Plan – America, Britain and the Reconstruction of Western Europe, 1947–1952* (Cambridge: 1987), pp. 427–45; Norman A. Graebner, 'Introduction: The Sources of Postwar Insecurity', Graebner (ed.) *The National Security – Its Theory and Practice, 1945–1960* (NY and Oxford: 1986), pp. 3–27.
5. Bert Zeeman, 'Britain and the Cold War: An Alternative Approach. The Treaty of Dunkirk Example', *European History Quarterly*, 16:3 (July 1986),

pp. 343–67; Fraser Harbutt, *The Iron Curtain – Churchill, America, and the Origins of the Cold War* (Oxford, 1986), pp. 117–241; Ann Deighton, 'The "Frozen Front": The Labour Government, the Division of Germany and the Origins of the Cold War, 1945–47', *International Affairs*, 63:3 (Summer 1987), pp. 449–65; Martin H. Folly, 'Breaking the Vicious Circle: Britain, the United States, and the Genesis of the North Atlantic Treaty', *Diplomatic History* 12:1 (Winter 1988), pp. 59–77.

6. Young, *Britain, France and the Unity of Europe 1945–1951* (Leicester: 1984); Warner, 'Britain and Europe in 1948: The View from the Cabinet' in Josef Becker and Franz Knipping (eds.), *Power in Europe? – Great Britain, France, Italy and Germany in a Postwar World, 1945–1950* (NY and Berlin: 1986), pp. 27–46.

7. See David Reynolds, 'Britain and the New Europe: The Search for Identity since 1940', *The Historical Journal* 31:1 (1988), pp. 231–2; Becker and Knipping (eds.), *Power in Europe?*; Wilfried Loth, *The Division of the World 1941–1955* (London: 1988); Josef Foschepoth, 'Einleitung', Foschepoth (ed.) *Kalte Krieg und Deutsche Frage-Deutschland im Widerstreit der Mächte 1945–1952* (Zürich: 1985), pp. 11–31; Lawrence S. Kaplin, 'The Cold War and European Revisionism' *Diplomatic History* 11:2 (Spring 1987), pp. 147–56; Timothy Ireland, *Creating the Entangling Alliance – The Origins of the North Atlantic Treaty Organization* (London: 1981).

8. D. C. Watt, 'Rethinking the Cold War: a Letter to à British Historian', *The Political Quarterly* 49:4 (1978), p. 455.

1 Initial plans to rearm West Germany

1. For the Attlee cabinet, see Richie Ovendale 'Introduction' in Ovendale (ed.) *The Foreign Policy of the British Labour Governments, 1945–1951* (Leicester: 1984), p. 2; Kenneth Morgan, *Labour in Power* (Oxford: 1984), pp. 7–8; Nicholas Henderson, *The Private Office* (London: 1984), pp. 29–32; Lord Strand, *Home and Abroad* (London: 1956), pp. 287, 293–5; H. J. Yasamee, 'Britain, Germany and Western European Integration' unpublished conference paper at Munich, 3–5 May 1988.

2. CP(46)186, CAB 129/9, Public Record Office (PRO, Kew); quoted also in Elisabeth Barker, *The British Between the Superpowers* (London: 1983), p. 64.

3. From Emanuel Shinwell's statement (the Minister of Fuel and Power) see 98th mtg, CAB 128/6. See also F. S. Northedge, *British Foreign Policy – The Process of Readjustment 1945–61* (London: 1962), pp. 68–74.

4. 17th mtg, CAB 128/5; 42nd mtg, CAB 128/9; CP(46)186, CAB 129/9; 1st and 63rd mtgs, CAB 128/9 and 10; CP(47)326, CAB 129/22; Jean Edward Smith (ed.), *The Papers of General Lucius D. Clay, Germany 1945–1949* (Bloomington and London: 1974) 1, pp. 343–4; R. Girault, 'The French Decision-Makers and their Perception of French Power in 1948' in *Power in Europe?* pp. 48–61 *passim*.

5. CP(48)5,6 and 72, CAB 129/23 and 25; 2nd and 19th mtgs, CAB 128/2 and 12; P. Dixon, *Double Diploma* (London: 1968), pp. 247–57.

6. PHP(44)17(0), CAB 79/78; Barker, *The British*, pp. 1–9; Victor Rothwell, *Britain and the Cold War 1941–1947* (London: 1982), p. 119; Julian Lewis, *Changing Direction – British Military Planning for Post-war Strategic Defence, 1942–1947* (London: 1988), ch. 4.

7. COS(46)105, CAB 80/101; COS (47)227, DEFE 5/6; CP(46)186, CAB 129/9.

8. CP(47)326, CP(48) 5 and 6, CP(49)208, CAB 129/22,23,23 and 37. Anthony Adamthwaite 'Britain and the World, 1945–1949: The View from the Foreign Office' in *Power in Europe?*, p. 14.

9. CP(48)6, CAB 129/23.

10. *Foreign Relations of United States* (FRUS), 1948, 3, pp. 18–19, 39; John Baylis, 'Britain, the Brussels Pact and the Continental Commitment', *International Affairs*, 60:4 (Autumn, 1984), p. 626; FO 371/73051 (7, 9, 10, 11 March 1948); FO 371/73052 (11, 12 March 1948); Folly, 'Breaking the Vicious Circle' p. 66; Allan K. Henrikson, 'The Creation of the North Atlantic Alliance, 1948–1952' *Naval War College Review* 32:3 (1980), p. 9.

11. *FRUS*, 1948, 3, p. 75; Alan Bullock, *Ernest Bevin: Foreign Secretary (1945–1951)* (London: 1983), pp. 541–2.

12. 81st and 82nd mtgs, CAB 128/13; 10th mtg, CAB 128/15; D. Cameron Watt, 'Germany' in Evan Luard (ed.) *In the Cold War – A Reappraisal* (London: 1964), p. 330; Hugh Dalton, *High Tide and After* (London: 1962), pp. 166–7, 269–70.

13. 16th and 18th mtgs, DEFE 4/10; 63rd mtg, CAB 128/13; Bullock, *Bevin*, p. 373.

14. 82nd mtg, CAB 128/13.

15. 16th and 18th mtgs. DEFE 4/10; Bullock, *Bevin*, p. 764.

16. CP(48)5,6, and 7, CAB 129/23; COS(47)173 and 227, DEFE 5/5 and 6; 151st mtg. DEFE 4/10; DO(48)46, CAB 131/6; DO(49)3, CAB 131/7.

17. 15th mtg. DEFE 4/10; JP(48)91(F), JP(49)85(F), DEFE 6/6 and 9; Kenneth W. Condit, *The History of the Joint Chiefs of Staff and National Policy 1945–1947*, 2 (Wilmington, DE: 1979), pp. 283–309.

18. DO(48)53, CAB 131/6; see also JP(48)91, DEFE 6/6.

19. COS(46)105, CAB 80/101; COS (47)227(O), DEFE 5/6; 16th and 18th mtgs. DEFE 4/10.

20. 16th and 18th mtgs, DEFE 4/10; John Baylis, 'The Evolution of British Defence Policy, 1945–86' in Martin Edmonds (ed.) *The Defence Equation* (London: 1986), p. 21.

21. 16th mtg. CAB 131/8.

22. See, for instance, 16th and 18th mtgs. DEFE 4/10.

23. Adamthwaite, *Power in Europe?*, pp. 12–15.

24. CP(48)6, CAB 129/23; Confidential annex to 19th mtg. CAB 129/14. This question of Bevin's enthusiasm for European unity in the context of Britain's global status is also discussed by Watt, *Succeeding John Bull – America in Britain's Place, 1900–1975* (London: 1984), p. 117; Warner, *Power in Europe?*, pp. 34–44; John Kent 'Bevin's Imperialism and the Idea of Euro-Africa, 1945–49; in M. L. Dockrill and John Young (eds.), *British Foreign Policy, 1945–1956* (London: 1989).

25. DO(46)40, CAB 131/2.

26. For Britain's earlier perceptions of her economic position, see G. C.

Peden, 'Economic Aspects of British Perceptions of Power on the Eve of the Cold War' in *Power in Europe?*, pp. 237–60; FO 371/62420 (12 February 1947); A. V. Alexander (Minister of Defence, July 1946–February 1950) note for his speech at Imperial College, 16 November 1947, Alexander papers, 12/247, Churchill College, Cambridge.

27. Britain offered military equipment and training facilities to the BPO. In June 1949, Britain also promised to send one infantry brigade group to support the Dutch armed forces in the event of war. See DO(49)2, 3, 7, 9, 33, 45 and 59, CAB 131/7.

28. For the American point of view see *FRUS*, 1948, 3, pp. 21–3, 84–5; see also Henrikson, 'The Creation of NATO', p. 14.

29. *FRUS*, 1948, 3, pp. 19, 88–9, 99–100; 18th mtg, DEFE 4/10; CP(48)249, CAB 129/30; Bullock, *Bevin*, pp. 531–654 *passim*; see also Folly, 'Breaking the Vicious Circle', p. 63.

30. Bullock, *Bevin*, p. 687.

31. CP(48)249, CAB 129/30; *FRUS*, 1948, 3, pp. 79–80, 138–9.

32. CP(49)208, CAB 129/37; PUSC(51)(F), CAB 21/1761; *FRUS*, 1950, 3, p. 875.

33. DO(50)20, CAB 131/9; Walter S. Poole, *The History of the Joint Chiefs of Staff*, 1950–2, (Wilmington: 1979), 4, p. 183.

34. JP(50)22, DEFE 6/12; DO(50)20, CAB 131/9; 5th mtg, CAB 131/8; Bullock, *Bevin*, p. 759; Dean Acheson, *Present at the Creation* (London: 1969); Robert J. Donovan, *Tumultuous Years – The Presidency of Harry S. Truman, 1949–1953* (London: 1982), pp. 98–104; Alfred Grosser, *The Western Alliance* (NY: 1980), pp. 82–95.

35. CO(50)20, CAB 131/9; 5th mtg, CAB 131/8; JP(50)22, DEFE 6/12.

36. Montgomery's speech at Fontainbleau (the BTO), 5 May 1950, (underlined in original), Air Chief Marshall, Sir James M. Robb papers, AC 71/9/123, RAF Museum, Hendon.

37. DO(50)31, CAB 131/9; 17th mtg, CAB 131/8; Lord Ismay, *NATO: The First Five Years 1949–1954* (Netherlands: 1954), p. 29; Poole, *JCS*, 4, p. 185.

38. Adenauer's military advisers, Lt Generals Dr Speidel and Adolf Heusinger, were those who had not compromised themselves during the Third Reich: see Manfred Messerschmidt, Christian Greiner and Norbert Wiggershaus, 'West Germany's Strategic Position and her Role in Defence Policy as Seen by the German Military, 1945–1949' in *Power in Europe?*, pp. 356–62; Hans Speidel, *Aus unserer Zeit-Erinnerungen* (Berlin: 1977), pp. 252–3.

39. Gunther Mai, *Westliche Sicherheitspolitik im Kalten Krieg der Korea-Krieg und die deutsche Wiederbewaffnung 1950 – Militärgeschichte seite*, 1945, 4, MGFA (ed.) (Boppard am Rhein: 1977) (hereafter cited as *MGFA*, 4), p. 113.

40. For German views on their defence contribution prior to the Korean War see Messerschmidt et al., *Power in Europe?*, pp. 353–67; Speidel, *Erinnerungen* pp. 249–66, 454–76; N. Wiggershaus, 'Zur Frage der Planung für die verdeckte Aufstellung westdeutscher Verteidigungskräfte in Konrad Adenauers sicherheitspoltischer Konzeption 1950' in MGFA

(ed.) *Dienstgruppen und westdeutscher Verteidigungsbeitrad – Militärges-chichte seite,* 1945, 6 (hereafter cited as *MGFA,* 6) (Boppard am Rhein: 1982), pp. 11–33; Christian Greiner, 'The Defence of Western Europe and the Rearmament of West Germany, 1947–1950' in *Western Security,* pp. 160–72.

41. Speidel, *Erinnergen,* pp. 250–4; For Adenauer's similar yearning for a European force, see Konrad Adenauer, *Konrad Adenauer Memoirs 1945–1953* trans. B. Rhum von Oppen (London: 1966), p. 268; McCloy to Acheson in Box 3389 (1 June 1950), Decimal File, RG59, National Archives Washington (hereafter cited as NAW).

42. Adenauer, *Memoirs 1945–1953,* p. 270; Manfred Overesch, 'Senior West German politicians and their Perception of the German Situation in Europe 1945–1949' in *Power in Europe?* pp. 118–9, 126–8; Wolfram F. Hanrieder, 'West German Foreign Policy, 1949–1979' in W. H. Hanrieder (ed.) *West German Foreign Policy, 1949–1979* (Colorado: 1980); Marc Cioc, *Pax Atomica: The Nuclear Defense Debate in West Germany During the Adenauer Era* (NY: 1988), pp. 13–15.

43. For Bonn's suspicions about NATO defence line, Adenauer, *Memoirs,* p. 267; Speidel, *Erinnerungen,* p. 255; JP(49)156, DEFE 6/11; COS(50)8, DEFE 5/19; *FRUS,* 1950, 4, p. 595. For Adenauer's interview, see Wiggershaus, in *MGFA* (ed.) 6, p. 127.

44. JP(49)156(F), DEFE 6/11; FO 371/85050 (17 August 1950); Nunley, tel 16, Box 3388 (6 January 1950), Decimal File, RG59, NAW; *FRUS,* 1948, 3, pp. 163–5, 201–5, 234–5, 237 and 242; *FRUS,* 1950, 3, pp. 860–1091.

45. Pierre Mélandri, *Les États-unis face a l'unification de l'Europe, 1945–1954* (Paris: 1980), p. 289; François Seydoux, *Mémoires-d'outre-Rhin* (Paris: 1975) pp. 155–7; René Massigli, *Une Comédie des erreurs 1943–1956 – Souvenirs et réflexions sur une de la construction européenne* (Paris: 1978) pp. 239–42; J. Frémaux and A. Martel, 'French Defence Policy 1947–1949' in *Western Security,* pp. 96–9; *FRUS,* 1948, 3, pp. 39, 142–3.

46. JP(49)156, DEFE 6/11; COS(50)8, DEFE 5/19; 52nd and 70th mtgs, DEFE 4/30, 31.

47. JP(49)156, DEFE 6/11; CP(50)80, CAB 129/39; PREM 8/1203 (2 May 1950).

48. 29th mtg, CAB 128/27; PUSC(51)(F), CAB 21/1761; 52nd mtg, DEFE 4/30; see also Sir Stafford Cripps's broadcast of 27 November 1949 (Chancellor of Exchequer and Minister of Economic Affairs), S. Cripps papers, 654/ 1043, Nuffield College, Oxford.

49. CP(48)249, CP(49)208, CAB 129/30,37; S. Newton, 'Britain, the Sterling Area and European Integration', 1945–50, *The Journal of Imperial and Commonwealth History,* 13: 3 (1985), pp. 163–82.

50. *Parl Deb H of C,* 446, col.395. See also Warner, 'The Labour Governments and the Unity of Western Europe' in *The British Labour Governments,* p. 68.

51. CP(50)92, CAB 129/39; 29th mtg, CAB 128/17.

52. CP(48)249, CAB 129/30; Watt, *Succeeding John Bull,* pp. 121–3.

53. CP(50)114, CAB 129/40; 29th mtg, CAB 128/17.

54. For the East German police force, see Cmd 9213, PREM 11/909; H. R. Külz, 'The Soviet Zone of Germany' *International Affairs,* 27:2 (April

1951) p. 161; JP(49)156, DEFE 6/11.

55. DO(50)67, CAB 131/9; CP(50)8, CAB 129/39.

56. PUSC(49)62, PREM 8/1203; CP(50)114, CAB 129/40.

57. JP(49)156, DEFE 6/11; PUSC(49)62, PREM 8/1203; 29th mtg, CAB 128/17.

58. This will be discussed in ch 6.

59. The PUSC was established in 1949 in order to examine British long-term foreign policies; see Adamthwaite, in *Power in Europe?*, pp. 16–19.

60. PUSC(49)62 and PUSC(50)9, PREM 8/1203.

61. DO(50)34 'Global Strategy', quoted in FO 371/85050 (12 July 1950).

62. CAB 21/1896 (9 June); PREM 8/1203 (13 June); FO 371/85050 (12, 13 July); CP(50)80, CAB 129/39; 29th mtg, CAB 128/17.

63. 70th mtg, DEFE 4/31.

64. 70th mtg, DEFE 4/31; CAB 21/1896 (24 August); Speidel, *Erinnerungen*, p. 255; Wiggershaus, 'The Decision for a West German Defence Contribution' in *Western Security*, p. 200; Julian Lider, *Origins and Development of West German Military Thought*, 1, 1946–66 (Aldershot: 1986) p. 240.

65. FO 371/85050 (5 July); FO 371/85088 (5 August); CP(50)80, CAB 129/39; JP(49)156, DEFE 6/11.

66. FO 371/85050 (12, 13 July).

67. John Lewis Gaddis, *The United States and the Origins of the Cold War 1941–1947* (NY: 1972), pp. 95–132; Ireland, *Creating*, pp. 42–7; Loth, *The Division of the World*, pp. 16–17.

68. General Records of the Central European Division, 1944–53, Box 1, Lot Files, RG59, NAW.

69. JCS 1067/17 (27 February 1946) in *Records of the Joint Chiefs of Staff*, part 2, 1946–53 (Maryland: a microfilm project of University Publications of America Inc., 1980) (hereafter cited as *RJCS*); see also JCS 1517/7 (20 May 1946), JCS 1517/10 (1 August 1946), and SWNCC 372/D (20 September 1946) all in *RJCS*; *FRUS* 1948, 2, pp. 1297–8, 1308–12; Acheson speech (18 January 1948), Acheson papers, Box 47, Series 3, Yale University, New Haven.

70. McGeehan, *The German Rearmament Question*, p. 13; Roger Morgan, *The United States and West Germany, 1945–1973* (London: 1974) p. 23; see also, Hogan, *The Marshall Plan*, pp. 1–17, 26–53, 128–34.

71. Michael Sherry, *Preparing for the Next War – American Plans for Postwar Defense 1941–45* (New Haven: 1977), chs. 1 and 6; James F. Schnabel, *The History of the Joints Chiefs of Staff and National Policy*, 1, 1945–7 (Wilmington: 1979) chs. 1,2, and 3.

72. J. L. Gaddis, 'The United States and the Question of a Sphere of Influence in Europe, 1945–1949' in *Western Security*, p. 67.

73. Forrest C. Pogue, *George C. Marshall: Statesman, 1945–1959* (NY: 1987), p. 289; Henrikson, 'The Creation of NATO', p. 8.

74. *FRUS*, 1947, 1, p. 740; see also, Laurence W. Martin, 'The American Decision to Rearm Germany' in Harold Stein (ed.), *American Civil–Military Decisions* (Alabama: 1963) pp. 643–66.

75. Harry S. Truman, *Memoirs: Years of Trial and Hope,* (NY: 1956), 2, pp. 245–9; NSC 9/3 (28 June 1948) in *Documents of the National Security Council 1947–1977* (Maryland: 1980) (hereafter cited as *DNSC*); PPS 23 (24 Febru-

ary 1948) in Thomas H. Etzold and J. L. Gaddis, *Containment: Documents on American Policy and Strategy 1945–1950* (NY: 1978), pp. 114–21, 135; George F. Kennan, *Memoirs, 1925–1950* (NY: 1967), pp. 415–48; Condit, *JCS*, 2, p. 374.

76. L. W. Martin, in *American Decisions*, p. 648; James L. Richardson, *Germany and the Atlantic Alliance* (Cambridge, Mass: 1966), pp. 18–19.
77. JCS 2124, *RJCS*; Poole, *JCS*, 4, p. 192.
78. NSC 71 (8 June 1950), *DNSC*.
79. *Ibid*.
80. NSC 71/1 (3 July 1950), *DNSC*, Poole, *JCS*, 4, p. 193.
81. L. W. Martin, in *American Decisions*, p. 651.
82. Gaddis Smith, *Dean Acheson – The American Secretaries of State and Their Diplomacy*, 16 (NY: 1972), p. 79.
83. NCS 71/1, *DNSC*; CP(50)114, CAB 129/40; *FRUS*, 1950, 3, pp. 869–1091 ff.
84. *FRUS*, 1950, 4, p. 681.
85. NSC 71/1, *DNSC*; Mélandri, *Les États-Unis Face*, pp. 278–9; Hogan, *The Marshall Plan*, pp. 26–53, 367–8.
86. *FRUS*, 1950, 3, pp. 60–2; Henrikson, 'The Creation of NATO', pp. 27–8.
87. *FRUS*, 1948, 3, pp. 1–351, ff; Pogue, *Marshall*, ch. 19; Ireland, *Creating*, chs. 2 and 3. On the American approach to NATO see also L. S. Kaplan, *The United States and NATO – The Formative Years* (Lexington: 1984), pp. 65–92; C. Wiebes and B. Zeeman, 'The Pentagon Negotiations, March 1948: The Launching of the North Atlantic Treaty', *International Affairs*, 59 (Summer 1983), pp. 351–63; N. Petersen, 'Who Pulled Whom and How Much? Britain, The United States and the Making of the North Atlantic Treaty', *Millennium: Journal of International Studies*, 11:2 (Summer 1982), pp. 93–114.
88. For US anxiety to limit her commitment to Europe: *FRUS* 1948, 3, pp. 78–9, 303; Henrikson, 'Creation of NATO', p. 14; Lundestad, *Scandinavia and the Cold War*, p. 195. For Canadian and British expectations see Escott Reid, *Time of Fear and Hope* (Toronto: 1977), pp. 29–34; PUSC (50)9, PREM 8/1203.
89. JIC report (18 May 1950), Bohlen papers, Lot Files, RG 59, NAW; *FRUS*, 1950, 3, pp. 63–5.
90. NSC 71/1, *DNSC*.
91. Bohlen papers, Box 2 (20 October 1949), Lot 74 D379, RG 59, NAW; J. L. Gaddis in *Western Security*, p. 81; *FRUS*, 1949, 4, pp. 343–5, 353–8; Charles Bohlen, *Witness to History, 1929–1969* (NY: 1973), pp. 288–9.
92. Bohlen papers (20 October 1949) (see Note 91); *FRUS*, 1949, 3, p. 343; *FRUS*, 1950, 3, p. 63–5, 875.
93. *FRUS*, 1950, 3, p. 63.
94. *Ibid*, p. 875; Bohlen papers (20 October 1949); CP(50)92, CAB 129/39.
95. 72nd mtg, CAB 128/16; 20th and 22nd mtgs, CAB 131/8; Bullock, *Bevin*, pp. 798–9; Kenneth Harris, *Attlee* (London: 1982), p. 455.
96. For the NSC-68 in *Containment: Documents*, pp. 383–443; Acheson, *Present*, p. 377; Poole, *JCS*, 4, pp. 4–14.
97. J. L. Gaddis, *Strategies of Containment* (NY and Oxford: 1982), p. 113; Poole, *JCS*, 4, p. 15.

2 The American Initiative in New York, September 1950

1. 53rd mtg, CAB 128/18; 126th mtg, DEFE 4/34; 14th and 17th mtgs, CAB 131/8; FO 371/84086 (4 July); PREM 8/1429 (29 August).
2. JIC 530/3 (22 August) *RJCS*; NSC 73/4 (25 August), *DNSC*; Box 1 (28 July), Lot File 52-316, RG 59, NAW; Poole, *JCS*, 4, pp. 48–51; Callum M. MacDonald, *Korea – The War Before Vietnam* (London: 1986), pp. 30–1.
3. 55th mtg, CAB 128/18; 117th mtg, DEFE 4/34; FO 800/483 (31 August); Maréchal Juin, *Mémoires, 1944–1958* (Paris: 1960), pp. 222–4; Massigli, *Une Comédie*, pp. 246–7; *FRUS*, 1950, 3, pp. 220–4, 229, 1382–3.
4. Acheson, *Present*, p. 436; *FRUS*, 1950, 3, pp. 228–30; Poole, *JCS*, 4, p. 190.
5. Bullock, *Bevin*, p. 793; FO 371/85050 (13 July).
6. 126th and 140th mtgs, DEFE 4/34,35; 17th mtg, CAB 131/8.
7. Ivone Kirkpatrick (UK High Commissioner for Germany from June 1950), *The Inner Circle* (London: 1959), p. 238; Mai, *MGFA*, 4, pp. 99–141; Speidel, *Erinnerungen*, pp. 267–9; Adenauer, *Memoirs*, p. 279; FO 371/85049 (29 June, 3, 12 and 15 July); FO 371/85050 (15 July); CAB 21/1896 (19, 24 August).
8. Wiggershaus in *MGFA*, 6, p. 29; Adenauer, *Memoirs*, pp. 272–3.
9. DO(50)66, CAB 131/9; Mai in *MGFA*, 4, p. 113.
10. Mai, *ibid.*, pp. 100–10; Speidel, *Erinnerungen*, pp. 268–9.
11. Speidel, *Erinnerungen*, pp. 257–69 ff.; CAB 21/1896 (24, 27 August); FO 371/85089 (18 September); PREM 8/1429 (29 August); Fursdon, *The EDC*, pp. 74–6.
12. Massigli, *Une Comédie*, p. 244; FO 371/89201 (tripartite discussion – UK, France and the US – in Paris of 3 and 4 August); FO 371/85050 (17 August); PREM 8/441 (12 August); CAB 21/1896 (19 August); Clarence C. Walton, 'Background for the European Defence Community', *Political Science Quarterly* 68 (March 1953), p. 47.
13. For the resolution see, *Documents on International Affairs 1949–1950* (London: 1953), p. 331.
14. CAB 21/1896 (26 August); WU 10711/4 (11 August) in Roger Bullen and M. E. Pelly (eds.), *Documents on British Policy Overseas* Series 2, 1 (London: 1986) hereafter cited as *DBPOI*, pp. 286–7; Adenauer *Memoirs*, p. 277.
15. Bullock, *Bevin*, p. 797.
16. Churchill to Attlee (6 August), FO 800/456; Martin Gilbert, *'Never Despair' Winston S. Churchill, 1945–1965* (London: 1988) pp. 542–5; see also *Parl Deb H of C*, 478, cols. 984–6.
17. DO(50)66 and 67, CAB 131/9.
18. DO(50)67, CAB 131/9.
19. FO371/85050 (17 August); DO(50)66, CAB 131/9; FO 371/85053 (30 August).
20. FO 371/85053 (30 August).
21. 70th mtg, DEFE 4/31; JP(50)46(S), DEFE 6/12; CAB 21/1896 (9 June).
22. FO 371/85050 (17 August); 130th mtg (Mallet present), DEFE 4/34; DO(50)66, CAB 131/9.

23. 130th and 139th mtgs, DEFE 4/34,35; FO 371/85050 (17 August); DO(50)66, CAB 131/9.
24. DO(50)66, CAB 131/9; 17th mtg, CAB 131/8; 56th mtg, CAB 128/18; COS(50)345, DEFE 5/23.
25. 17th mtg, CAB 131/8; 56th mtg, CAB 128/18; FO 371/85050 (15 July).
26. CAB 21/1896 (24 August); Wiggershaus, in *MGFA*, 6, p. 49.
27. Adenauer, *Memoirs*, p. 275; DO(50)66, CAB 131/9.
28. 139th mtg, DEFE 4/35; DO(50)66, CAB 131/9.
29. PREM 8/1429 (29 August); DO(50)66, CAB 131/9.
30. CAB 21/1896 (24, 26 August); FO 371/85053 (7 September).
31. CAB 21/1896 (24, 25, 27 and 29 August); Seydoux, *Mémoires*, pp. 158–9; Massigli, *Une Comédie*, p. 244.
32. Acheson, *Present*, p. 437.
33. JCS 2124/9 (20 July) and JCS 2124/11 (27 July) both in *RJCS*.
34. Acheson, *Present*, p. 437.
35. *FRUS*, 1950, 3, pp. 167–8.
36. *FRUS*, 1950, 3, pp. 190–2. For the State Department proposal see *ibid.*, pp. 211–19.
37. *Ibid.*, pp. 216.
38. *FRUS*, 1950, 3, pp. 220–4; Massigli, *Une Comédie*, pp. 246–7.
39. Box l (25 August), Lot file 52-316, RG 59, NAW; Poole, *JCS*, 4, p. 196; L. S. Kaplan, *A Community of Interests: NATO and the Military Assistance Program, 1948–1951* (Washington, D.C.: 1980), pp. 108–9.
40. CAB 21/1896 (8 September).
41. JCS 2124/6 (26 August), JSPC 876/173 (28 August), JCS 2124/18 (1 September), JCS 2073/61 (3 September), JCS 2124/10 (6 September), all in *RJCS*; Poole, pp. 194–7.
42. *FRUS*, 1950, 3, p. 213; Dean Acheson, *Sketches from Life of Men I Have Known* (London: 1961), p. 33.
43. Acheson, *Present*, p. 437; Poole, *JCS*, 4, p. 195.
44. Acheson, *ibid.*, p. 438; Poole, *ibid*, pp. 198–200; David S. McLellan, *Dean Acheson – The State Department Years* (NY: 1976), p. 239.
45. For the joint agreement see *FRUS*, 1950, 3, pp. 273–8.
46. *Ibid.*, pp. 273–6; see also, JCS 2124/18 (1 September) and JSPC 876/173 (28 August) both in *RJCS*.
47. L. Martin, *American Decisions*, p. 656; JCS 2124/18, *RJCS*.
48. A copy of the US memorandum is in FO 800/449.
49. JCS 2124/18 (1 September), *RJCS*.
50. See the US memorandum presented to the NATO Council in FO 800/449.
51. *FRUS*, 1950, 3, pp. 277–8; Acheson, *Sketches*, pp. 26–7; L. Martin, *American Decisions*, p. 657.
52. C. C. Schweitzer et al. (ed.) *Basic Documents: Politics and Government in the Federal Republic of Germany* (Leamington Spa: 1984), pp. 318–20.
53. Omar Bradley and C. Blair, *A General's Life* (London: 1983), p. 557.
54. JCS 2073/57 (17 August) and JSC 2073/53 (17 August) both in *RJCS*.
55. Truman, *Memoirs*, p. 252; Acheson, *Present*, pp. 438–9; Ronald Caridi,

The Korean War and American Politics (Philadelphia: 1968), pp. 7, 17–18; David Rees, *Korea: the Limited War* (London: 1964), pp. 58, 200–1.

56. JCS 2073/53 (17 August), JSPC 876/173 (28 August), JCS 2073/61 (3 September) all in *RJCS*; Poole, *JCS*, 4, p. 186.

57. L. Martin, *American Decisions*, p. 656; see also JCS 2073/28 (24 May 1950), *RJCS*; L. Kaplan, *A Community of Interests*, p. 139.

58. Bradley and Blair, *A General's Life*, p. 581,544; NSC 68/1 (21 September), *DNSC*; 206th mtg, DEFE 4/38; Poole, *JCS*, 4, p. 65.

59. Acheson, *Present*, p. 438.

60. For the record of the New York conference, see FO 800/499 and *FRUS*, 1950, 3, pp. 207–354; Poole, pp. 203–7.

61. FO 371/85050 (13 September).

62. FO 800/465 (2 December).

63. FO 371/85053 (13 September).

64. 58th and 59th mtgs, CAB 128/18.

65. FO 371/85054 (15 September).

66. FO 371/85055 (18 September).

67. FO 371/85054 (14 September).

68. Mélandri, *Les États-Unis Face*, pp. 297–8; Massigli, *Une Comédie*, pp. 248–9; FO 371/15054 (15 and 16 September).

69. Jules Noch, *Histoire de Réarmement Allemand depuis 1950* (Paris: 1965), pp. 61–87 ff; Elliot papers, sec 1/4/1, The Liddell Hart Centre for Military Archives, King's College London.

70. Acheson, *Present*, p. 444; Poole, *JCS*, 4, pp. 60–2.

71. FO 371/85055 (23 September); FO 800/467 (3 October); 155th mtg, DEFE 4/36.

72. DO(50)80, CAB 131/9; 155th mtg, DEFE 4/36.

73. FO 371/85055 (22, 23 September).

74. FO 800/449 (22 September).

75. FO 800/467 (3 October).

76. FO 800/449 (26 September).

77. FO 800/499 (18, 19 September); CP(50)222, CAB 129/42; FO 371/85056 (5 October).

78. Adenauer, *Memoirs*, pp. 283-8; FO 371/85055 (23 September); FO 371/85341 (23 September); Armand Bérard, *Un Ambassadeur se Souvient – Washington et Bonn, 1945–1955* (Paris: 1978), p. 345.

79. Speidel, *Erinnerungen*, pp. 257, 269, 494–5; Adenauer, *Memoirs*, p. 292; Karl Deutsch and Lewis Edinger, *Germany Rejoins the Powers* (Stanford, CA: 1959), pp. 29–30; FO 371/85054 (18 September); FO 371/85055 (18,23 September); FO 371/85056 (28 September); FO 371/85057 (22 November).

80. See ch. 2, pp. 36–7.

81. FO 371/85089 (18 September); FO 371/85056 (30 September, 4, 7, and 11 October).

82. FO 371/85056 (7 October); CAB 21/1898 (18 November); *FRUS*, 1950, 4, p. 726; *DBPO Series 2, 3 German Rearmament Question September–December 1950* Bullen and Pelly (eds.), London: 1989) (hereafter cited as *DBPO*, 3), pp. 286–8.

83. For the aftermath of the police force issue see Cmd 8213, PREM 11/909.

84. Messerschmidt, et al. in *Power in Europe?*, pp. 358–9; CAJB 21/1898 (16 November).

3 The search for allied agreement

1. CAB 21/1897 (9 October).
2. Massigli, *Une Comédie*, p. 254; Moch, *Histoire*, pp. 90–1; FO 371/85089 (18 September and 19 October).
3. Jean Monnet, *Memoirs* (London: 1978) trans. Richard Mayne, p. 345; Seydoux, *Mémoires*, pp. 159–63.
4. Monnet, *Memoirs*, pp. 345–6; Mélandri, *Les États-Unis Face*, p. 299.
5. *Ibid.*, p. 300; Monnet, *Memoirs*, p. 347; CAB 131/9 (7 November); CAB 21/1898 (24,25 October); PREM 8/1429 (28 October); see also *DBPO*, 3, pp. 206–12; Hervé Alphand, *L'Étonnement d'être Journal 1939–1973* (Paris: 1977), pp. 219–20.
6. CAB 131/9 (7 November); Moch, *Histoire*, p. 94; PREM 8/1429 (28 and 29 October).
7. PREM 8/1429 (28 October); *FRUS*, 1950, 3, pp. 411–12.
8. Moch, *Histoire*, pp. 145–7; Seydoux, *Mémoires*, pp. 159–63; Hans-Jürgen Rautenberg in MGFA (ed.), *Angänge westdeutscher Sicherheitspolitik 1945–1956 – Von der Kapitulation bis zum Pleven-Plan* (München: 1982), pp. 778–9.
9. Herbert Blankenhorn, *Verständnis und Verständigung – Blätter eines Politischen Tagebuchs 1949 bis 1979* (Frankfurt: 1980), pp. 115–16; Anselm Doering-Manteuffel, *Die Bundesrepublik Deutschland in der Ära Adenauer –Außenpolitic und innere Entwicklung, 1949–1963* (Darmstadt; 1983), p. 57; Wiggershaus, in *Kapitulation*, pp. 393–400; Seydoux, *Mémoires*, p. 160.
10. FO 800/483 (25 October); PREM 8/1429 (29 October); *DBPO*, 3, pp. 217–20; Acheson, *Present*, p. 459; Poole, *JCS* 4, p. 212.
11. *Parl. Deb H of C* vol. 480, col. 33; *FRUS*, 1950, 3, pp. 412–13; Fursdon, *The EDC*, p. 91; McGeehan, *The German Rearmament Question*, pp. 75–6.
12. Poole, *JCS*, 4, pp. 209–16 ff; *FRUS*, 1950, 3, pp. 373,1384 and 1690; Bradley and Blair, *A General's Life*, p. 577; Acheson, *Present*, p. 459.
13. Truman, *Memoirs*, p. 257; Stephen Ambrose, *Eisenhower-Soldier-General of the Army-President Elect, 1890–1952* (London: 1984), 1, p. 496.
14. *FRUS*, 1950, 3, p. 409 (author's italics); *ibid.*, pp. 356–7, 372–7, 381–2; Ted Galen Carpenter, 'United States' NATO Policy at the Crossroads: The 'Great Debate' of 1950–1951' *The International History Review*, 8:3 (August 1986), p. 396.
15. *FRUS*, 1950, 3, pp. 1689–90, 404–6, 426–7; CAB 21/1898 (25 October).
16. CAB 21/1784 (1 November); FO 800/483 (25 October).
17. *FRUS*, 1950, 3, p. 427; Moch, *Histoire*, pp. 159–64.
18. PREM 8/1429 (28 and 29 October); CAB 131/9 (7 November); *FRUS*, 1950, 3, pp. 415–27, 431–2, 439–40.
19. PREM 8/1429 (1 and 25 November); *FRUS*, 1950, 3, p. 423.
20. Monnet, *Memoirs*, p. 348; Massigli, *Une Comédie*, p. 255; *DBPO*, 3, pp. 206–7, 228–9; Young, *Britain, France*, p. 172.

21. PREM 8/1429 (31 October).
22. 69th mtg, CAB 128/18; *FRUS*, 1950, 3, pp. 435–6.
23. FO 371/85089 (13 October); FO 371/85057 (28 and 31 October, 6 and 22 November); CAB 21/1898 (16 November).
24. Hans-Peter Schwarz, *Adenauer – Der Aufstieg: 1876–1952* (Stuttgart: 1986), pp. 763–8, 71–5; Bérard, *Un Ambassadeur*, pp. 351–2.
25. Frank K. Roberts, 'Ernest Bevin as Foreign Secretary' in *The British Labour Governments*, p. 35; *The Observer* (7 September 1986).
26. McGeehan, *The German Rearmament Question*, p. 73; Lewis J. Edinger, *Kurt Schumacher – A Study in Personality and Political Behaviour* (Stanford and Oxford: 1965), pp. 14–15, 230–3; Cioc, *Pax Atomica*, pp. 16–17; Deutsch and Edinger, *Germany Rejoins*, p. 70.
27. Edinger, *Schumacher*, p. 232; Speidel, *Erinnerungen*, p. 289.
28. H. Schwartz, *Der Aufstieg*, pp. 776–8; Edinger, *Schumacher*, p. 230; Adenauer, *Memoirs*, pp. 300–1.
29. *Ibid.*, pp. 302–4; FO 371/85057 (17 November).
30. FO 371/85057 (21 and 22 November); FO 371/85341 (1 December).
31. FO 371/85057 (18 and 20 November).
32. FO 371/85057 (16 November).
33. *Ibid.*, (16, 20 November).
34. *Ibid.*, (21 November).
35. JP(50)161, DEFE 6/15; COS(50)474, DEFE 5/25; 177th mtg, DEFE 4/37.
36. The NATO Council of Deputies was set up in London in order to discuss and determine policy between meetings of the NATO Council: see DO(51)35, CAB 131/11.
37. Annex A to CP(50)311, CAB 129/43; *FRUS*, 1950, 3, pp. 457–61, 501–5, 517–21, 531–47; Poole, *JCS*, 4, pp. 213–14, 218–19.
38. *FRUS*, 1950, 3, pp. 518–19, 572–3, 756 and 1749.
39. *Ibid.*, pp. 446–8, 454–5, 484–5, 491; CAB 21/1899 (29, 30 November and 2 December).
40. CAB 21/1784 (26 October).
41. 177th mtg, DEFE 4/37.
42. *FRUS*, 1950, 3, pp. 457, 519; PREM 8/1429 (25 November).
43. PREM 8/1429 (25 November).
44. 177th mtg, DEFE 4/37.
45. DO(50)100, PREM 8/1429.
46. *Ibid.*; FO 371/85057 (16 November); 186th mtg, DEFE 4/37; PREM 8/1429 (25 November).
47. *Ibid.*
48. 22nd mtg, CAB 131/8; PREM 8/1429 (25 November); 186th mtg, DEFE 4/37; DO(50)100, PREM 8/1429; CP(51)43, CAB 129/44.
49. 22nd mtg, CAB 131/8; *FRUS*, 1950, 3, pp. 493, 507. See also, A. W. DePorte, *Europe between the Superpowers* (New Haven and London: 1979), pp. 162–3.
50. For the 19th note, see PREM 8/1433 (23 October); for the 21st Prague Resolutions, see Ruhm von Oppen (ed.) *Documents on Germany under Occupation 1945–1954* (London: 1955), pp. 522–7.
51. For the 3 November note, see *FRUS*, 1950, 4, pp. 902–3 and for Britain's

response see 71st and 73rd mtgs, CAB 128/18; PREM 8/1433 (5 November); CP(50)266, CAB 129/43.

52. 71st mtg, CAB 128/18; CP(50)266, CAB 129/43; G. Smith, *Acheson*, pp. 254; McLellan, *Acheson*, p. 336.

53. FO 800/465 (23 October); FO 371/85089 (25 October); FO 371/85090 (26 October); Moch, *Histoire*, pp. 229–32.

54. FO 800/503 (22 November); FO 800/564 (2 December); 73rd mtg, CAB 128/18; FO 371/85089 (25 October); FO 371/85090 (26 October); PREM 8/1433 (5 November); *DBPO*, 3, pp. 255–6.

55. DO(50)99, CAB 131/9.

56. Broadcast by Sir Oliver Franks in Washington, 17 May 1951, Elliot papers, 3/3/2; Poole, *JCS*, 4, pp. 66–73.

57. See MPs' protests, 30 November, Attlee papers 114, Nuffield College, Oxford; Dalton Diaries, 30 November, Dalton papers, part I/38, British Library of Political and Economic Science, London School of Economics and Science (LSE) and the American denial of this, 80th mtg, CAB 128/18; Bullock, *Bevin*, p. 823; Bradley and Blair, *A General's Life*, p. 605.

58. For Attlee's Washington talks, see Lord Attlee in conversation with Francis-Williams, edited by Richard Cawston, 3 January 1959, Francis-Williams papers I/15, Churchill College, Cambridge; PREM 8/1200 (December, 1950); FO 371/81637 (9, 10 December); *FRUS*, 1950, 3, pp. 1698–789; Attlee, *As It Happened* (London: 1954), p. 201; Truman, *Memoirs*, pp. 396–418; Harris, *Attlee*, pp. 461–7.

59. CP(50)311, CAB 129/43.

60. 193rd mtg, DEFE 4/38; *DBPO*, 3, pp. 327–8.

61. CP(50)311, CAB 129/43; 194th and 197th (Kelly present) mtgs, DEFE 4/38; 82nd, 84th and 86th mtgs, CAB 128/18.

62. For the record of the talks in PREM 8/1200; 85th mtg, CAB 128/18; *FRUS*, 1950, 3, p. 1748; NSC 93, *DNSC*; Poole, *JCS*, 4, p. 217.

63. 206th mtg, DEFE 4/38.

64. 193rd, 194th, 195th and 198th mtgs, DEFE 4/38.

65. 198th mtg, DEFE 4/38; FO 800/456 (6 December); *DBPO*, 3, pp. 341–5.

66. *Ibid.*, pp. 345–8; see also Ireland, *Creating*, pp. 206–7.

67. FO 800/456 (7 December); CP(50)311, CAB 129/43.

68. See ch. 3, p. 44.

69. *FRUS*, 1950, 3, pp. 505–6.

70. PREM 8/1200; *FRUS*, 1950, 3, p. 1761.

71. *FRUS*, 1950, 3, pp. 584–5.

72. CP(51)1,43, CAB 129/44; FO 800/483 (19 December); *DBPO* 3, pp. 386–90; *FRUS*, 1950, 3, pp. 585–605 ff; Poole, *JCS*, 4, pp. 218–20.

73. CP(51)1, CAB 129/44; Oppen (ed.), *Documents on Germany*, p. 541.

74. *DBPO*, 3, pp. 398–9; *FRUS*, 1950, 3, pp. 496–8, 520.

75. Adenauer, *Memoirs*, p. 307; Speidel, *Erinnerungen*, p. 288; CAB 21/1899 (9 December).

76. CP(50)311 and CP(51)43, CAB 129/43,44; Anthony Mann, *Come Back Germany 1945–1952* (London: 1980), pp. 202–3; Fursdon, *The EDC*, p. 96.

77. McLellan, *Acheson*, p. 335; *FRUS*, 1950, 3, pp. 580–2; CAB 21/1899 (16 December); *DBPO*, 3, pp. 396–7.

78. *FRUS*, 1950, 3, p. 578.
79. CP(51)1,43 and 74, CAB 129/44; FO 371/93445 (21 December); FO 371/93376 (23 February 1951).
80. CP(51)74, CAB 129/44; FO 371/93376 (23 February).
81. See chapter 4, sections 1 and 2.
82. 10th and 12th mtgs, CAB 128/19; FO 371/93315 (1 and 23 January 1951).
83. Kenneth Younger diaries, 4 February 1951; 12th mtg, CAB 128/19.
84. Dalton diaries, 31 December 1950, Dalton papers, Part 1/38; Douglas Hill (ed.) *Tribune 40* (London: 1977), pp. 93–4; transcripts of interviews between Kenneth Younger and Richard Rose, 27 December 1961, Younger papers, Nuffield College; Philip Williams, *Hugh Gaitskell* (Oxford: 1982), p. 168.
85. Younger diaries, 4 February 1951.
86. For NSC 100, see *FRUS*, 1951, 1, pp. 7–18; for the great debates, see Acheson, *Present*, pp. 488–9; Phil Williams, *The Senate and US Troops in Europe* (London: 1985), pp. 43–69; Carpenter, 'Great Debate', pp. 398–415; Ireland, *Creating*, pp. 183–220.

4 The decision to support the Pleven plan

1. Petersberg, a mountain resort overlooking Bonn, was the HQ of the Allied High Commission. The three allied deputies were John Ward (UK), Armand Bérard (France) and Maj. Gen. George Hays (US), see *FRUS*, 1951, 3, p. 990; G. Mayer in *Kapitulation*, p. 729.
2. FO 371/93381 (9, 16 May).
3. Rautenberg in *Kapitulation*, p. 813.
4. FO 371/93445 (21 December); Oppen (ed.), *Documents on Germany*, p. 542.
5. Paul Weymar, *The Authorised Biography – Adenauer* (London: 1957) ed. and trans. P. Mendelssohn, p. 389; *FRUS*, 1951, 3, pp. 1001–3, 1013–14; CP(51)43, CAB 129/44.
6. CAB 21/1784 (27 January).
7. For the American record of the Bonn talks, see *FRUS*, 1950, 3, pp. 990–1047. No equivalent record can be found in the British archives, but the following are useful: CAB 21/1899 (9 January and 18, 19 February 1951); PREM 8/1429 (3 February); CP(51)43, CAB 129/44; 31st mtg, DEFE 4/40; CP(51)74, CAB 129/44. See also Speidel, *Erinnerungen*, pp. 287–90 ff.
8. See ch. 1, p. 11.
9. H. J. Rautenberg and N. Wiggershaus *Die 'Himmeroder Denkschrift' vom Oktoker 1950* (Freiberg; MGFA, 1985); *FRUS*, 1950, 3, pp. 1016–20, 1032–5; Paul Noack, *Das Sheitern Der Europäischen Verteidigungsgemeinschaft-Entscheidungsprozesse vor und nach dem 30 August 1954* (Düsseldorf: 1977) pp. 152.
10. *FRUS*, 1951, 3, p. 1023–4.
11. Rautenberg and Wiggershaus, 'Himmeroder' pp. 27–8; *FRUS*, 1951, 3, p. 1032.
12. *Ibid.*, pp. 992–4; Rautenberg and Wiggershaus, 'Himmeroder', pp. 28, 43.

13. Messerschmidt et al. in *Power in Europe?*, pp. 354–6, 363; DO(50)89, CAB 131/9.
14. JP(51)119 and 141, DEFE 6/17,18; *FRUS*, 1951, 3, pp. 1017–18.
15. See the summary of the Spofford plan in CP(50)311, CAB 129/43.
16. JP(51)119 and 141, DEFE 6/17,18.
17. *FRUS*, 1951, 3, pp. 1038–9.
18. *FRUS*, 1951, 3, pp. 1013–14; Speidel, *Errinerungen*, p. 290; CAB 21/1896 (9 January); Messerschmidt et al. in *Power in Europe?*, pp. 354–6, 363–5.
19. Robert H. Ferrell (ed.) *The Eisenhower Diaries* (NY: 1981), pp. 185–90; Nigel Hamilton, *Monty – The Field-Marshal 1944–1976* (London: 1986), pp. 779–800.
20. Poole, *JCS*, 4, p. 92.
21. CP(51)128, CAB 129/45; 48th, 52nd and 54th mtgs, DEFE 4/41.
22. PREM 8/1429 (3 February); 52nd and 54th mtgs, DEFE 4/41; COS (51)44 and 55, DEFE 5/28; *FRUS*, 1951, 3, pp. 1038–43.
23. No full text of the Bonn report can be found in either the American or British sources, but for a summary, see *FRUS*, 1951, 3, pp. 1044–7; CAB 21/1789 (15 September).
24. For the record of the main plenary sessions of the Paris conference between February and June 1951, see *FRUS*, 1951, 3, pp. 755–98; for the less complete reports from Harvey, see CAB 21/1784; see also Massigli, *Une Comédie*, pp. 270–1.
25. Jan van der Harst, 'The Netherlands and the European Defence Community', unpublished paper for a conference at the European University Institute, Florence, 13–14 February 1986. See also CAB 21/1784 (9, 13 and 20 February).
26. FO 800/465 (31 January 1951); *FRUS*, 1951, 3, pp. 763–4.
27. *Ibid.*, 766–7, 790–1, 793(FN.2); CAB 21/1784 (27 January and 16 February); Weymar, *Adenauer*, p. 412; Speidel, *Erinnerungen*, pp. 290–1.
28. *FRUS*, 1951, 3, p. 777.
29. *Ibid.*, pp. 775–9. CAB 21/1784 (9 and 16 March, 14 April).
30. Monnet, *Memoirs*, p. 357; *FRUS*, 1951, 3,1 pp. 1029–30; *DBPO*, 3, p. 229.
31. Speidel, *Erinnerungen*, p. 291; *FRUS*, 1951, 3, pp. 769–72, 794; CAB 21/1784 (23 February).
32. *Ibid.* (23 February, 13, 30 April); *FRUS*, 1951, 3, pp. 783–4. See also Antonio Varsori, 'De Gasperi, Nenni, Sforza and their role in post-war Italian foreign policy' in *Power in Europe?*, pp. 84–114.
33. CAB 21/1784 (14 April).
34. CP(51)74 and 240, CAB 129/44 and 47; Weymar, *Adenauer*, p. 414; Oppen (ed.), *Documents on Germany*, pp. 550–3.
35. FO 371/93376 (16 February).
36. *FRUS*, 1951, 3, pp. 813–14, 1014–16, 1030–2, 1038–9.
37. CP(51)74, CAB 129/44; FO 371/93381 (16 May); FO 371/93376 (18 and 19 January, 23 February).
38. CP(50)311, CAB 129/43; Cabinet 86th mtg (14 December 1950) and 12th mtg (8 February 1951), both in PREM 8/1429; CP(51)43, 74 and 128, CAB 129/44, 45.
39. CP(51)43, CAB 129/44; see also 48th and 54th mtgs, DEFE 4/41.

40. 31st mtg (Kirkpatrick present), DEFE 4/40; CAB 21/1784 (12 March).
41. CP(51)128, CAB 129/45.
42. FO 371/93341 (23 May); 35th mtg, CAB 128/19; see also Davies report on the talks, FO 371/93349 (29 June).
43. 40th, 43rd, 44th mtgs, CAB 128/19; Dixon minute and Davies report both in FO 371/93349 (29 June).
44. Davies report, FO 371/93349; CP(51)115, CAB 129/45; 40th and 43rd mtgs, CAB 128/19; Bohlen, *Witness to History*, p. 297.
45. CP(51)239, CAB 129/47; FO 37193349 (30 June).
46. *FRUS*, 1951, 3, pp. 1002–3, 1014–16.
47. *Ibid.* pp. 837, 1020–1.
48. *Ibid.* p. 802.
49. See ch. 1, pp. 18–19 for earlier US views on this.
50. *FRUS*, 1951, 3, pp. 803, 813–19; CAB 21/1784 (6, 11 July).
51. *FRUS*, 1951, 3, pp. 785–9, 798–9, 800, 832; CAB 21/1784 (22 June).
52. CP(51)233, CAB 129/47; CAB 21/1784 (6 July).
53. *FRUS*, 1951, 3, pp. 813–19, 837; CP(51)240, CAB 129/47.
54. *FRUS*, 1951, 3, pp. 832–7 ff.
55. *Ibid.*, p. 837.
56. CAB 21/1784 (6 July); CP(51)233, CAB 129/47; Berard, *Un Ambassadeur*, p. 375; see also M. Michel, 'German Rearmament as a factor in Anglo-West German Relations 1949–1955' unpublished PhD thesis, London University (LSE) (1963), ch. 3.
57. For earlier German views on European unity, ch. 1, p. 11; H. Schwartz, *Der Aufstieg*, pp. 846–7; Weymar, *Adenauer*, pp. 418–20.
58. CAB 21/1784 (6 July); *FRUS*, 1951, 3, pp. 824–6; Wiggershaus, in *Kapitulation*, pp. 400–2; Speidel, *Erinnerungen*, pp. 294–5; H. Schwartz, *Der Aufstieg*, p. 873.
59. Bérard, *Un Ambassadeur*, p. 375; Massigli, *Une Comédie*, p. 282–3; CAB 21/1784 (6 July).
60. *FRUS*, 1951, 3, pp. 806.
61. *Ibid.* pp. 805–12, 838–41.
62. Elliot papers, 3/4/2; Massigli, *Une Comédie*, pp. 281–2.
63. CAB 21/1784 (15 February).
64. Fred Greenstein, *The Hidden-Hand Presidency: Eisenhower as Leader* (NY: 1982) pp. 46–7, 66–72, 124–38; Robert F. Burk, *Dwight D. Eisenhower – Hero and Politician* (Boston: 1986) pp. 18–20, 103, 146; Ambrose, *Eisenhower*, 1, pp. 501–7.
65. Thomas A. Schwartz, 'From Occupation to Alliance: John J. McCloy and the Allied High Commission in the Federal Republic of Germany 1949–1952' unpublished Ph.D. thesis, Harvard University, (1985) see pp. 545–52.
66. Ambrose, *Eisenhower*, 1, p. 508; Ferrell, *The Eisenhower Diaries*, p. 194; Bohlen, *Witness to History*, p. 296; *FRUS*, 1951, 3, pp. 838–9.
67. *FRUS*, 1951, 3, pp. 837, 839, 842–6, 856–65; CAB 21/1784 (23 July).
68. *Ibid.*, pp. 843–6, 856–62; CP(51)266, CAB 129/47.
69. *Ibid.*, pp. 800, 856–8; Massigli, *Une Comédie*, p. 280.
70. *FRUS*, 1951, 3, pp. 803, 1035–6; JCS 2123/52 (6 August 1951), *RJCS*.

71. *FRUS*, 1951, 3, p. 845.
72. Speidel, *Erinnerungen*, pp. 292–3; H. Schwartz *Der Aufstieg, p. 873;* *FRUS*, 1951, 3, pp. 856–8.
73. Mélandri, 'France and the Atlantic Alliance, 1950–1953' in *Western Security*, p. 272; Adenauer, *Memoirs*, p. 315; Poole, *JCS*, 4, pp. 85–6, 93, 109; Michel, 'German Rearmament', ch. 3.
74. H. Schwartz, *Der Aufstieg*, pp. 833–49; Adenauer, *Memoirs*, pp. 315–20; *FRUS*, 1951, 3, pp. 1008–9.
75. Eisenhower also suggested this idea, see *FRUS*, 1951, 3, pp. 820–1, p. 837 (FN 2); T. Schwartz, 'John McCloy', p. 568.
76. *FRUS*, 1951, 3, pp. 849–52; CAB 21/1784 (11 July); CP(51)240, CAB 129/47.
77. John Campbell, *Nye Bevan and the Mirage of British Socialism* (London: 1987), pp. 232–71; Ben Pimlott, *Hugh Dalton* (London: 1986), p. 598; Harris, *Attlee*, pp. 475–8.
78. CP(51)239, CAB 129/47.
79. Massigli, *Une Comédie*, pp. 283–4; *DBPO*, 1, pp. 393–9; CP(51)230, CAB 129/47.
80. CP(51)239, CAB 129/47; 58th mtg, CAB 128/20; for Morrison see Pimlott, *Dalton*, p. 596; Young, *Britain, France*, pp. 177–8; Morgan, *Labour in Power*, pp. 464–6.
81. 20th mtg, CAB 131/10; 56th mtg, CAB 128/20.
82. 56th mtg, CAB 128/20; see also Dalton to Attlee and Dalton to Morrison (10 July), Dalton papers, 2 C; comment on a Tribune pamphlet, Bevan's 'One Way Only', *Daily Telegraph* (10 July), Attlee papers, 134.
83. 118th mtg (Shuckburgh present), DEFE 4/45; CP(51)233, CAB 129/47.
84. CP(51)233 and 240, CAB 129/47.
85. For the virtues of the French scheme see, *ibid.*; 56th and 58th mtgs, CAB 128/20; PREM 8/1430 (3 September).
86. CP(51)239, CAB 129/47; 58th mtg, CAB 128/20.
87. *Ibid.*; CP(51)240, CAB 129/47.
88. *FRUS*, 1951, 3, pp. 843–6, 856–65.
89. 58th mtg, CAB 128/20.
90. CAB 21/1898 (24 October); CP(51)240, 266, CAB 129/47.
91. FO 371/94147 (12 January); *FRUS*, 1951, 3, pp. 1027–9, 1274–7; FO 371/93392 (17 September); 137th mtg, DEFE 4/46; CP(51)238, CAB 129/47.
92. CP(51)238, CAB 129/47.
93. CP(51)240, *ibid.*
94. *FRUS*, 1951, 3, pp. 1274–7; FO 371/93392 (17 September).
95. *Ibid.*
96. CP(51)238, CAB 129/47; FO 371/93392 (17 September).
97. *DBPO*, 1, pp. 723–4; Massigli, *Une Comédie*, p. 290.
98. CAB 21/2281 (13 September); CP(51)266, CAB 129/47.
99. CAB 21/1789 (15 September); 142nd and 156th mtgs, DEFE 4/46,47.
100. *FRUS*, 1951, 3, pp. 871–2; Schuman to Attlee, CP(51)240, CAB 129/47.
101. Oppen (ed.), *Documents on Germany*, p. 516; CAB 21/1789 (15 September); CP(51)266, CAB 129/47.
102. *Ibid.*; CAB 21/1789 (15 September).

103. CP(51)266, CAB 129/47; *FRUS*, 1951, 3, p. 878; Harst, 'The Netherlands and the EDC'.
104. *Ibid.*; *FRUS*, 1951, 3, pp. 885–6, 888–91.
105. Massigli, *Une Comédie*, p. 280; Mélandri, *Les États-Unis Face*, p. 329; *idem.*, in *Western Security*, p. 274.

5 The signature of the EDC treaty in May 1952

1. On this, see Michael Charlton (ed.), *The Price of Victory* (London: 1983).
2. Lord Moran, *Winston Churchill – The Struggle for Survival 1940–1965* (London: 1966), p. 353; John Colville, *The Fringes of Power – Downing Street Diaries, 1939–1955* (London: 1985), p. 633.
3. Harold Macmillan, *Tides of Fortune, 1945–1955* (London: 1969), p. 491; Peter Boyle, 'The "Special Relationship" with Washington' in *Churchill's Peacetime Administration*, pp. 38–43.
4. C(51)32, CAB 129/48; see also Gilbert, *Never Despair*, p. 661; Anthony Seldon, *Churchill's Indian Summer – The Conservative Government, 1951–55* (London: 1981), pp. 26–30 ff; Colville, *The Fringes of Power*, p. 633.
5. Quoted in Charlton, *The Price of Victory*, p. 20; see also Michel, 'German Rearmament', p. 158.
6. C(51)32, CAB 129/48.
7. *Ibid.*; PREM 11/373 (7 December 1951); Gilbert, *Never Despair*, p. 682; see also Churchill's meetings with Eisenhower and Lester Pearson in *FRUS*, 1951, 3, pp. 974–5; Pearson, *Memoirs 1948–1957*, (eds.) John Munro and A. I. Inglis (London: 1974), p. 86.
8. For his earlier concept, see ch. 2, pp. 23–24; for his present ideas, see, C(51)32, CAB 129/48; COS(51)733, DEFE 5/35; *Parl. Deb. H of C* vol. 494, col.2595. 'Record of Talks at Paris on 17 Dec. 1951', CAB 21/1792.
9. *Ibid.*, CAB 21/1792.
10. COS(51)733, DEFE 5/35; JP(51)215; DEFE 6/19.
11. C(51)32, CAB 129/48.
12. CAB 21/1792 (17 December).
13. FO 371/93456 (4 December); C(51)32, CAB 129/48; Moran, *Churchill*, p. 362; Charlton, *The Price of Victory*, p. 27.
14. Norman Book in John Wheeler Bennett (ed.), *Action This Day – Working With Churchill* (London: 1968), p. 40; Acheson, *Present*, p. 595; Charlton, *The Price of Victory*, p. 129; Gilbert, *Never Despair*, pp. 661–2.
15. Colville in *Action This Day*, p. 132; Gilbert, *Never Despair*, pp. 659–60; Colville, *The Fringes of Power*, p. 632; David Carlton, *Anthony Eden – A Biography* (London: 1981), p. 294.
16. Charlton, *Price of Victory*, pp. 35, 147.
17. Oliver Harvey Diaries, 15 July 1944, Harvey papers, Additional MSS, 22, 564000. British Library, London; Carlton, *Eden*, pp. 184–7.
18. Evelyn Shuckburgh, *Descent to Suez – Diaries 1951–56* (London: 1986), p. 17; Robert Rhodes James, *Anthony Eden* (London: 1986), p. 347.
19. Anthony Eden, *Memoirs – Full Circle* (London: 1960), p. 5; Shuckburgh, *Descent to Suez*, pp. 15–17; James, *Eden*, pp. 293, 319, 333 and 336; *DBPO*, 1, p. 792.

20. *Parl. Deb. H of C*, vol. 481, col. 1183 and vol. 484, cols. 49–50; Massigli, *Une Comédie*, pp. 260, 270.
21. PM/51/137, PREM 11/373.
22. *Ibid.*; Cabinet 16th mtg, *ibid.*
23. Eden, *Full Circle*, p. 32; James, *Eden*, p. 347; Pearson, *Memoirs*, p. 86.
24. *FRUS*, 1951, 3, p. 701.
25. Shuckburgh, *Descent to Suez*, p. 18; see also Eden, *Full Circle*, p. 9; Carlton, *Eden*, p. 299; Charlton, *The Price of Victory*, p. 152.
26. *Ibid.*, p. 140; Carlton, *Eden*, pp. 299–300; Shuckburgh, *Descent to Suez*, p. 18; H. J. Yasamee, 'Anthony Eden and Europe, November 1951' *Foreign & Commonwealth Office Historical Branch Occasional Papers*, no. 1 (November 1987), pp. 40–1.
27. *DBPO*, 1, p. 752.
28. *Parl. Deb. H of C*, vol. 493, cols. 7–8 and vol. 494, col. 40.
29. *DBPO*, 1, p. 809; for the record of the Strasbourg discussions see *ibid.*, pp. 762–8.
30. Seldon, *Indian Summer*, p. 41; Alistair Horne, *Macmillan, 1894–1956*, vol. 1 of the Official Biography (London: 1988), p. 313.
31. Eden, *Full Circle*, p. 29; *DBPO*, 1, pp. 759–60; James, *Eden*, pp. 352–3; for British public opinion see, *DBPO*, 1, p. 787; Charlton, *The Price of Victory*, pp. 131 and 135.
32. *DBPO*, 1, p. 759, fn 2.
33. *Ibid.*, pp. 759–60; 10th mtg, CAB 128/23.
34. *DBPO*, 1, p. 770; see also Earl of Kilmuir (Sir David Maxwell-Fyfe), *Memoirs – Political Adventure* (London: 1964), p. 187.
35. See *DBPO*, 1, p. 766.
36. *Ibid.*, pp. 769–72 and 779–81; Lord Boothby, *Boothby – Recollections of a Rebel* (London: 1978), pp. 222–3.
37. Kilmuir, *Memoirs*, p. 186–7; Anthony Nutting, *Europe Will Not Wait* (London: 1960), p. 41.
38. Eden to Churchill, PREM 11/373 (5 December).
39. Reynaud to Churchill, PREM 11/373 (29 November); *DBPO*, 1, p. 768.
40. Box 3394, Decimal File, 740.00, RG 59, NAW.
41. Young, in *Churchill's Peacetime Administration*, pp. 101–2 and Yasamee, 'Eden and Europe', pp. 39–48 both support Eden's point.
42. Carlton, *Eden*, p. 311.
43. *DBPO*, 1, pp. 769–72.
44. *Ibid.*, see also pp. 779–81 in *ibid.*; for Macmillan's views, see Macmillan, *Memoirs*, pp. 468–70; Horne, *Macmillan*, pp. 321–3, 348–51; C (52)56, CAB 129/50; Macmillan to Churchill, PREM 11/373 (17 May 1951).
45. PREM 11/373 (13 December).
46. Kilmuir, *Memoirs*, p. 187; *DBPO*, 1, pp. 769–72.
47. *FRUS*, 1951, 3, p. 747.
48. Shuckburgh, *Descent to Suez*, p. 18; James, *Eden*, p. 614.
49. *DBPO*, 1, p. 765, fn 1.
50. *FRUS*, 1951, 3, p. 966; Nutting, *Europe*, p. 41.
51. The three wise men were Averell Harriman (US), Edwin Plowden (UK) and Jean Monnet (France).

52. CP(51)251, 266, CAB 129/47; FO brief for Rome conference of the Council of NATO, unsigned and undated, PREM 11/369.
53. C (51)15, CAB 129/48; PREM 11/373 (24 November); *FRUS*, 1951, 3, pp. 883–5, 903–5, 933–46; Speidel, *Erinnerungen*, pp. 301–7.
54. Harst, 'The Netherlands and the EDC', Massigli, *Une Comédie*, pp. 294–5; Eisenhower's mtg with Van Zeeland of 15 November 1951, Box 2, Lot 55D115, RG59, NAW; *FRUS*, 1951, 3, pp. 906, 960–7, 985–89; *FRUS*, 1952–4, 5, pp. 572–6.
55. *FRUS*, 1951, 3, pp. 931–2, 955; *FRUS*, 1952–4, 5, pp. 581, 586, 590; Harst, 'The Netherlands and the EDC'.
56. *FRUS*, 1951, 3, pp. 931–2, 965; *FRUS*, 1952–4, 5, pp. 584, 586–7.
57. PREM 11/373 (5 December 1951); Mélandri, *Les États-Unis Face*, p. 344.
58. *FRUS*, 1952–4, 5, p. 586.
59. 199th mtg, DEFE 4/50; FO minute in COS(51)733, DEFE 5/35; JP(51)213, DEFE 6/19.
60. *FRUS*, 1951, 3, p. 982; see also COS(51)733, DEFE 5/35.
61. *Ibid.*, DEFE 5/35; unsigned FO brief for Paris visit by PM and Eden, CAB 21/1792; JP(51)215, DEFE 6/19.
62. COS(51)733, DEFE 5/35; FO brief (see fn 61 above); JP(51)213, DEFE 6/19; 202nd mtg, DEFE 4/50; C(51)62, CAB 129/48.
63. *Ibid.*, in CAB 129/48; 192nd mtg, DEFE 4/49.
64. Fourteen American Congressmen participated in the Assembly of the Council of Europe at Strasbourg 19–23 November 1951, see *DBPO*, 1, pp. 762–5; PREM 11/153 (5, 13 and 15 December); PREM 11/373 (15 and 22 December).
65. PREM 11/373 (24 November and 5, 13 December); see also Seydoux, *Mémoires*, p. 162.
66. *FRUS*, 1951, 3, pp. 746–7; PREM 11/373 (6, 8 December).
67. COS(51)733, DEFE 5/35.
68. C(51)62, CAB 129/48.
69. *FRUS*, 1951, 3, pp. 974–5.
70. FO 800/777 (27 November 1951); PREM 11/373 (6, 8 December 1951); Eden, *Full Circle*, p. 35; *FRUS*, 1951, 3, pp. 746–7.
71. Author's italics. FO 371/101737 (23 January); Carlton, *Eden*, p. 311; *FRUS*, 1951, 3, pp. 970–3, 977.
72. PREM 11/373 (8 December).
73. *FRUS*, 1952–4, 5, pp. 580–5, 598.
74. *Ibid.*, pp. 597–604.
75. For the EDC treaty, see RIIA (ed.) *Documents on Int. Affairs 1952*, pp. 116–62; Cmd 9127 (London: HMSO, 1954).
76. *FRUS*, 1951, 3, pp. 963–6, 985–9; *FRUS*, 1952–4, 5, pp. 236, 600; Fursdon, *The EDC*, p. 156.
77. FO 371/97737 (24, 26 January); C(52)31, PREM 11/679; C(52)47, CAB 129/49; *FRUS*, 1952–4, 5, pp. 595–6, 604–5; Bérard, *Un Ambassadeur*, p. 388.
78. West German *Bundestag* resolution on the Saar (8 February 1952), *Documents on Int. Affairs 1952*, p. 77; Adenauer, *Memoirs*, p. 404; Weymar, *Adenauer*, p. 462; Mélandri, *Les États-Unis Face*, pp. 355–6.

79. FO 371/101737 (29 January, 2 February); FO 371/101729 (13 February); *FRUS*, 1952–4, 5, pp. 612–5; Massigli, *Une Comédie*, p. 306; Vincent Auriol, *Journal de Septennat 1947–1954*, 6, 1952 (Paris: 1978), pp. 105–6.
80. C(52)31, PREM 11/679; FO 371/97580 (2 February); for the record of the London talks, see *FRUS*, 1952–4, 5, pp. 36–106; also see PREM 11/679 (19 February).
81. PREM 11/373 (6 December); Eden, *Full Circle*, p. 40.
82. 17th mtg, PREM 11/373.
83. *FRUS*, 1952–4, 5, pp. 42, 46, 57, 79 and 621; PREM 11/679 (19 February).
84. *FRUS*, 1952–4, 5, p. 42; Massigli, *Une Comédie*, pp. 307–8.
85. Cabinet 18th mtg, PREM 11/373.
86. For the tripartite communiqué of 19 February, see PREM 11/679.
87. *FRUS*, 1952–4, 5, pp. 42, 52 and 78–86; Acheson, *Present*, p. 615.
88. Alphand, *Journal*, pp. 227–8; Massigli, *Une Comédie*, pp. 308–10; Auriol, *Journal*, pp. 117, 127; PREM 11/373 (16 and 17 February); FO 371/101729 (16 January and 27 February); C(52)90, PREM 11/165; PREM 11/373 (17 February).
89. *FRUS*, 1952–4, 5, pp. 80, 132.
90. *Ibid.*, pp. 132 (fn 4), 139; Massigli, *Une Comédie*, p. 313.
91. See Article 107, sec 4(a) in the EDC treaty.
92. See London talks, pp. 68–9 and 83 in *FRUS*, 1952–4, 5.
93. *Ibid.*, pp. 64–71 and 82–85 ff; 18th mtg, PREM 11/373; Manteuffel, *Die Bundesrepublik*, p. 57.
94. *FRUS*, 1952–4, 5, p. 137; for the final report, see *ibid.*, pp. 230–46.
95. *Ibid.*, pp. 627–34; Harst, 'The Netherlands and the EDC'; Eden, *Full Circle*, pp. 42–3; C(52)92, CAB 129/50.
96. *FRUS*, 5, 1952–4, p. 631; Messerschmidt et al. in *Power in Europe?*, pp. 357–63; Speidel, *Erinnerungen*, p. 250.
97. Cmd 8512 (April 1952) in PREM 11/373; *FRUS*, 1952–4, 5, p. 631.
98. C(52)92, CAB 129/50.
99. *FRUS*, 1952–4, 5, p. 631; Eden, *Full Circle*, pp. 42–3; Massigli, *Une Comédie*, p. 313.
100. C(52)92, CAB 129/50; *FRUS*, 1952–4, 5, pp. 627–8.
101. C(52)92, CAB 129/50.
102. Cabinet 35th and 37th mtgs, PREM 11/373; C(52)92, CAB 129/50.
103. *FRUS*, 1952–4, 5, p. 638; COS(52)211, DEFE 5/38.
104. C(51)15, CAB 129/48; C(52)106, CAB 129/51.
105. C(51)15, C(52)36, 106 and 141, CAB 129/48, 49, 51; PREM 11/679 (5 May 1952); FO 371/100034 (16 May); C(52)384, PREM 11/170; C(53)112, CAB 129/60.
106. C(52)141, CAB 12/51; 53rd mtg, CAB 128/25; Poole, *JCS*, 4, pp. 114–16.
107. 4th mtg, CAB 128/24; Shuckburgh, *Descent to Suez*, pp. 3–4.
108. FO 371/100029 (28 April); 182nd mtg, DEFE 4/49; C(51)15, CAB 129/48; C(52)141, CAB 129/51.
109. Ronald Lewin, *Slim: The Standard Bearer* (London: 1976), pp. 278–9; Lawrence Freedman, *The Evolution of Nuclear Strategy* (London: 1983), pp. 79–80.
110. Folder 3F, 23 December 1951, personal papers of Sir John Slessor, Air

Historical Branch, Ministry of Defence, London; see also Folder 3G, 17 November 1952, *ibid.*

111. Lewis, *Slim*, p. 279; COS(53)584, DEFE 5/50.
112. C(52)141, CAB 129/51; *FRUS*, 1952–4, 5, pp. 252–4.
113. FO 371/100029.
114. PREM 11/373 (23 May); Harst, 'The Netherlands and the EDC'; *FRUS*, 1952–4, 5, pp. 663–8.
115. *Ibid.*, pp. 674–5; for the EDC treaty, see Cmd 9127.
116. Author's italics, PREM 11/373 (24 May); *FRUS*, 1952–4, 5, pp. 677–9; Auriol, *Journal 1952*, pp. 264–5, 311–12, 351–3; Alphand, *Journal*, p. 229.
117. Author's italics. See *Documents on Int. Affairs, 1952*, p. 169.
118. PREM 11/373 (25 May); *FRUS*, 1952–4, 5, pp. 679–80.
119. For West Germany's economic recovery, see Balfour, *West Germany*, p. 280; Alan S. Milward, *The Reconstruction of Western Europe, 1945–51* (London: 1984), pp. 354–8; FO371/105831 (24 March).
120. PREM 11/373.

6 The fate of the EDC project

1. Air Vice Marshal J. W. Merer attended the EDC Interim Committee as the Head of the UK military delegation, see his reports COS(52)343, 376, 401, DEFE 5/40; COS(52)604, DEFE 5/42; see also *FRUS*, 1952–4, 5, pp. 685, 719; Fursdon, *The EDC*, pp. 198–9.
2. FO 371/97767 (10, 12, 18, 22 December); 102nd mtg, CAB 128/25; *FRUS*, 1952–4, 5, p. 698.
3. *Ibid.*, pp. 692–7 ff; Harst, 'The Netherlands and the EDC'; FO 371/97762 (25 September, 26 November).
4. Auriol, *Journal 1952*, pp. 645–6; Seydoux, *Mémoires*, pp. 168–70; FO 371/ 101737 (21 October); *FRUS*, 1952–4, 5, pp. 688–9, 697.
5. FO 371/101741 (12, 25 November).
6. 102nd mtg, CAB 128/25; C(52)434, CAB 129/57; FO 371/101741 (10 November); FO 371/101743 (16 December).
7. Auriol, *Journal 1952*, pp. 106–7; Seydoux, *Mémoires*, pp. 162–3; Alfred Grosser, 'A la recherche de la spécificité de la politique extérieure de Pierre Mendès France' in F. Bédarida and J. P. Rioux, (eds.) *Pierre Mendès France et le Mendésisme-L'Expérience Gouvernementale et sa Postérité 1954–1955* (Paris: 1985), p. 249.
8. Slessor papers, Folder 14 D; see also Slessor (Paris) to John Harding (CIGS), 11 December 1952, *ibid.*, Folder 25 C.
9. Hamilton, *Monty*, pp. 826–7; PREM 11/373.
10. Healey minute, undated (February–March 1953?). Noel-Baker papers, NBKR 4/301, Churchill College, Cambridge.
11. C(53)108, CAB 129/60; see also, C(52)56, CAB 129/50.
12. C(52)434, CAB 129/57; PREM 11/373 (26 February 1953).
13. 'Impressions from my Continental Tour', Sir Basil Liddell Hart papers, 11/1952/12, The Liddell Hart Centre of Military Archives, King's College London.

14. Auriol, *Journal 1952*, pp. 804–8; FO 371/101743.
15. C(52)434, CAB 129/57.
16. For the FO plan for a remodelled NATO in COS(52)658, DEFE 5/43; C(52)434, CAB 129/57.
17. FO 371/101743; Auriol, *Journal, 1953–4*, pp. 62–3; Massigli, *Une Comédie*, pp. 352–4.
18. FO 371/97767 (11 December); FO 371/101743 (16, 30 December); C(52)434, CAB 129/57; *FRUS*, 1952–4, 5, p. 697.
19. For recent studies on the Eisenhower presidency: see J. L. Gaddis, *Strategies of Containment*, pp. 127–30; Richard A. Melanson, 'The Foundations of Eisenhower's Foreign Policy – Continuity, Community, and Consensus' in Melanson and David Mayers (eds.) *Reevaluating Eisenhower – American Foreign Policy in the Fifties* (Urbana and Chicago: 1989), pp. 31–64; Greenstein, 'Eisenhower as an Activist President; A Look at New Evidence' *Political Science Quarterly* 94 (Winter, 1979–80).
20. See for instance, E. N. Clark to DDE (5 September 1952) Box 9 and Eisenhower to Churchill (8 May 1953) Box 16 both in International Series, Ann Whitman File, the Eisenhower Library, Abeline (hereafter cited DDEL); Dulles to Jean Monnet (3 January 1951, Box 54, Dulles' speech (15 September 1952), Box 59, J. F. Dulles papers. The Seeley Mudd Library, Princeton University.
21. Ambrose, *Eisenhower*, 2, pp. 21, 50; undated minute by Dulles(?), Box 73, Dulles papers; Louis L. Gerson, *John Foster Dulles American Secretaries of State and their Diplomacy*, (NY: 1967), 17, pp. 86–8, 98 and 214; Townsend Hoopes, *The Devil and John Foster Dulles* (Boston and Toronto: 1973), pp. 64, 142–3; see also *FRUS*, 1952–4, 5, pp. 712, 765.
22. *Ibid.*, p. 709; Draper to DDE (30 December 1952) Box 8, Subject Series, Dulles papers, DDEL.
23. *The New York Times* (28 January), FO 371/103512.
24. *FRUS*, 1952–4, 5, p. 713.
25. Wolf minute (15 December 1952), Box 2, Lot 55D 115, RG 59, NAW.
26. JCS 2124/84 (20 March 1953), *RJCS*.
27. Wolf's minute (see fn 25 above); Eisenhower diary (6 January), Box 9, DDE diary series, Ann Whitman file, DDEL; *FRUS*, 1952–4, 5, pp. 709, 713, 1555–6.
28. *FRUS*, 1952–4, 5, p. 715.
29. *Ibid.*, pp. 694, 709; Dunn to Dulles, Box 8, Subject Series, Dulles papers, DDEL.
30. *FRUS*, 1952–4, 5, pp. 733, 1548–81.
31. Seydoux, *Mémoires*, pp. 172–5; Bérard, *Un Ambassadeur*, p. 423; Decimal file, 762.00/1-1453 (14 January 1953), RG 59, NAW; FO 371/107434 (1 January); PREM 11/438 (9 January).
32. Massigli, *Une Comédie*, pp. 352–5; Auriol, *Journal 1953–4*, pp. 31–2; Alphand, *Journal*, pp. 233–4; Seydoux, *Mémoires*, p. 173; PREM 11/438 (12 January).
33. COS(53)135, DEFE 5/45; PREM 11/438 (10 January); *FRUS*, 1952–4, 5, pp. 702–3, 719–26; Auriol, *Journal 1953–4*, p. 54.

34. *FRUS*, 1952–4, 5, pp. 719–21, 730, 1551–6 ff, 1569 and 1573; Speidel, *Erinnerungen*, pp. 312–13.
35. *FRUS*, 1952–4, 5, pp. 728,1555–6.
36. COS(53)167, DEFE 5/45.
37. FO 371/107443; Alphand, *Journal*, pp. 234–5.
38. C(53)73, CAB 129/59; Massigli, *Une Comédie*, pp. 359–61; PREM 11/373 (27 February).
39. JP(53)25, DEFE 6/21; C(53)112, CAB 129/60; PREM 11/373 (7 January).
40. 14th mtg, CAB 128/26.
41. C(53)73, CAB 129/59.
42. COS(52)662 and COS(53)304, DEFE 5/43 and 47.
43. 15th mtg, CAB 128/26; C(53)73 and 111, CAB 129/59 and 60.
44. C(53)111, CAB 129/60; see also FO 800/777 (Eden–Schuman talks on 19 December 1952).
45. PREM 11/373 (6 January 1953); PREM 11/422 (7 April); *FRUS*, 1952–4, 5, pp. 708, 1565.
46. Shuckburgh, *Descent to Suez*, p. 231; Boyle, in *Churchill's Peacetime Administration*, p. 32.
47. 102nd mtg, CAB 128/25; *FRUS*, 1952–4, 5, p. 750.
48. Leonard Mosley, *Dulles: A Biography of Eleanor, Allen and John Foster Dulles and Their Family Network* (London: 1978), p. 353; Gerson, *Dulles*, p. 71.
49. C(53)73, CAB 129/59; *FRUS*, 1952–4, 5, pp. 747, 754.
50. C(53)158, CAB 129/61; 32nd mtg, CAB 128/26; see also 39th mtg, CAB 128/26; C(53)332, CAB 129/64; Auriol, *Journal, 1953–4*, p. 78.
51. This will be discussed in the next chapter.
52. *FRUS*, 1952–4, 5, p. 754.
53. C(53)111, CAB 129/60.
54. FO 371/107443 (28 and 30 March).
55. Adenauer, *Memoirs*, pp. 442–9 ff; FO 371/103951 (10 April); *FRUS*, 1952–4, 5, pp. 782, 786–7.
56. *Ibid.*, pp. 750, 757.
57. *Ibid.*, pp. 750, 757–61, 767, 795, 1576; Harst, 'The Netherlands and the EDC'; COS(53)301, DEFE 5/47; Fursdon, *EDC*, pp. 210–21.
58. *FRUS*, 1952–4, 5, pp. 767, 776–8, 790–1; Adenauer, *Memoirs*, p. 435; FO 371/103945 (1 May); FO 371/103705 (20 May).
59. Stalin note of 10 March in PREM 11/168.
60. Poole, *JCS*, 4, p. 293; Mélandri, *Les États-Unis Face*, p. 362.
61. For Acheson's statement see Reinhard Neebe, 'Wahlen als Test: Eine gescheiterte Initiative des Politischen Planungsstabs im State Department zur Stalin-Note vom März 1952', *Militärgeschichtliche Mitteilungen* 1 (1989), p. 151; see also Box 3829 (5, 10, 19, 20 March) Decimal files, 762.00/3,10,RG59, NAW; *FRUS*, 1952–4, 7, pp. 173–9.
62. Cabinet 29th mtg, PREM 11/168; 38th, 40th and 47th mtgs, DEFE 4/52, 53.
63. Loth, *The Division of the World*, pp. 262–4; Speidel, *Erinnerungen*, pp. 311–12; Blankenhorn, *Verständnis*, p. 132–3; FO 371/97877 (11 and 12 March).

64. Auriol, *Journal, 1952*, pp. 201, 211; Mélandri, *Les États-Unis Face*, p. 362–3; FO 371/97877 (12 March); FO 371/101737 (15 April).
65. Unsigned FO paper, FO 371/103680 (24 September).
66. Eden, *Full Circle*, p. 45.
67. For instance, Rolf Steininger suggests that Stalin was serious, but that the Western leaders, especially Adenauer, failed to take advantage of the opportunity for reunification, see Steininger, 'Die Stalin-Note vom März – eine chance zur Wiedervereinigung Deutschlands?' in *Kalte Krieg und Deutsche Frage*, pp. 362–79; *idem.*, *Eine vertane Chance – Die Stalin-Note vom 10 März 1952 und Wiedervereinigung* (Berlin and Bonn: 1986). See also P. Windsor, *City on Leave – A History of Berlin* (London: 1963), p. 187. In opposition to these views see Hermann Graml, 'Die Legende von verpassten Gelegenheit zur Sowjetischen Notenkampagne des Jahres 1952', *Vierteljahrshefte für Zeitgeschichte* 29:3 (1981), pp. 307–41. For a more cautious view of the Stalin note, see Loth, *The Division of the World*, pp. 258–67.
68. For similar arguments about whether the Stalin note was attractive to the West, see T. Schwartz 'The Stalin Note of March 1952 and German Reunification' unpublished conference paper at Harvard University, 3–5 December 1987.
69. Acheson minute (12 April), Box 3829, Decimal File 762.00/4, RG 59, NAW; FO 371/103685 (22 October).
70. 102nd mtg, CAB 128/25; FO 371/106524 (23 December 1952, 12 January 1953); FO 371/103658 (25 February).
71. FO 371/106524 (20, 23 March); FO 371/106525 (22 April); FO 371/106538 (25 April); *FRUS*, 1952–4, 5, pp. 365, 371–8 and 395; *FRUS*, 1952–4, 8, pp. 1108–11, 1156–9; M. Steven Fish, 'After Stalin's Death: The Anglo-American Debate over a New Cold War' *Diplomatic History* 10:4 (Autumn 1986), pp. 333–5.
72. FO 371/106524 (8 April); the US State Dept liked the FO paper, see FO 371/106525 (27 April); for French views, see FO 371/106537 (13 April).
73. For the Austrian peace treaty see Günter Bischof, ' "Austria and Moscow's Wiles": The Western Powers, Neutrality and the Austrian Peace Treaty' unpublished conference paper at Harvard University, 3–5 December 1987.
74. FO 800/794 (8 April 1953).
75. Hamilton, *Monty*, p. 831; COS 189th and 191st mtgs, DEFE 4/49.
76. Ambrose, *Eisenhower*, 2, p. 89; JCS 2101/79 (10 November 1952) and JIC 636/2 (11 June 1953) both in *RJCS*.
77. D(53)3, 45, CAB 131/13.
78. *Parl. Deb. H of C*, vol. 515, cols. 883–98; GIlbert, *Never Despair*, pp. 829–32.
79. FO 371/103665 (17 June); Blankenhorn, *Verständnis*, pp. 148–9; Josef Forschepoth, 'Churchill, Adenauer und die Neutraliserung Deutschlands' *Deutschland Archiv* 17 (December 1984), pp. 1290–1; *FRUS*, 1952–4, 7, pp. 460–1.
80. Piers Brendon, *Ike – The Life and Times of Dwight D. Eisenhower* (London: 1987), p. 255; Bohlen, *Witness to History*, p. 371; see also *Docs on Int.*

Affairs, 1953 (London: 1956), pp. 51–7.

81. Churchill to Eisenhower (22 April), *FRUS*, 1952–4, 6, p. 975; Eisenhower to Churchill (25 April), Box 16, Int. Series, Ann Whitman File, DDEL.

82. Churchill to Eisenhower (4, 7 May), Box 16, Int. Series, Ann Whitman File, DDEL; Carlton, *Eden*, pp. 327–8; Shuckburgh, *Descent to Suez*, pp. 85–95 f.

83. James, *Eden*, pp. 364–5.

84. FO 371/103660 (30 May).

85. C (53)194, CAB 129/61.

86. Slessor papers (19 November), Folder 15/A

87. PREM 11/370 (2 July).

88. PREM 11/449 (13 June); see also the PM's concern about West Germany's possible production of nuclear weapons in Churchill to Lord Cherwell (10 May 1952) and Cherwell to Churchill (12 May 1952) both in Lord Cherwell papers, J.3, Nuffield College, Oxford.

89. FO 371/106538 (25 April); FO 371/103666 (29 June); PREM 11/373 (7 May); FO 371/103668 (3, 4 July); 40th mtg, CAB 128/26; Auriol, *Journal, 1953–4*, pp. 163–5; Seydoux, *Mémoires*, pp. 176–7.

90. Young, 'Churchill, the Russians and the Western Alliance: the three-power conference at Bermuda, December 1953' *English Historical Review* (October 1986), p. 889; 33rd mtg, CAB 128/26; Gilbert, *Never Despair*, p. 833; for Eisenhower's views, see PREM 11/520 (21 May), unsigned memo (3 June) and Eisenhower to Churchill (30 May and 19 June) all in Box 16, Int. Series, Ann Whitman File, DDEL.

91. PREM 11/428 (11 June); James, *Eden*, pp. 364–5.

92. FO 371/106538 (29 May, 3 June).

93. C(53)187, 194, CAB 129/61; 39th mtg, CAB 128/26.

94. For the record of the Washington talks, see PREM 11/425, 419 and 373; see also *FRUS*, 1952–4, 5 pp. 1582–1768 ff.

95. For the *Bundestag* resolution see PREM 11/449. See also *FRUS*, 1952–4, 5, p. 1617.

96. *Ibid.*, pp. 1587–9; Blankenhorn, *Verständnis*, p. 152; Dulles minute, Box 13 (6 July), Int. Series, Ann Whitman File, DDEL; Forschepoth, 'Churchill und die Neutralisierung', pp. 1294–5.

97. PREM 11/425 (10 July).

98. 42nd mtg, CAB 128/26; *FRUS*, 1952–4, 5, pp. 1673–5; Auriol, *Journal, 1953–4*, pp. 290–1.

99. For instance, the record of the Dulles–Adenauer mtg of 7 February 1953, FO 371/103928; Eisenhower to Adenauer, FO 371/103670 (23 July); see also FO 371/103960 (25, 30 June); Hermann-Josef Rupieper, 'Deutsche Frage und europäische Sicherheit: Politisch-strategische überlegungen 1953/1955', B. Thoss & H. E. Volkmann, *Zwischen Kaltem Krieg und Entspannung-Sicherheits und Deutschlandpolitik der Bundesrepublik im Mächte-system der Jahre 1953–1956* (Boppard am Rhein: 1988), pp. 179–90.

100. Loth, *The Division of the World*, pp. 267–72; Speidel, *Erinnerungen*, p. 318; PREM 11/673 (17 June); *FRUS*, 1952–4, 7, pp. 487–90; Fish, 'After Stalin's Death', pp. 339–42.

101. FO 371/103665.

102. For this apparent decrease in Russian interest in reunification after the East German uprising and also after the fall of Beria, see Henry A. Turner, Jr, *The Two Germanies Since 1945* (New Haven and London: 1987), pp. 123–4.

103. *FRUS*, 1952–4, 5, p. 800; Eden minute (undated) in PREM 11/426; see also PREM 11/618 (6 November).

104. *FRUS*, 1952–4, 5, pp. 802–3, 808–12, 817, 822, 870–1; COS (53)588, DEFE 5/50.

105. PREM 11/434 (27 November); PREM 11/618 (28 November and 1 December); FO 371/107446 (20 May); Auriol, *Journal, 1953–4*, pp. 536–7; Massigli, *Une Comédie*, pp. 400–4; G. H. Soutou, 'La France, L'Allemagne et les accords de Paris' *Relations Internationales*, 52 (Winter 1987), p. 451; for the Soviet note of 26 November 1953 see Cmd 9022 in PREM 11/664.

106. Moran, *Churchill*, p. 540; Horne, *Macmillan*, p. 348.

107. Gilbert, *Never Despair*, p. 876.

108. 42nd mtg, CAB 128/26.

109. PREM 11/418 (5, 7 and 10 November); 64th and 65th mtgs, CAB 128/26; Churchill to Eisenhower (12 November), Box 17, Int. Series, Ann Whitman File, DDEL.

110. For the record of the Bermuda conference see *FRUS*, 1952–4, 5, pp. 1710–847 ff; see also the British record (not complete) in PREM 11/418, 618 and 664.

111. *FRUS*, 1952–4, 5, p. 1759; Gilbert, *Never Despair*, pp. 917–17, 921–3.

112. Box 9 (6 January 1953), DDE Diary Series, Ann Whitman File, DDEL.

113. *FRUS*, 1952–4, 5, p. 1761.

114. UK note of 8 December see Cmd 9022, PREM 11/664; 77th mtg, CAB 128/26.

115. *FRUS*, 1952–4, 5, pp. 792–7 ff; Box 5 (7 September), DDE Diary Series, Ann Whitman File, DDEL.

116. Alphand, *Journal*, pp. 238–401; Auriol, *Journal, 1953–4*, pp. 557–8.

117. *FRUS*, 1952–4, 5, p. 1903; Gilbert, *Never Despair*, p. 918.

118. *FRUS*, 1952–4, 5, p. 868.

119. Mélandri, *Les États-Unis Face*, p. 429; *FRUS*, 1952–4, 5, pp. 827–9, 1771.

7 Eden's successful alternative

1. See ch. 5, pp. 91–2.

2. COS(52)480, DEFE 5/41; 33rd mtg (Lord Hood, the Foreign Office, was present), DEFE 4/69.

3. See Annex to C(53)332, CAB 129/64.

4. 31st mtg, DEFE 4/69.

5. COS(52)480, DEFE 5/41.

6. PREM 11/618.

7. Mélandri, *Les États-Unis Face*, pp. 419–22; Juin, *Mémoires*, pp. 255–6; Auriol, *Journal, 1953–4*, p. 571; *FRUS*, 1952–4, 5, pp. 887, 960.

8. See, for instance, Dulles's policy statement at NY on 12 January 1954 in FO 371/109112; General Gruenther's speech at SHAPE on 11 January

1954 in PREM 11/771. See also recent studies on this issue by Samuel F. Wells jun., 'The Origins of Massive Retaliation' 96:1 (Spring 1981), p. 31–52 and Richard M. Saunders, 'Military Force in the Foreign Policy of the Eisenhower Presidency', 100:1 (Spring 1985), pp. 97–116 both in *Political Science Quarterly*.

9. *FRUS*, 1952–4, 5, pp. 873–4, 1772–3, 1795–1802; C(54)93, CAB 21/66; Mélandri, États-Unis Face, pp. 424–5; Massigli, *Une Comédie*, pp. 420–1.

10. 2nd mtg (Hood present), DEFE 4/68.

11. C(54)93, CAB 129/66; 17th mtg, CAB 128/27; see also Cmd 9126 (13 April 1954).

12. C(54)93, CAB 129/66; Cmd 9126; Massigli, *Une Comédie*, pp. 442–5 ff.

13. *Parl. Deb. H of C* vol. 526, cols. 1141–7; Shuckburgh, *Descent to Suez*, p. 165.

14. The Parliamentary Committee of the Labour party minute (3 May 1952), Noel-Baker papers, NBKR 4/301, Churchill College; Attlee's views on this subject in *Daily Herald* (6 March 1952) and Dalton's speech in the H of C (1 August 1952) both in Dalton papers, part 2 C/9/27. See also *Daily Telegraph* 15 April, FO 371/109762; *The Guardian* (4 May), FO 371/109641; Nutting, *Europe*, p. 163.

15. C(54)93, CAB 129/66.

16. JP(54) Note 10, DEFE 6/28; 2nd mtg, DEFE 4/69; see also Slim's lecture on British strategy in the United States, April 1952, Slim papers, 314, Churchill College.

17. Earl Alexander to Eden (23 December 1953), PREM 11/618.

18. 17th mtg, CAB 128/27.

19. 22nd mtg, DEFE 4/69.

20. *FRUS*, 1952–4, 5, p. 928.

21. *Ibid.*

22. *Ibid.*, pp. 886–7.

23. For the importance of the European allies to the US, see Eisenhower to Churchill (19 June 1953, 9 February 1954), Boxes 16, 17, Int. Series, Ann Whitman File, DDEL; see also George Herring and Richard Immerman, 'Eisenhower, Dulles and Dienbienphu: "The Day We Didn't Go to War" Revisited', *The Journal of American History*, 71 (September 1984), pp. 359–61.

24. *FRUS*, 1952–4, 5, pp. 890–3, 960.

25. Massigli, *Une Comédie*, p. 423; Alphand, *Journal*, pp. 246–7.

26. Mélandri, 'Introduction' to part 3 in *Mendésisme*, pp. 231–3; Seydoux, *Mémoires*, pp. 185–6; Jean Lacouture, *Pierre Mendès-France*, trans. George Holoch (London: 1984), pp. 6, 266–7. There was and continues to be speculation about a secret deal between Molotov and Mendès-France at Geneva about the Indochina settlement and France's rejection of the EDC. Lord Jebb (then British ambassador to France) denied this in *The Memoirs of Lord Gladwyn* (London: 1972), p. 272. French historians are equally dismissive. See R. Girault, 'La France dans les rapports Est–Ouest au temps de Pierre Mendés France' in *Mendésisme*, pp. 255–8; Sotou, 'Les Accords de Paris', pp. 452–3.

27. For the French additional protocols, see PREM 11/618 (16 August);

FRUS, 1952–4, 5 pp. 1033–6; see also Bérard, *Un Ambassadeur*, p. 567.

28. For the record of the Brussels conference see PREM 11/618 and *FRUS*, 1952–4, 5 pp. 1652–70; see also Bérard, *Un Ambassadeur*, pp. 564–71; Blankenhorn, *Verständnis*, pp. 191–3; Paul Henri Spaak, *The Continuing Battle* (London: 1971) pp. 166–71.

29. Mélandri, *Les États-Unis Face*, p. 235; Lacouture, *Mendès-France*, pp. 266–7.

30. PREM 11/618 (23 August); Massigli, *Une Comédie*, pp. 449–50.

31. Mérandri, in *Mendèsisme*, p. 239; see also Jacques Fauvet, 'Birth and Death of a Treaty' in Raymond Aron and D. Lerner (eds.), *France Defeats EDC* (London: 1957), pp. 160–4.

32. FO 37109576 (21, 22 June); FO 371/109577 (22 June).

33. PREM 11/618 (27 June); 47th mtg, CAB 128/27; C(54)214, 226, CAB 129/69; for the record of the Anglo-US Study Group see PREM 11/618, FO 371/109578 (10 July) and *FRUS*, 1952–4, 5, pp. 997–1016 ff.

34. C(54)231, CAB 129/69; FO 371/109579 (15 July).

35. PREM 11/909 (2, 3 September); FO 371/109581 (1, 2 September); Blankenhorn, *Verständnis*, pp. 194–5; Bérard, *Un Ambassadeur*, p. 571; Noack, *Das Sheitern der EVG*, p. 85.

36. FO 371/109571 (13 July); *FRUS*, 1952–4, 5, p. 975–8; R. Steininger, 'Das Scheitern der EVG und der Beitritt der Bundesrepublik zur NATO' *Aus Politik und Zeitgeschichte* 17 (April 1985), p. 10; Spaak, *The Continuing Battle*, pp. 159–61.

37. PREM 11/618 (24 June); FO 371/109578 (1 July); C(54)276, CAB 129/70; R. Cutler minute (20 July), Box 10, Administration Series, Ann Whitman File, DDEL.

38. Hoopes, *Dulles*, p. 246; *FRUS*, 1952–4, 5, pp. 1114–16, 1118–19, 1120–2.

39. *Ibid.*, pp. 1179–80.

40. Box 8, DDE Diaries, Ann Whitman File, DDEL.

41. *FRUS*, 1952–4, 5, pp. 1145–6, 1160–1, 1170–7, 1205–9, 1265–6.

42. DDE to Churchill (7 September), Box 8, DDE Diaries, Ann Whitman File, DDEL; Dulles(?) minute (for NATO mtg in May 1955), Box 96, Dulles papers, The Seeley Mudd Library; see also M. L. Dockrill, 'Britain and the First Chinese Off-Shore Islands Crisis, 1954–5' in *British Foreign Policy, 1945–56*, pp. 176–7; Leonard Gordon, 'United States Opposition to Use of Force in the Taiwan Strait, 1954–1962' *The Journal of American History*, 72 (December 1985), pp. 637–44.

43. PREM 11/909 (1 September); 58th mtg, CAB 128/27; Eden, *Full Circle*, p. 149; Moran, *Churchill*, pp. 595, 601.

44. *FRUS*, 1952–4, 5, p. 1151.

45. Adenauer, *Erinnerungen, 1953–5* (Stuttgart: 1966), pp. 305–7; Blankenhorn, *Verständnis*, pp. 195–7; Bérard, *Un Ambassadeur*, p. 576. For Churchill to Adenauer, FO 800/795 (1 September), *FRUS*, 1952–4, 5, pp. 1144–5; Adenauer's reply to this letter is in PREM 11/909 (4 September).

46. PREM 11/679 (8 September); *FRUS*, 1952–4, 5, pp. 1198–9.

47. PREM 11/909 (1 September); 59th mtg, CAB 128/27.

48. James, *Eden*, p. 387; PREM 11/909 (7 September); *FRUS*, 1952–4, 5, pp. 1103–1, 1154–5.

49. *Ibid.*, pp. 1155, 1218.
50. PREM 11/909 (3 September), 59th mtg, CAB 128/27; *FRUS*, 1952–4, 5, pp. 1155–6, 1218.
51. 60th, 61st mtgs, CAB 128/27; PREM 11/909 (12 September); *FRUS*, 1952–4, 5, pp. 1184–8, 1194–1294 ff, 1210–13; Eden, *Full Circle*, pp. 151, 163; Adenauer, *Erinnerungen*, pp. 307–8; Lacouture, *Mendès-France*, pp. 279–80; Maurice Vaïsse, 'La Grande-Bretagne, une partenaire privilégiée?' in *Mendésisme*, p. 283.
52. *FRUS*, 1952–4, 5, pp. 1192–4, 1213–21; Eden, *Full Circle*, p. 164.
53. *Ibid.*, pp. 164–5; James, *Eden*, p. 388.
54. For the record of the London conference, see *FRUS*, 1952–4, 5, pp. 1294–364; and also FO 371/109774, 109751 and 109538.
55. See Article of Protocol 2 in Cmd 9498. For the detailed composition of German forces, see JP(55)150, DEFE 6/32.
56. See Cmd 9498 and *FRUS*, 1952–4, 5, p. 1325; see also Noack, *Das Scheitern der EVG*, pp. 112–120 ff.
57. Cmd 9498 and Cmd 9289.
58. *FRUS*, 1952–4, 5, p. 1317; 'Final Act' in Cmd 9289.
59. *FRUS*, 1952–4, 5, p. 1381.
60. FO 371/109582 (13, 14, 15 September); COS(54)329, DEFE 5/54.
61. C(54)298, CAB 129/70; Eden, *Full Circle*, pp. 165–6.
62. *FRUS*, 1952–4, 5, pp. 1312–13; Cmd 9289. For the US guarantee to the WEU see Cmd 9408, in PREM 11/845.
63. 54th mtg, CAB 128/27; *FRUS*, 1952–54, 5, p. 1331; Cmd 9306.
64. Eden, *Full Circle*, p. 151; Charlton, *The Price of Victory*, p. 163–5; 57th mtg, CAB 128/27; Macmillan, *Memoirs*, p. 481.
65. Harst, 'The Netherlands and the EDC'; C(52)434, CAB 129/57.
66. Bérard, *Un Ambassadeur*, p. 561; Vaïsse, in *Mendésisme*, pp. 279–81; *FRUS*, 1952–4, 5, p. 1024.
67. 57th, 59th and 60th mtgs, CAB 128/27; FO 800/794 (10 September); see also a FO paper in COS(54)41, DEFE 5/51.
68. *FRUS*, 1952–4, pp. 1366–7; Blankenhorn, *Verständnis*, p. 199; see also Spaak, *The Continuing Battle*, pp. 182–6.
69. Cmd 9289 and Cmd 9498. Author's italics.
70. F. W. Mulley, *The Politics of Western Defence*, (London: 1962), pp. 132–3; Paul Gore-Booth, *With Great Truth and Respect* (London: 1974), pp. 235–6; Hugh Beach, 'British Forces in Germany, 1945–1985' in *The Defence Equation*, p. 164.
71. 107th mtg, DEFE 4/73; C(54)302, CAB 129/71; James, *Eden*, p. 388; *Parl. Deb. H of C*, vol. 533, cols. 397–520, 573–694; *FRUS*, 1952–4, 5, pp. 1485–6.
72. R. Steininger's recent article reaches a similar conclusion, see 'John Foster Dulles, the European Defence Community, and the German Question' ch. 3 in Richard Immerman (ed.), *Foreign Policy of John Foster Dulles* (title provisional – forthcoming).
73. A NATO Council mtg in December 1954 agreed to take account of the use of nuclear weapons in future planning, see *FRUS*, 1952–4, 5, pp. 554–9, 560–2; see also *ibid.*, pp. 532–7, 541–8 ff.

74. Mélandri, p. 240, Vaîsse, pp. 280–4, Girault, pp. 251–4, all in *Mendésisme*; Soutou, 'Les Accords de Paris', p. 457.
75. PREM 11/909 (12 September); 62nd mtg, CAB 128/27; Eden, *Full Circle*, p. 158.
76. *FRUS*, 1952–4, 5, p. 1525; Eden, *Full Circle*, p. 171.
77. Jebb, *Memoirs*, p. 274; Mendès-France to Churchill, FO 371/118195 (5 January 1955); Massigli, *Une Comédie*, pp. 490–1.
78. *FRUS*, 1955–7, 4, pp. 19–22.
79. *Ibid.*, pp. 279, 289–90; see also H. J. Küsters, 'Adenauers Europapolitik in der Gründungsphase der Europäischen Wirtschaftsgemeineschaft' *Vierteljahrshefte für Zeitgeschichte* 31:4 (1983), pp. 646–7; Nutting, *Europe*, pp. 82–6.

Conclusion

1. See Alfred Grosser, in *Mendésisme*, p. 249.
2. Michael Howard in *Western Security*, p. 14.
3. See Carlton, *Eden*, p. 303; Watt, *Succeeding John Bull*, p. 129; Boyle in *Churchill's Peacetime Administration*, pp. 30–4.
4. Box 16, Administration Series, Ann Whitman File, DDEL.

SELECT BIBLIOGRAPHY

British government official sources

1. Public Record Office, Kew
CAB 21: Cabinet office registered files, 1950–1
CAB 128, 129: Cabinet meetings and memoranda, 1945–55
CAB 130: Ad Hoc Committee of the Cabinet, 1950–52
CAB 131: Defence Committee's meetings and memoranda, 1946–55
PREM 8, 11: Prime Minister's office, 1948–55
FO 371: Files of the Foreign Office, 1947–55
FO 800: Bevin's papers, 1948–51; Eden's papers, 1951–5
CAB 79, 80: Chiefs of Staff meetings and memoranda, 1944–6
DEFE 4, 5: Chiefs of Staff meetings and memoranda, 1947–55
DEFE 6: Reports of the Joint Planning Staff, 1947–55
2. Command Papers (London: Her Majesty's Stationery Office (HMSO), 1952–5) for Cmd 8501, 8610, 9126, 9127, 9289, 9304, 9368, 9498, and 9501
3. Hansard, House of Commons, 5th series (London, 1947–55)
4. *Documents on British Policy Overseas, Series 2, Vols. 1 and 3* (London, 1986, 1989)

United States government official sources

1. National Archives, Washington
Department of State, Decimal Files, RG 59
——, Lot Files, RG 59
2. *Foreign Relations of the United States (FRUS)*, volumes for 1947–57 (Washington, D.C.: USGPO, 1973–88)
3. *Records of the Joint Chiefs of Staff part 2, 1946–1953* (Maryland: a Microfilm Project of University Publications of American Inc., 1980)
4. *Documents of the National Security Council, 1947–1977* (Maryland: a Microfilm Project of University Publications of American Inc., 1980)

Private papers

Dean C. Acheson papers, Yale University, New Haven
C. R. Attlee papers, Bodleian Library, Oxford
Lord Cherwell papers, Nuffield College, Oxford
Sir Stafford Cripps papers, Nuffield College, Oxford

Hugh Dalton papers and diaries, The British Library of Political and Economic Science, London

John F. Dulles papers, The Seeley Mudd Library, Princeton University, New Jersey

John F. Dulles papers, Dwight D. Eisenhower Library, Kansas

Dwight D. Eisenhower papers (Ann Whitman File), Dwight D. Eisenhower Library, Kansas

Sir W. Elliot papers, The Liddell Hart Centre for Military Archives, King's College London, London

Lord Francis-Williams papers, Churchill College, Cambridge

Sir Basil Liddell Hart papers, The Liddell Hart Centre for Military Archives, King's College London

Oliver Harvey diaries, The British Library, London

Field-Marshall Montgomery papers, The Imperial War Museum, London

Air Chief Marshal, Sir James Robb papers, RAF Museum, Hendon

Sir John Slessor papers, The Air Historical Branch, the Ministry of Defence, London

Field-Marshal, Sir William Slim papers, Churchill College, Cambridge

Kenneth Younger interview transcript, Nuffield College, Oxford

Kenneth Younger diaries, by kind permission of Lady Younger

Published biographies and memoirs

Acheson, D. *Present at the Creation* (London: Hamish Hamilton, 1970)

Adenauer, K. *Memoirs 1945–1953* (London: Weidenfeld and Nicolson, 1966) trans. Beate Rhun von Oppen

——, *Erinnerungen, 1953–55* (Stuttgart: Deutsche Verlags-Anstalt, 1966)

Alphand, H. *L'Etonnement d'être* Journal 1939–73 (Paris: Fayard, 1977)

Ambrose, S. E. *Eisenhower*, 1, 2 (London: George Allen & Unwin, 1984)

Attlee, C. R. *As It Happened* (London: William Heinemann Ltd, 1954)

Auriol, V. *Journal de Septennat* 6, 7 (Paris: Librairie Armand Colin, 1971, 1978)

Bérard, A. *Un Ambassadeur se Souvient* (Paris: Plon, 1978)

Blankenhorn, H. *Verständnis und Verständigung* (Frankfurt: Ullstein, 1980)

Bohlen, C. E. *Witness to History* (NY: W. W. Norton & Company Inc., 1973)

Lord Boothby, *Boothby* (London: Hutchinson & Co. Ltd, 1978)

Bradley, O. and Blair, C. *A General's Life* (London: Sidgwick & Jackson, 1983)

Bullock, A. *Ernest Bevin* (London: William Heinemann Ltd, 1983)

Campbell, J. *Nye Bevan* (London: Weidenfeld and Nicolson, 1987)

Carlton, D. *Anthony Eden* (London: Allen Lane, 1981)

Colville, J. *The Fringes of Power* (London: Hodder and Stoughton, 1985)

Dalton, H. *High Tide and After* (London: Frederick Muller Limited, (1962)

Dixon, P. *Double Diploma* (London: Hutchinson, 1968)

Eden, A. *Full Circle* (London: Cassell, 1960)

Edinger, L. *Kurt Schumacher* (California: Stanford University Press, 1965)

Ferrell, R. H. *The Eisenhower Diaries* (NY and London: W. W. Norton & Company, 1981)

Gilbert, M. *'Never Despair' Winston S. Churchill* (London: Heinemann, 1988)

Lord Gladwyn, *The Memoirs of Lord Gladwyn* (London: Weidenfeld and Nicolson, 1972)

Hamilton, N. *Monty – The Field Marshal 1944–1976* (London: Hamish Hamilton, 1986)

Harris, K. *Attlee* (London: Weidenfeld and Nicolson, 1982)

Henderson, N. *The Private Office* (London: Weidenfeld and Nicolson, 1984)

Hoopes, T. *The Devil and John Foster Dulles* (Boston: Little Brown and Company, 1973)

Horne, A. *Macmillan 1894–1956*, 1. (London: Macmillan, 1988)

. James, R. R. *Anthony Eden* (London: Weidenfeld and Nicolson, 1986)

Maréchal Juin, *Mémoires* (Paris: Fayard, 1960)

Earl of Kilmuir, *Memoirs* (London: Weidenfeld and Nicolson, 1964)

Kirkpatrick, I. *The Inner Circle* (London: Macmillan & Co. Ltd, 1959)

Lacouture, J. *Pierre Mendès-France* (NY and London: Holmes & Meier, 1984) trans. George Holoch

Lewis, R. *Slim* (London: Leo Cooper Ltd, 1976)

Macmillan, H. *Tides of Fortune* (London: Macmillan, 1969)

Massigli, R. *Une Comédie des Erreurs* (Paris: Plon, 1978)

McLellan, D. S. *Dean Acheson* (NY: Dodd, Mead & Company, 1976)

Moch, J. *Histoire de Réarmement Allemand depuis 1950* (Paris: Robert Laffont, 1965)

Monnet, J. *Memoirs* (London: Collins, 1978) trans. Richard Mayne

Lord Moran, *Winston Churchill* (London: Sphere Books Ltd, 1966)

Nutting, A. *Europe Will Not Wait* (London: Hollis & Carter, 1960)

Pimlott, B. *Hugh Dalton* (London: Papermac, a division of Macmillan Publishers Ltd, 1986)

Pogue, F. C. *George C. Marshall 1954–1959* (NY: Viking, 1987)

Reid, E. *Time of Fear and Hope* (Toronto: McClelland and Stewart Limited, 1977)

Schwartz, H. P. *Adenauer – Der Aufstieg* (Stuttgart: Deutsche Verlags-Anstalt, 1986)

Seydoux, F. *Mémoires* (Paris: Bernard Grasset, 1975)

Shuckburgh, E. *Descent to Suez – Diaries 1951–1956* (London: Weidenfeld and Nicolson, 1986)

Smith, G. *Dean Acheson* (NY: Square Publishers, Inc., 1972)

Spaak, P. H. *The Continuing Battle* (London: Weidenfeld and Nicolson, 1971)

Speidel, H. *Aus unserer Zeit-Erinnerungen* (Berlin: Ullstein, 1977)

Lord Strand, *Home and Abroad* (London: Andre Deutsch, 1956)

Truman, H. S. *Years of Trial and Hope* (NY: Doubleday & Company Inc, 1956)

Weymar, P. *The Authorised Biography – Adenauer* (London: Andre Deutsch, 1957) ed. and trans. Peter de Mendelssohn

Williams, M. P. *Hugh Gaitskell* (Oxford and NY: Oxford University Press, 1982)

Other published works

Aron, R. and Lerner, D. (eds.) *France Defeats EDC* (London: Thames and Hudson, 1957)

193

Barker, E. *The British between the Superpowers* (London: Macmillan, 1983)

Becker, J. and Knipping, F. (eds.) *Power in Europe?* (Berlin and NY: Walter de Gruyter, 1986)

Bédarida, F. and Rioux, J. *Pierre Mendès France et le Mendésisme* (Paris: Fayard, 1985)

Cioc, M. *Pax Atomica* (NY: Columbia University Press, 1988)

Deutsch, K. and Edinger L. *Germany Rejoins the Powers* (Calif.: Stanford University Press, 1959)

Dockrill M. and Young, J. (eds.) *British Foreign Policy, 1945–1956* (London: Macmillan, 1989)

Doering-Manteuffel, A. *Die Bundesrepublik Deutschland in der Ära Adenauer* (Darmstadt: Wissenschaftliche Buchgesellschaft, 1983)

Donovan, R. *Tumultuous Years* (NY and London: W. W. Norton & Company, 1982)

Foschepoth, J. (ed.) *Kalte Krieg und Deutsche Frage* (Zurich: Vandenhoeck & Ruprecht, 1985)

Fursdon, E. *The European Defence Community* (London: Macmillan, 1980)

Gaddis, J. *Strategies of Containment* (Oxford and NY: Oxford University Press 1982)

Graebner, N. (ed.) *The National Security* (Oxford and NY: Oxford University Press, 1986)

Grosser, A. *The Western Alliance* (NY: Macmillan, 1980)

Hogan, M. J. *The Marshall Plan* (Cambridge and NY: Cambridge University Press, 1987)

Harbutt, F. The Iron Curtain (Oxford and NY: Oxford University Press, 1986)

Ireland, T. *Creating the Entangling Alliance* (London: Aldwych Press Ltd, 1981)

Kaplan, L. *A Community of Interests* (Washington, D.C.: The Office of the Secretary of Defense, Historical Office, 1980)

——, *The United States and NATO* (Lexington: The University Press of Kentucky, 1984)

Lewis, J. *Changing Direction* (London: The Sherwood Press, 1988)

Loth, W. *The Division of the World* (NY: Routledge, 1988)

McGeehan, R. *The German Rearmament Question* (Urbana: University of Illinois Press, 1971)

Mélandri, P. *Les États-Unis Face a L'unification de L'Europe, 1945–1954* (Paris: Pedone, 1980)

Melanson, R. & Mayers, D. *Reevaluating Eisenhower* (Urbana: University of Illinois Press, 1989)

Militärgeschichtliches Forschungsamt(MGFA) (ed.), Mai, G. *Westliche Sicherheitspolitik im Kalten Krieg- Militärgeschichte seite 1945* vol. 4 (Boppard: Harald Boldt Verlag, 1977)

—— (ed.), *Dienstgruppen und westdeutscher Verteidigungsbeitrag Militärgeschichte seite 1945* vol. 6 (Boppard: Harald Boldt Verlag, 1982)

——. *Anfänge westdeutscher Sicherheitspolitik 1945–1956 – Von der Kapitulation bis zum Pleven-Plan* (München: R. Oldenbourg Verlag, 1982)

Morgan, K. *Labour in Power* (Oxford: Clarendon Press, 1984)

Noack, P. *Das Scheitern Der Europäischen Verteidigungsgemeinschaft* (Düsseldorf: Droste Verlag, 1977)

194

Northedge, F. S. *British Foreign Policy* (London: George Allen & Unwin, 1962)

Ovendale, R. (ed.) *The Foreign Policy of the British Labour Governments, 1945–1951* (Leicester: Leicester University Press, 1984)

Pelling, H. *The Labour Governments, 1945–1951* (London: Macmillan, 1984)

Poole, W. *The History of the Joint Chiefs of Staff*, 4 (Wilmington: Michael Glazier Inc, 1979)

Richardson, J. *Germany and the Atlantic Alliance* (Cambridge, MA: Harvard University Press, 1966)

Riste, O. (ed.), *Western Security: The Formative Years* (Olso: Norwegian University Press, 1985)

Rothwell, V. *Britain and the Cold War, 1941–1947* (London: Jonathan Cape, 1982)

Seldon, A. *Churchill's Indian Summer* (London: Hodder and Stoughton, 1981)

Stein, H. *American Civil–Military Decision* (Alabama: University of Alabama Press, 1963)

Steininger, R. *Eine vertane Chance* (Berlin and Bonn: Verlag J. H. W. Dietz Nachf, 1985)

Turner, H. Jr. *The Two Germanies since 1945* (New Haven: Yale University Press, 1987)

Watt, D. C. *Succeeding John Bull* (Cambridge and NY: Cambridge University Press, 1984)

Windsor, P. *City on Leave* (London: Chatto & Windus, 1963)

Young, J. *Britain, France and the Unity of Europe* (Leicester: Leicester University Press, 1984)

——, (ed.), *The Foreign Policy of Churchill's Peacetime Administration, 1951–1955* (Leicester: Leicester University Press, 1988)

195

INDEX

Acheson, Dean, 18, 70, 84, 163n, 165n, 166n, 168n, 169n, 170n, 173n, 177n, 180n
  and Britain's membership of EDC, 93
  and Eden, 157
  and London Talks, February, 1952, 95–6
  and Paris conference on European army, 88
  and Pleven plan, 42
  and rearmament of Western European allies, 22
  and Stalin note, 121
  and US package proposal, 28, 30–3
  and West German attitudes to their rearmament, 56
  and West German rearmament, 68
  chairs NATO Council Conference, New York, 34–7ff
  support for EDC, 72–3, 79
  suspicion of consummation of EDC project, 68–9
Achillers, Theodore, 119
Adamthwaite, Anthony, 162n
Adenauer, Dr Konrad, 11, 60, 124, 141, 164n, 167n, 168n, 169n, 171n, 172n, 179n, 183n, 188n, 189n
  and Churchill's call for summit talks, 124, 126
  and Churchill's European army concept, August 1950, 24
  and EDC, 140
  and four-power talks on Germany, 124, 127–8
  and France, 38, 141
  and internal party politics, 45, 116
  and London Conference, September 1954, 144
  and London Talks, February 1952, 95–7
  and NATO solution, 142
  and Pleven plan, 42
  and Saar question, 119–20
  and Spofford plan, 55, 58

  and Washington talks, July 1953, 127
  and West German federal police force, 27, 32, 39–40
  and West Germany's ratification of the EDC treaty, 105, 129
  anxiety to integrate West Germany into the West, 10–11, 104, 124
  approach to post-EDC Europe, 141
  approach to Western occupying powers, 22, 46–7, 59
  concern to restore West Germany's sovereignty, 10–11, 59, 66, 141
  readiness to compromise over negotiations on Allied settlement over a future West Germany, political and military, 97, 142
  attitudes to EDC, 70, 72
  support for West Germany's defence contribution to the West, 11, 59, 70, 152
  support for EDC, 127
  support for European unity, 70, 150
  victory in general election (1953), 129
aid, US, financial and military: to Europe, 21, 29, 30, 33, 63, 68, 69, 72, 94, 100–1, 104, 116: to Indochina, 113, 120
Alexander, A. V. (Labour), 163n
Alexander of Tunis, 135
Allen, W. D., 46
Allied Control Council, 4
Allied High Commission, 27
Allied High Commissioners 10, 15, 22, 32, 38–9, 46, 55, 140–1
Allied Military Governors, 10
Alphand, Hervé, 64–5, 99, 105, 170n, 180n, 181n, 183n, 186n, 187n
Ambrose, Stephen, 170n, 175n, 182n, 184n
Amery, Julian, 85
Aron, Reymond, 188n
Article 51 of the UN Charter, 99
Atlantic Confederate Force, Bevin, the concept of, 49–50, 58, 110, 155